PSYCHOLOGICAL PERSPECTIVES IN YOUTH SPORTS

THE SERIES IN CLINICAL AND COMMUNITY PSYCHOLOGY

CONSULTING EDITORS:

CHARLES D. SPIELBERGER and IRWIN G. SARASON

Averill	Patterns of Psychological Thought: Readings in Historical and Contemporary Texts
Becker	Depression: Theory and Research
Bermant, Kelman, and Warwick	The Ethics of Social Intervention
Brehm	The Application of Social Psychology to Clinical Practice
Cattell and Dreger	Handbook of Modern Personality Theory
Endler and Magnusson	Interactional Psychology and Personality
Friedman and Katz	The Psychology of Depression: Contemporary Theory and Research
Iscoe, Bloom, and Spielberger	Community Psychology in Transition
Janisse	Pupillometry: The Psychology of the Pupillary Response
Kissen	From Group Dynamics to Group Psychoanalysis: Therapeutic Applications of Group Dynamic Understanding
Klopfer and Reed	Problems in Psychotherapy: An Eclectic Approach
London	Personality: A New Look at Metatheories
Manschreck and Kleinman	Renewal in Psychiatry: A Critical Rational Perspective
Olweus	Aggression in the Schools: Bullies and Whipping Boys
Reitan and Davison	Clinical Neuropsychology: Current Status and Applications
Smoll and Smith	Psychological Perspectives in Youth Sports
Spielberger and Diaz-Guerrero	Cross-Cultural Anxiety
Spielberger and Sarason	Stress and Anxiety, volume 1
Sarason and Spielberger	Stress and Anxiety, volume 2
Sarason and Spielberger	Stress and Anxiety, volume 3
Spielberger and Sarason	Stress and Anxiety, volume 4
Spielberger and Sarason	Stress and Anxiety, volume 5
Ulmer	On the Development of a Token Economy Mental Hospital Treatment Program

IN PREPARATION

Cohen and Ross	Biology and Psychopathology
Krohne and Laux	Achievement, Stress, and Anxiety

PSYCHOLOGICAL PERSPECTIVES IN YOUTH SPORTS

EDITED BY **FRANK L. SMOLL**
RONALD E. SMITH

both of the University of Washington, Seattle

HEMISPHERE PUBLISHING CORPORATION

Washington   **London**

A HALSTED PRESS BOOK
JOHN WILEY & SONS

New York   **London**   **Sydney**   **Toronto**

Hemisphere Publishing Corporation
1025 Vermont Ave., N.W., Washington, D.C. 20005

Distributed solely by Halsted Press, a Division of John Wiley & Sons, Inc.,
New York.

1 2 3 4 5 6 7 8 9 0   D O D O   7 8 3 2 1 0 9 8

Library of Congress Cataloging in Publication Data

Main entry under title:

Psychological perspectives in youth sports.

    (The Series in clinical and community psychology)
    Includes indexes.
    1. Sports—Psychological aspects—Addresses,
essays, lectures. 2. Sports for children—Psychologi-
cal aspects—Addresses, essays, lectures. I. Smoll,
Frank L. II. Smith, Ronald Edward, date
GV706.4.P68   796'.01   78-7535
ISBN 0-470-26383-0

CONTENTS

    Ronald E. Smith, Frank L. Smoll, and Bill Curtis   173

    Method   174
    Subjects   182
    Results and Discussion   182
    Development of Experimental Coaching Clinics   198
    References   200

9   Cooperative Games: Systematic Analysis and Cooperative Impact
    T. D. Orlick, Jane McNally, and Tom O'Hara   203

    Component Structure of Games   204
    Behavior Observation   206
    Assessments of Liking   209
    Kindergarten Study   211
    Concluding Comments   224
    References   224

IV SPORT AND THE HANDICAPPED CHILD

10 Adult Reactions to the Special Olympics
    G. Lawrence Rarick   229

    Method   230
    Results   234
    Summary and Conclusions   245
    References   247

11 Significant Others and Sport Socialization of the Handicapped Child
    John H. Lewko   249

    Teacher Expectancy   250
    Attribution Theory and the Significant Other   253
    Teacher Attribution of Student Performance   253
    Attribution Awareness Training   258
    General Discussion   273
    References   274

    Author Index   279

    Subject Index   285

CONTRIBUTORS

David Blievernicht, Division of Health and Physical Education, Wayne State University, Detroit, Michigan

Russell Bruce, Department of Physical Education, Lake Superior State College, Sault St. Marie, Michigan

Bill Curtis, Department of Psychology, University of Washington, Seattle, Washington

Thomas Gilliam, Department of Physical Education, University of Michigan, Ann Arbor, Michigan

John H. Lewko, Department of Physical Education and Institute for Child Behavior and Development, University of Illinois, Champaign, Illinois

Robert M. Malina, Department of Anthropology and Department of Physical Education, University of Texas, Austin, Texas

Jane McNally, Department of Kinanthropology, University of Ottawa, Ottawa, Ontario, Canada

Karan A. H. Moss, Department of Physical Education, University of Texas, Austin, Texas

Tom O'Hara, Department of Kinanthropology, University of Ottawa, Ottawa, Ontario, Canada

T. D. Orlick, Department of Kinanthropology, University of Ottawa, Ottawa, Ontario, Canada

Michael W. Passer, Department of Physical Education, University of Washington, Seattle, Washington

G. Lawrence Rarick, Department of Physical Education, University of California, Berkeley, California

Glyn C. Roberts, Department of Physical Education and Institute for Child Behavior and Development, University of Illinois, Champaign, Illinois

Tara K. Scanlan, Department of Kinesiology, University of California, Los Angeles, California

Vern D. Seefeldt, Department of Health, Physical Education, and Recreation, Michigan State University, East Lansing, Michigan

Michael D. Smith, Department of Physical Education and Department of Sociology, York University, Toronto, Ontario, Canada

Ronald E. Smith, Department of Psychology, University of Washington, Seattle, Washington

Frank L. Smoll, Department of Physical Education, University of Washington, Seattle, Washington

L. Keith Tennant, College of Physical Education, Health, and Recreation, University of Florida, Gainesville, Florida

Jerry R. Thomas, Department of Health, Physical, and Recreation Education, Louisiana State University, Baton Rouge, Louisiana

FOREWORD

The symposium from which this volume originated was a joint undertaking of the Department of Psychology and the Department of Physical Education at the University of Washington. The flavor of the conference seemed to reflect the interdisciplinary cooperation in research that will have to become much more widespread if scholars and scientists are to come to grips, in real terms, with the whole spectrum of sport in the life of contemporary societies.

The graduate school of the University of Washington and the Safeco Insurance Company generously provided the funds that made the meeting possible. Though one might expect the graduate school of a major university to support such an undertaking, it is not common practice for a business firm to underwrite this aspect of the sport phenomenon. This is an interesting paradox, for we are all too familiar with the involvement of business and industry in supporting athletic teams and sport tournaments and in sponsoring the televising of major sports events, which now take place almost daily. Sport sponsorship, even to the tune of a million dollars, is a well-recognized avenue for advertising one's business products. Why then do business and industry usually not underwrite the cost of sport research? The answer is that there is not, as yet, an identifiable consumer market for sport research. Thus, there is no guarantee of even a minimal return on a dollar invested to promote such work. Society would profit greatly, however, if public concern for sport resulted in an awareness of the need to know more about how sport operates and how it affects the lives of players and nonplayers alike. Thus, private industry and business could indeed find a suitable return for their dollar investment in the sponsorship of sport research. After all, almost every other facet of human behavior—including economic, domestic, sexual, and political behavior—has been the focus of intensive scholarly inquiry, for which there are varying but extensive sources of funding from both private and corporate sources.

The phenomena of play, games, and sport have yet to achieve widespread serious recognition on either the academic or the fiscal front. And this is unfortunate, for our lives are permeated with play and we are surrounded by sport. During the past decade, questions about the impact of highly organized sport on the lives of young people have been raised with increasing frequency. Yet, in the absence of real information derived from systematic research, such questions must remain unanswered. For centuries, in the best Western tradition, sport has been something that people with the time, energy, and inclination took up in the lighter moments of their lives. In the space of a few decades, however, that idyllic pattern has changed.

The lure of sport, particularly for the very young, is now well recognized, especially by politicians, churchleaders, teachers, and generals, all of whom exploit sports' power of attraction without thought for the consequences of such actions of the player participants or sport itself as long as the ends of their own systems are served. The transformation of sport from pastime to institution has gone on unchecked and virtually unnoticed except by a few scholars, such as Johan Huizinga, Paul Weiss, and Jessie Bernard who, together with a handful of educators such as Pierre de Coubertin, Homer Babbidge, and James Conant, foresaw the impact, in humanistic terms, of institutionalized sport on the life of humans. But no matter how eloquently these scholars have argued their point, their concerns have gone unheeded. They are, after all, idealists and antiquarians whose reasoning is unsupported by scientific information and whose outlook on life is not in step with the exploitive rhythm of the times. The public is unlikely to be concerned about the impact of institutionalized sport until there are sufficient objective data about human behavior and the complex phenomenon of sport. Until recently, knowledge about sport was in the hands of the coach and the sports buff. The one was content with pragmatic and traditional knowledge of technique; and the other, with mastery of sporting trivia. In such a sacred sphere, the scientist-scholar was as rare as the female athlete.

It is not surprising, then, that our extant knowledge of sport involvement and practices has evolved but little beyond what has been known for centuries. Whether we choose to acknowledge it, we are forced to recognize, for instance, that our knowledge of athletic training and conditioning has advanced little beyond what has been handed down to us by Galen, whose knowledge was derived from his care and observation of gladiators. Similarly, our understanding of motivation and control of the athlete by coaches seems but little advanced beyond the principles adopted by the legendary Ikos, onetime winner of the pentathlon in the 75th Olympic Games. And, finally, an understanding of spectators and their role in the athletic drama seems little better than the penetrating and perhaps scathing criticisms of either Euripedes or Diogenes.

In this last quarter of the 20th century, organized sport has permeated the social structure even more than it did in the late Roman Empire. Obviously, it is time we understood this phenomenon much more thoroughly; it is in this direction that this volume directs a significant step.

W. Robert Morford
Department of Physical Education
University of Washington

PREFACE

A symposium entitled "Contemporary Research on Youth Sports" was held at the University of Washington on March 23–24, 1977. The purpose of the conference was to provide an opportunity for researchers from the United States and Canada to exchange information regarding research projects in the area of youth sports and to discuss possible directions for future research and theory development.

The field of sport psychology is fragmented, and communication of current knowledge is an important factor in its future growth. This symposium was designed to foster such communication. It departed from previous youth sport symposia in that all presentations were data based. This volume includes papers selected from those reports.

We wish to gratefully acknowledge the financial support provided by the Safeco Insurance Company, as well as the continuing concern this organization has demonstrated for the physical and psychological well-being of children and youth. We also wish to acknowledge financial support provided by the graduate school of the University of Washington. Finally, we wish to thank the conference participants for providing a stimulating forum for the exchange of information and ideas.

Frank L. Smoll
Ronald E. Smith

I

PSYCHOLOGICAL FRONTIERS IN YOUTH SPORTS

SPORT AND THE CHILD
Conceptual and Research Perspectives

Ronald E. Smith and Frank L. Smoll

Few phenomena in contemporary society touch as many people, both vicariously and directly, as does sport. Sport has become an increasingly integral part of Western culture and must be regarded as a social institution of major import. Although children have always engaged in play, the past half century has witnessed the development of increasingly organized youth sport programs. In moving from the sandlot to the more formalized programs that now exist, youth sports have come to involve a broadening range of community participation. Estimates of the number of children involved in these programs range as high as 20 million, and the social system of youth sports has become increasingly more complex with the greater degree of involvement of parents, businessmen, and other people in the community. The expanding scope of community involvement has increased the complexity of the socialization process that always existed in children's sports. The traditional course of childhood has been markedly changed by high levels of involvement in highly structured and adult-supervised athletic programs. To an increasing degree, the psychological concomitants of involvement are coming under the scrutiny of the researcher. Indeed, the research emphasis on youth sports has become a significant trend in the emerging subdiscipline of sport psychology.

Youth sports are an important part of our daily lives. They are firmly entrenched in our social and cultural milieu. Despite this, the desirability of youth sports is a topic of controversy and bitter debate. Proponents of youth sport programs maintain that the programs provide a medium for the development of desirable psychosocial attributes such as cooperativeness, persistence, delay of gratification, achievement motivation, self-assertiveness, and coping skills. Advocates generally view youth sports as miniature life situations in which children can learn to cope with realities they will face in later life. In addition, the advocates point out, lifelong patterns of physical activity that promote health and fitness can be established in childhood through sports involvement. Critics counter by raising the possibility that excessive physical and psychological demands are placed on children. They also contend that the increasing encroachment of adults into the world of the child diminishes the value of play as a free and spontaneous outlet for expression. Some insist that youth sports are conducted primarily for the self-serving needs of parents and adult supervisors and suggest that children would benefit far more if adults simply left them alone to participate in self-organized activities (Devereux, 1976).

Unfortunately, neither proponents nor critics of youth sports have much in the way of solid scientific evidence to support their claims. There has been an abundance of opinion and pontification and a paucity of soundly designed empirical research. At present, the major substance of the subdiscipline of sport psychology consists of literature from the field of physical education and extrapolation from social psychological laboratory research. Sport psychology conferences and symposia have been characterized by presentations primarily speculative in nature; these reports draw heavily on psychological theories (e.g., psychoanalytic theory and social learning theory) to formulate hypotheses concerning effects of sport participation. There is no shortage of hypotheses, but there is a great need for soundly designed empirical tests of them. It is equally clear that few psychologists have been attracted to this potentially fertile area of human behavior. As Whiting (1976) noted:

> While there are undoubtedly within sports psychology organizations many sport-oriented people with psychological qualifications, it is doubtful if there are many psychologists with academic interests in sport. . . . national bodies like the British Psychological Society or the American Psychological Association do not have an established sub-division entitled Sports Psychology and there is little evidence that they would welcome such a development. (pp. 8–9)

It is unfortunate that so few psychologists have been attracted to the area of sport psychology, since, by virtue of their training, they are equipped to contribute to the badly needed data base. As the list of contributors to this volume attests, the research burden is presently being borne by a relatively small group of faculty in physical education and kinesiology departments who have psychological interests and training.

Future advances in sport psychology will be dependent not only on soundly designed empirical investigations, but also on the concomitant development and testing of theoretical frameworks and models that can serve as a source of testable hypotheses. In the remainder of this chapter, we hope to chart some of the directions in which psychological research in youth sports might proceed and some of the forms that it might take. Many areas of psychology are relevant to research on youth sports, including the burgeoning area of community psychology. The youth sport system provides a naturalistic laboratory that offers unique opportunities to advance knowledge about human behavior while at the same time having clear-cut applications that can contribute to human betterment.

RESEARCH APPROACHES IN YOUTH SPORTS

Of the many behavioral research approaches, several are particularly applicable to the study of youth sports. Because of the complexity of the phenomenon in question, a variety of complementary approaches will be required to provide the needed theoretical developments and body of empirical knowledge.

Descriptive Research

As noted previously, much of the current knowledge in psychology is in the form of laboratory studies in which an attempt has been made to isolate and control various aspects of the environment. Although this approach is certainly an important one in achieving understanding of behavioral determinants, we must acknowledge the fact that youth sports are carried on in a complex physical and social environment. Roger Barker (1969) pointed out that psychology has learned a great deal about human behavior under artificial and highly controlled conditions, but it knows relatively little about behavior in the natural environment, where the interplay between internal and external factors is particularly important. The ecological approach Barker used in the development of his theory of behavior settings seems to have extraordinary application to the study of youth sports. In stressing the interrelationships among psychological phenomena, social norms, and the environments in which they apply, Barker showed how an analysis of behavior settings can provide critically important information on the causes of behavior. This approach seems entirely consistent with the recent emphasis within the psychology of personality on the study of interactions between individual difference variables and situational factors (Endler & Magnusson, 1976).

Barker and Gump (1964) showed that a sandlot baseball game in which there are four players to a side is a significantly different behavior setting than one in which there are nine players to a side. In the former instance, the players enjoy special privileges such as batting more frequently, and also special burdens such as being responsible for covering a larger area of the field. To carry their analysis still further, the behavior setting of a Little League baseball game may satisfy or frustrate the different needs that arise within it. The player who performs well satisfies one set of psychological needs, parents watching in the stands may receive a different set of satisfactions, and the coach and teammates are satisfied in still other ways. The physical and psychological setting also sets important constraints on the range of behaviors deemed appropriate or even possible. Though the complexities of the behavior setting pose formidable methodological problems, the resulting epistemic yield appears to justify greater use of this approach. Methodological developments in the area of behavioral assessment are providing a technical capability with which to observe, code, and analyze sport-related behaviors in their natural settings (Rushall, 1976; Salmela, 1977; Smith, Smoll, & Hunt, 1977).

Descriptive research has the potential to provide data relevant to a number of current controversies in youth sports. For example, little league baseball critics maintain that many coaches engage in extremely high frequencies of punitive behaviors. A behavioral analysis of coaches, such as that reported by Smith, Smoll, and Curtis (this volume), can help to shed light on the frequencies with which coaches do in fact engage in certain classes of behaviors. Such data can then be related to children's reactions to their organized sport experiences. Through the use of behavioral assessment, it is also possible to identify the behavioral patterns of highly successful and, also, unsuccessful coaches. Tharp and Gallimore (1976) reported a behavioral analysis of former UCLA basketball coach John Wooden, and they use these data as a basis for recommendations for teachers.

It is our belief that much valuable knowledge can be gained by developing classification systems not only for individuals and for behaviors, but also for situations (Magnusson, 1971). Kelly (1969) pointed out that functional variations in environments result in differences in the development and control of social norms and in requirements for adaptation within those settings. By specifying the situational parameters of presumed importance, it is possible to use descriptive research for hypothesis testing. For example, one can identify behavioral differences associated with such parameters as whether parents are present and whether the team is winning.

Epidemiological research constitutes yet another form of descriptive research. The unit of analysis in epidemiology is the target population rather than the individual. Descriptive epidemiology involves the measurement of disease frequency, ideally in groups similar to each other with respect to all significant variables but one. Though this is a basically descriptive approach, it can be used for hypothesis testing by defining situational or individual parameters. For example, Bramwell, Requa, and Garrick (1972) compared the frequency and nature of high school football injuries on synthetic turf as opposed to natural turf. It is clear that many of the effects, both harmful and beneficial, of youth sport participation could be specified in greater detail through careful epidemiological studies. To date, the research that has been done in this manner has primarily concerned physical injuries. From a psychological point of view, of even greater significance would be epidemiological studies of stress reactions and other psychological responses to particular kinds of conditions. Lowe (1973) was able to specify situational factors that significantly affected physiologically measured stress responses in Little League baseball players. It is clear that this kind of epidemiological research can form the basis for recommendations designed to prevent or reduce untoward effects of sports participation.

Systems Research

The general systems approach (von Bertalanffy, 1968) to studying organizational structures also seems relevant to the study of youth sports because it is concerned with interrelationships between components within a particular system and the interrelationships of the system with related systems. Youth sports involve the extensive interplay of a variety of systems and subsystems. Although the increased involvement of adults in youth sports has increased the complexity of these systems, this development also affords the opportunity to study the functioning of an intact system having specifiable boundaries.

Because the systems approach is concerned with the dynamic relationships that exist between the components of a system, it provides a useful conceptual framework for the study of the complex patterns of social influence that are exchanged within the athletic context. The socialization forces that impinge on (and are initiated by) the child athlete do not occur in a vacuum; they interact with other socialization factors (e.g., familial and academic). Whereas a systems approach presents such severe methodological challenges that its range of application has thus far been fairly limited, its heuristic promise for the study of sport systems clearly warrants the attention of researchers. The system comprising child, coach, and parents, or that consisting of players and coach, are examples of systems that might be studied fruitfully. A first step would be the designation of the system and its subsystems, and of the indexes of change to be studied. Efforts would then focus on (a) how the system changes and the factors that cause the change and (b) on the development of a model, either mathematical or graphic, that describes the observed causal patterns. Finally, (c) the elements of the model might be manipulated to test the effect of theoretical changes. Hutcheson and Krause (1969) discussed the manner in which the systems approach might be applied to the development of optimally effective delivery and prevention programs in the area of mental health. The same strategies might be applied to the development of carefully specified youth sport experiences that are tailored to the needs of certain kinds of children coming from certain kinds of backgrounds and current environments. This ideal may never be realized, but we are certain to learn a great deal about the functioning of social systems in the process of trying.

Evaluation Research

It seems that the age of accountability is here, and increasingly greater emphasis is being placed on evaluating the effects of programs and services. A new area of *program evaluation* has emerged during the past decade, and extensive handbooks of evaluation techniques have appeared (e.g., Struening & Guttentag, 1975). In actuality, however, evaluation research and *basic research* bear great similarity to one another. The same principles of research design and hypothesis testing apply to the community as to the laboratory, and the aim of both approaches is to eliminate plausible alternatives by hypotheses that might account for the observed relationships. In both laboratory and community, methodology must be tailored to the problem to be studied and the circumstances under which the study is to be carried out. The major difference between evaluation research and basic research is not so much subject matter or methodology, but rather the purpose for which the study is done (Heller & Monahan, 1977). Whereas basic research is directed toward accretion of knowledge for its own sake, evaluation is explicitly geared toward immediate application. Typically, the questions are derived from the nature and intent of the program and are designed to provide information that decision makers can use to make more rational decisions. Applying this distinction to youth sports, the basic researcher might assess the effects of participation in a particular program to gain information on how children are affected by the specified experiences that constitute the program. The same study done for evaluation purposes would be designed to determine if the explicit goals of the program are being attained to an extent that justifies continuation of the program, as opposed to alternative experiences. The answer to this question would determine whether attempts would be made to change the program.

Empirical techniques are increasingly being employed to evaluate programs on the organizational and community level. In the area of youth sports, many of the current controversies concerning the desirability of organized and adult-supervised programs could be addressed by well-designed evaluation studies. No large-scale evaluation research has been performed on the programs of national youth sport organizations despite the fact that some of them have been in existence for nearly four decades. Those who would undertake such research, however, should not expect to be greeted with open arms. Many leaders of youth sport organizations have understandably become suspicious and hostile toward social scientists. For years, social scientists critical of such programs have been drawing negative "scientific" conclusions in the mass media in the absence of anything approximating acceptable scientific data. Overcoming the resulting resistance to evaluation may pose a greater challenge than conducting the research itself. Our own experience indicates that if a commitment is made to work with the organization to help improve its program, cooperation is far more likely to occur. In other words, the research should be construed as being in the service of the organization rather than as a challenge to it.

Given the scope and importance of youth sports, the need for program evaluation is an urgent one. Well-conducted evaluations not only can have practical benefits, but also can produce the strong scientific data base that is the goal of basic research.

Laboratory Research

To this point we have emphasized the desirability and need for research conducted in naturalistic settings. Much information in sport psychology texts consists of extrapolation from laboratory research in personality and social psychology. It is critically important to confirm the external validity of such findings by replication in naturalistic settings. The relationship between laboratory and field research is ideally a reciprocal one, with the tradeoff being the control and precision of measurement available in the laboratory versus the ecological validity of the natural behavior setting. There is a great need for this reciprocal relationship in sport psychology (as in other areas of psychology). Findings consistent under both laboratory and naturalistic conditions inspire more confidence than findings in either setting alone. In this volume, Scanlan and Passer report a successful attempt to replicate, in a field setting, relationships previously established under controlled laboratory conditions. More research of this type is needed.

We earlier emphasized the importance of theory construction in the development of a scientific discipline of sport psychology. Construction of sound theories is most likely to occur if the theory is developed and its validity assessed under both laboratory and naturalistic conditions. More than one psychological theory has had to be modified after being tested in a new setting. In this volume, for example, Roberts discusses some apparently needed alterations in Weiner's (1974) attribution theory of achievement when applied to a youth sport setting.

COMMUNITY PSYCHOLOGY AND YOUTH SPORTS

In May 1965, a conference was held in Swampscott, Massachusetts, which is widely regarded as the event that marked the birth of community psychology. The primary goal of the professionals who attended was to establish directions for the development of a community orientation, particularly within the mental health field. Community psychologists were characterized as "change agents, social systems analysts, consultants in community affairs, and students generally of the whole man in relation to all his environments" (Bennett, 1965, p. 833). Many participants maintained that community psychologists should assume an activist role and use their scientific training to generate and disseminate knowledge and to promote social change.

Though most of the participants in the Swampscott conference primarily were concerned with the development of community-based programs for the mentally ill, and although there has been a strong emphasis in this direction during the intervening years, community psychology has a much broader scope. There is general agreement that psychology ought to have increased concern for the healthy adaptation of the majority of the population, which never will require psychological treatment.

The area of youth sports appears to be an appropriate subject of attention for the community psychologist. Most youth sport programs are explicitly intended to facilitate the healthy physical and psychological development of the child. Most of the areas of research and practice discussed previously are the natural bailiwick of the community psychologist. The need for evaluation, consultation, and program development is evident in youth sports. Sport programs constitute an important community subsystem. And yet, we have searched in vain for any reference to the community psychologist's potential role as it pertains to youth sports. It is our hope that this volume, published as part of the Series in Clinical and Community Psychology, will serve to stimulate attention to the potential role community psychologists can play in the area of youth sports. In view of the importance of sport as a socialization force, the demand for knowledge regarding its psychological aspects is an urgent one indeed.

AN OVERVIEW OF THIS VOLUME

The symposium from which this volume emanated provided a unique forum for the exchange of scientific information on the status and effects of sport participation on the physical and psychosocial development of children. The 10 research reports that follow are divided into three major sections. The first section, entitled "Participatory Patterns and Characteristics of Youth Athletes," contains two reports. In the first, Vern D. Seefeldt, Thomas Gilliam, David Blievernicht, and Russell Bruce review existing evidence on physical and psychosocial traits studied in relation to youth sport participation. They then present the results of a large-scale study of the incidence and frequency of participation of more than 90,000 boys and girls in Michigan. This is the most comprehensive project that has been undertaken to study patterns of participation. The second report, by Robert M. Malina and Karan A. H. Moss, deals with age at menarche and selected family characteristics of a triracial sample of high school athletes and nonathletes. The comprehensive study includes comparisons between this sample and female athletes who competed in the 1976 Olympic Games.

The second section, "The Impact of Sports on Psychosocial Development," contains six reports. Michael D. Smith presents a study on social learning of violence by child and adolescent hockey players in Canada. Smith's analysis indicates the importance of cultural factors, including the mass media, in presenting sports violence in a favorable light and transmitting specific information on how to perform similar acts. Consideration is given to the impact of these experiences on the child's social development.

Tara K. Scanlan and Michael W. Passer describe a field study of anxiety-inducing factors in youth soccer players. Among other important findings, they discovered that children's precompetition state anxiety was related to a number of intrapersonal factors, such as trait anxiety and expectation of individual and team success, whereas postcompetition anxiety was most strongly related to several situational factors, such as the game outcome (win-loss) and the closeness of the game.

A report by Jerry R. Thomas and L. Keith Tennant deals with the way in which external rewards for athletic task performance can affect children's intrinsic motivation for participating in that task. These findings have important implications for the practice of rewarding performance with trophies, medals, and so forth.

Glyn C. Roberts presents an analysis of factors that influence the way in which children perceive the causes of winning and losing. Following an analysis of the relevance of attribution theory to children's sports, data are presented suggesting that this influential theory needs to be modified in important ways if applied to youth sports. Roberts suggests theoretical modifications that will expand the scope of the theory.

The report by Ronald E. Smith, Frank L. Smoll, and Bill Curtis presents the results of a research project dealing with the effects of coaching behaviors on child athletes. Specifically, the goals of the project are to (a) assess the relationships between specific coaching behaviors and the reactions of children to organized athletic experiences, and (b) develop and evaluate the effectiveness of a behavioral training program designed to help coaches provide a more positive athletic experience for children.

T. D. Orlick, Jane McNally, and Tom O'Hara describe a program designed to strengthen cooperative behaviors through participation in games having a cooperative, rather than competitive, structure. Their results show that modification of game structure and goals serve to increase cooperative social interactions both within and outside of physical education settings. This program represents a departure from traditional sport approaches, which serve to develop competitive tendencies in children, and shows how games can be used to increase cooperative tendencies.

Physically and mentally handicapped children have traditionally been excluded from sport participation. However, recent federal legislation has mandated the involvement of handicapped children in physical education and sport activities. The final section of the book, "Sport and the Handicapped Child," contains two studies involving handicapped children. G. Lawrence Rarick presents the findings of a study of adult reactions to the Special Olympics for mentally retarded children. The findings show how children in the Seattle and San Diego areas were introduced into the program and indicates that parents, teachers, and coaches viewed the program as having a positive effect on the participants in such areas as interest in physical activity, attitudes toward schoolwork, and acceptance by peers. Based on the findings, recommendations are presented for strengthening the program and increasing the scope of involvement for mentally handicapped children.

The second report, by John H. Lewko, describes a series of experimental studies in which attribution theory was used to analyze the socialization of physically handicapped children. The manner in which significant others (peers, teachers, coaches, and parents) react to success and failure as well as the handicapped child's own reactions to such outcomes is assumed to be of great importance. Findings from two studies showed that significant others who attributed low performance to stable factors (e.g., ability and task difficulty) had low expectancies for the child's future performance. The tendency toward making stable attributions for low performance, as well as the vague reasoning behind the type of feedback given to handicapped children, indicates the need to increase the sensitivity of significant others to the potential consequences of their perceptions of and responses to the child.

REFERENCES

Barker, R. G. Wanted: An eco-behavioral science. In E. P. Willems & H. L. Raush (Eds.), *Naturalistic viewpoints in psychological research.* New York: Holt, Rinehart, & Winston, 1969.

Barker, R. G., & Gump, P. *Big school, small school.* Stanford: Stanford University Press, 1964.

Bennett, C. C. Community psychology: Impressions of the Boston conference on the education of psychologists for community mental health. *American Psychologist,* 1965, *20,* 832–835.

Bramwell, S. T., Requa, R. K., & Garrick, J. G. High school football injuries: A pilot comparison of playing surfaces. *Medicine and Science in Sports,* 1972, *4,* 166–169.

Devereux, E. G. Backyard versus Little League baseball: Some observations on the impoverishment of children's games in contemporary America. In A. Yiannakis, T. D. McIntyre, M. J. Melnick, & D. P. Hart (Eds.), *Sport sociology: Contemporary themes.* Dubuque, Iowa: Kendall-Hunt, 1976.

Endler, N. S., & Magnusson, D. (Eds.). *Interactional psychology and personality.* Washington: Hemisphere, 1976.

Heller, K., & Monahan, J. *Psychology and community change.* Homewood, Ill.: Dorsey Press, 1977.

Hutcheson, B. R., & Krause, E. A. Systems analysis and mental health services. *Community Mental Health Journal,* 1969, *5,* 29–45.

Kelly, J. G. Naturalistic observations in contrasting social environments. In E. P. Willems & H. L. Raush (Eds.), *Naturalistic viewpoints in psychological research.* New York: Holt, Rinehart, & Winston, 1969.

Lowe, R. *Stress, arousal, and task performance of Little League baseball players.* Unpublished doctoral dissertation, University of Illinois, 1973.

Magnusson, D. An analysis of situational dimensions. *Perceptual and Motor Skills*, 1971, *32*, 851–867.

Rushall, B. S. A direction for contemporary sport psychology. *Canadian Journal of Applied Sport Sciences*, 1976, *1*, 13–21.

Salmela, J. H. *Behavioral assessment of post-performance affective reactions of Olympic gymnasts.* Paper presented at the meeting of the North American Society for the Psychology of Sport and Physical Activity, Ithaca, New York, May 1977.

Smith, R. E., Smoll, F. L., & Hunt, E. A system for the behavioral assessment of athletic coaches. *Research Quarterly*, 1977, *48*, 401–407.

Struening, E., & Guttentag, M. (Eds.). *Handbook of evaluation research* (2 vols.). Beverly Hills: Sage Publications, 1975.

Tharp, R. G., & Gallimore, R. What a coach can teach a teacher. *Psychology Today*, 1976, *9*, 75–78.

von Bertalanffy, L. *Organismic psychology and systems theory.* Worcester, Mass.: Clark University Press, 1968.

Weiner, B. *Achievement motivation and attribution theory.* Morristown, N.J.: General Learning Press, 1974.

Whiting, H. T. A. Sports psychology—State of the field. *Canadian Journal of Applied Sport Sciences*, 1976, *1*, 7–11.

II

PARTICIPATORY
PATTERNS AND
CHARACTERISTICS
OF YOUTH ATHLETES

2

SCOPE OF YOUTH SPORTS PROGRAMS IN THE STATE OF MICHIGAN

Vern D. Seefeldt, Thomas Gilliam, David Blievernicht, and Russell Bruce

A longitudinal study of youth sports programs was initiated by the State Legislature of Michigan in 1975. The study resulted from the concern of certain legislators that involvement in highly organized, agency-sponsored sports programs could be detrimental to the health of youthful participants. This concern was articulated to personnel at various institutions of higher learning, who then formed a consortium of four universities to study the problem. Faculty members from Michigan State University, Wayne State University, and Northern Michigan University met periodically during the spring and summer of 1975 for the purpose of formulating a comprehensive plan to study the involvement of Michigan's youth in a variety of sports programs. These planning sessions resulted in a written proposal to the Michigan State Legislature, requesting that the four universities be permitted to join together in a 3-year effort to study the problem. The proposal was approved in July 1975. Financial support was granted on a year-to-year basis to cover the period from July 1, 1975, to June 30, 1978.

This chapter is divided into four sections: (1) a review of the pertinent literature dealing with developmental, physiological, and psychological issues in sports for children; (2) an overview of the Michigan Youth Sports Study; (3) the procedures incorporated in the first year of the study; and (4) the results and interpretation of Phase I of this study.

REVIEW OF THE LITERATURE

The proliferation of youth sports programs in the United States is a phenomenon that is unique to the second half of the 20th century. Not only have youth sports programs emulated the previously established interscholastic programs of the public schools, but there is some evidence that agency-sponsored programs have become substitutes or replacements for school-sponsored athletic events. This occurrence presents a paradox concerning the values that parents hold for physical activity. On the one hand, there has been a steady decline in the support for programs of physical education at the elementary school level, whereas agency-sponsored athletic programs have increased in scope and in the numbers of participants who are enrolled in each sport.

The transfer of athletic programs from the exclusive domain of the public schools to agencies with state or national affiliations has raised a number of controversial issues. In lieu of the personalized local or regional control of sports programs, regulations are now commonly formulated and programs are being administered by impersonal governing bodies. Coaching, officiating, and administrative positions are filled by volunteers, thus reducing the amount of control that can be exercised concerning the qualifications of those who are primarily responsible for conducting the programs. Objectives of the programs are sometimes at odds with those commonly stated by educational institutions. These marked departures from commonly accepted attitudes surrounding athletic competition have raised the question, "What is the influence of physical activity on the youthful participant?" The following sections review the scientific literature pertaining to influences of physical activity on the growth and development, physiological function, and psychological development of children.

Physical Growth and Biological Maturation

The beneficial effects of physical activity on human growth and development have been a matter of scientific record for decades. Excellent reviews of this topic by Steinhaus (1933), Espenschade (1960), Malina (1969), and Rarick (1973) underscore the fact that bones, muscles, and nervous tissues must be stimulated through activity to maintain their integrity. Research evidence provides little information, however, concerning the kinds and amounts of activity that are essential for normal growth during the periods of infancy, childhood, and adolescence. Aside from a general lack of information on growth per se, the literature provides two perplexing problems for those who are interested in the relationship between activity and the growth of children and youths: (1) Most of the longitudinal studies were conducted using lower forms of life as subjects. It is evident that generalizations to human growth cannot be made from such experiments. (2)

Reports on human beings are essentially cross-sectional or of short duration. Subjects in the latter situations have generally come from highly specialized groups, usually involving athletes from team sports. Thus, it is evident that there is an insufficient body of information from which to draw valid conclusions concerning the beneficial or detrimental effects of stressful activity on the growing human organism.

This review includes only those reports that pertain to human growth and development as they relate to stressful competitive physical activity. Rarick (1973) suggested that there are three categories into which the hazards of activity can be conveniently grouped. They are as follows:

(1) The physical demands and psychological stresses of highly competitive athletics may be great enough to affect adversely growth and development; (2) repeated stress resulting from a particular movement peculiar to a sport may in some instances be sufficiently great to introduce trauma to a body part, thus impairing normal growth; and (3) a blow or forceful impact may be sufficiently great to be fatal or to do permanent damage to a growing structure. (p. 372)

There is fragmentary evidence that activity programs of modest and high intensity do not impair growth and may even be influencial in its acceleration. Ekblom (1969) reported that young people who participated in a program of long-distance running for a 32-month period (between the chronological ages of 11 and 14 years) had greater increments in height and weight during this period than had their inactive counterparts who served as a control group. Parizkova (1968) concluded that a physical-training program was responsible for increased shoulder width, decreased hip width and lower levels of adipose tissue in a group of boys studied between the ages of 11 and 15 years. Of four groups, categorized according to activity level, only those in the group with high-activity routines showed significant differences in body structure and shape from the other groups. She noted that no significant differences were noted between any of the groups in height, weight, and biological maturity. Theoretically, the contractile force of the muscles in the lower extremities caused the development of narrower pelves in the most active group of boys.

The most complete data available in published form on the influence of strenuous activity on physical growth were reported by Astrand, Engstrom, Eriksson, Karlberg, Nylander, Saltin, and Thoren (1963). In an investigation involving 30 girl swimmers, they noted that the growth of the girls during the training period was normal for most of them and accelerated in others. That no detrimental influence of stressful activity on growth was noted, however, may be attributable to the activity chosen for investigation. Swimming does not involve direct weight bearing on the long bones and hence would be less likely to interfere with long bone growth than would activities such as running.

Evidence from young people involved in competitive athletics suggests that the intensive regimens of some sports impair the physical growth of their participants. Rowe (1933) and Fait (1951) reported that intensive interscholastic programs of 6 months' duration had a curtailing effect on the growth in height of young athletes. Shuck (1962) reported a differential effect of athletics on growth of seventh-, eighth-, and ninth-grade boys, depending on the length of the season. Boys who played a 12-game schedule of basketball did not differ in standing height from their nonparticipating peers, but those who completed a 17-game season had a reduction in incremental growth over that period of time.

Controversial results were obtained from two reports pertaining to the influence of wrestling on physical growth. Practices in wrestling are of particular interest for two reasons: (1) the activity is regarded as unusually strenuous, and (2) performers are frequently asked to refrain from their normal caloric intake. Thus, young wrestlers may be subjected to two stressors that influence growth. K. C. Clarke (1974) reported that the wrestlers in his study made no significant gains in standing height during the course of a season; and Tipton and Tcheng's (1970) group of high school wrestlers showed a mean gain in standing height of only 1.5 cm over a 6-month period. These data are of particular interest when one considers that the annual mean gain in standing height for boys between the ages of 13 and 17 years is 7.0 cm, with many showing increments of 10-12 cm during the year of peak height velocity.

The rate of biological maturation in youthful performers has been the subject of numerous reports. Hale (1956) noted that 45% of the boys who participated in the 1955 Little League World Series were postpubescent in terms of secondary sex characteristics. Krogman (1959) concluded that the Little League baseball players in his study were successful because of their advanced biological ages. Similarly, Rochelle, Kelliher, and Thornton (1961) and Cumming, Garand, and Borysky (1972) found that skeletal age was a better predictor of success in football and track, respectively, than other measures of motor performance or growth. However, the pertinent question for this review involves the influence of physical activity on the rate of maturation. Do physically mature children gravitate toward competitive sports situations, or does participation in stressful activities hasten the maturational process? A partial answer to the question was provided by Adams (1965, 1966), who studied the structure of the throwing arms and shoulders in Little League baseball players. In 76 of 80 pitchers he noted varying degrees of epiphysitis, osteochondritis, and accelerated growth. These conditions were not present in the nonthrowing arms of pitchers, nor were they present in 41 of the 47 nonpitchers in the study. Evidently, the continued stress of a repetive movement can cause structural and functional changes that adversely affect young athletes.

A major concern of advisory committees to youth sports programs has been the incidence and severity of injuries sustained during the course of practices and participation. Perhaps the most vulnerable part of the growing body to the stresses of activity are the joints of the elbow, shoulder, knee, and ankle. Numerous medical authorities have suggested that the epiphyses of young athletes are the most susceptible of all tissues to injury, because the ligaments and fibrous capsules that surround the joints are more resistant than the epiphyses to the twisting and shearing forces to which they are subjected (Krogman, 1959; Larson, R. L., & McMahan, 1966; Sigmond, 1960). However, medical records and statistics on injury incidence provided by Little League officials suggest that the problem is not as great as opponents of youth sports programs have implied. R. L. Larson and McMahan (1966) noted that of 1,338 athletic injuries, treated by four orthopedists over a 10-year period, only 20% occurred in athletes who were 14 years and under. Of these only 1.7% involved the epiphyses. Hale (1961) reported that of over 5 million Little League baseball players, only 2% received injuries that required medical attention. Of these, 19% were fractures and 18% were sprains. None of the other categories involved injuries to the joints of the long bones.

Two reports suggest that the incidence of athletic injuries may be related to specific sports and the conditions under which the sports are conducted. Adams' (1965) report of the trauma inflicted on the elbows and shoulders of young baseball players underscores the vulnerability of the epiphyseal areas to injury when stresses are of a repetitive nature. The 11.2% incidence of injuries sustained by junior high school football players, as reported by Emerson (1964), raises some questions concerning the selection of sports for competitive purposes and the conditions under which certain programs are conducted.

In summary, a review of the literature pertaining to the influence of physical activity on growth reveals that young athletes are unlikely to suffer growth retardation as a result of participation in competitive athletics. Exceptions to this general statement include situations in which athletes are (a) repeatedly stressed to exhaustion, (b) required to refrain from their normal caloric intake, and (c) involved in stressful repetitive patterns of movement. Injuries to the epiphyses occur infrequently and generally can be treated with little likelihood of permanent damage. The incidence and severity of injuries is directly related to the conditions under which youth sports programs are conducted.

Physiological Effects

The physiological effects of physical training on young children have been studied by several investigators. The physiological measure that is regarded as most indicative of endurance (aerobic) capacity is maximum oxygen consumption (max $\dot{V}O_2$). In physiological terms, this is defined as the maximum rate of oxygen utilization during intense work. Max $\dot{V}O_2$ is measured in liters of oxygen per minute (l/min). It appears that the range for max $\dot{V}O_2$ in normal active children is 0.80 to 2.75 l/min. Another physiological effect studied is cardiac output ($\dot{Q}$), which is expressed in terms of liters of blood per minute. This is defined as the volume of blood pumped by the heart per minute, usually 4–15 l/min for healthy, active children. Static dimensions, such as size of the heart (volume), blood hemoglobin (Hb) concentration, and lung volume, also have been used to measure physiological efficiency.

The use of muscle biopsies has proven useful in determining the effects of training on muscle tissue. By studying the biochemical or histochemical makeup of a muscle, one can determine if the muscle has increased its potential to perform aerobically or anaerobically. Anaerobic (glycolytic) work is high-intensity, short-duration activity, such as the 100-yard dash, swinging a golf club, or serving a tennis ball. Aerobic (oxidative) work is low-intensity, long-duration activity, such as the 1-mile run or cross-country skiing. Enzymes such as succinic dehydrogenase (SDH) and reduced diphosphopyridine and nucleotide-diaphorase (DPNH-diaphorase) are indicative of oxidative potential. Conversely, phosphofructose kinase (PFK), a rate-limiting step in glycolytic activity, and lactate concentrations are measures of anaerobic potential.

Maximum oxygen consumption, cardiac output, and related measures

Several studies reported increases in maximum oxygen consumption for boys and girls 11–15 years of age through intensive training programs (Astrand et al., 1963; Ekblom, 1969; Eriksson, 1972). Changes from 1.93 l/min to 2.05 l/min in max $\dot{V}O_2$ were found for 11–13-year-old boys when compared with a control group. This increase, in relative terms, was similar to that achieved by adults with corresponding training. In another study, Eriksson, Gollnick, and Saltin (1973) reported max $\dot{V}O_2$ increases in eight boys who were between 11–13 years of age, following 4 months of training. In a similar study by Ekblom (1969), six 11-year-old boys increased their max $\dot{V}O_2$ by .43 l/min following a 6-month training program. No changes were reported for the control group. When five of the six boys continued to train for an additional 26 months, a mean increase of 1.26 l/min was reported for their max $\dot{V}O_2$, as compared with 0.55 l/min for the control group. The increase of max $\dot{V}O_2$ in the training group was greater than expected on the basis of age-dependent increases for certain anthropometric measures (Ekblom, 1969). This was not true for the control group.

Most studies showing increases in max $\dot{V}O_2$ in children due to training have involved children who were 11 years or older. Will similar increases, as a result of training, occur in younger children? Schmucker and Hollman (1974) studied the effects of training on children as young as 6 years of age. They reported that changes in max $\dot{V}O_2$, other than those related to normal growth and development, could not be expected until the age of 12 years. However,

Brown, Harrower, and Deeter (1972) reported increases in max $\dot{V}O_2$ in two 8-9-year-old girls following 6 weeks of training, with a leveling off occurring between 6 and 12 weeks. Admittedly, a sample size of two makes it difficult to draw valid conclusions, but the data may provide some insight as to what might be expected under similar conditions with a larger sample. It does appear, however, that max $\dot{V}O_2$ can be increased as a result of training in boys and girls older than 11 years of age. The effect of training on max $\dot{V}O_2$ in children younger than 11 years of age requires additional study.

Maximum cardiac output (max $\dot{Q}$), and heart volume were reported to increase in children 11-14 years of age. Eriksson (1972) reported a 17% increase in max $\dot{Q}$ (from 12.5 l/min to 14.6 l/min) as the result of a 16-week training program. Heart volume when corrected for growth did not change. Ekblom (1969), however, showed a 43% increase in heart volume following a 6-month training program, as compared with a 26% increase for a control group. In the opinion of authors, these inconsistent results were due to differences in the duration of the studies.

Increases in the maximum oxygen uptake have been attributed to increases in cardiac output. The stroke volume of the heart was increased significantly in boys 11-13 years of age (Eriksson, 1972). A factor in this increase may have been the increase in total blood volume and total hemoglobin observed as a result of training (Astrand, 1976; Astrand et al., 1963). When corrected for body size, posttraining stroke volume was found to be comparable with that of sedentary adults (Eriksson, 1972). Because the arteriovenous difference and the relative hemoglobin are not changed by training, the increase in stroke volume appears to be the determining factor in the increases found in cardiac output as the result of training.

Fiber composition and enzyme activity
in skeletal muscle

From results of earlier studies, it appears that local adaptations occur in the skeletal muscle of boys 11-15 years of age as a result of training (Eriksson et al., 1973). Most changes are similar to those reported for adults, but some differences are specific to boys of this age. A search of the literature revealed that no data on fiber composition and enzyme activity are available on boys under the age of 11 years or for girls of any age.

Biopsies of the vastus lateralis in five 11-year-old boys revealed a muscle composition of 55% slow-twitch and 45% fast-twitch fibers before training, with no significant change following 6 weeks of training on the bicycle ergometer (Eriksson, Gollnick, & Saltin, 1974). Changes in the oxidative and glycolytic potential of children's muscle fibers, however, were reported by Eriksson et al. (1973). Succinic dehydrogenase (SDH) activity was reported at 5.4 mol/g · min before training and was increased to 7.0 mol/g · min following training (Eriksson et al., 1973). It should be noted that the SKH activity found in boys was greater than that in most sedentary adults.

Reduced diphosphopyridine nucleotide-diaphorase (DPNH-diaphorase) staining, which is indicative of oxidative capacity and mitochrondrial density, also was more pronounced following the training period. Both SDH activity and DPNH-diaphorase staining are indicators of aerobic potential. Thus, it appears that the training program had a positive effect on the aerobic capacity of 11–13-year-old boys.

The phosphofructose kinase (PFK) activity of children was reported to be 40%–50% of that usually found in adults (Eriksson, 1972). Also, when compared with adults, children have lower muscle lactate concentrations and oxygen deficits (Eriksson, 1972). These data help explain why children have a relatively low anaerobic capability. Training has a positive effect on these variables, however, in that a 75%–80% increase in PFK activity and significant increases in muscle lactate concentration and oxygen deficit were reported (Eriksson, 1972). Even after training, the PFK activity of children was still less than that of adults. Training also brought about increases in the resting levels of the high-energy compounds of adenosine triphosphate (ATP) and creatine phosphate (CP).

Other physiological considerations

It has been hypothesized that physically active prepubertal children will have greater physiological upper limits (i.e., max $\dot{V}O_2$) as adults because of their involvement in strenuous activity programs during their growing years (Ekblom, 1969). The rationale for this hypothesis is based on some indications that growth hormone plays an important role in hypertrophy of the heart and other organs after exercise (Beznak, 1960). During growth and physical activity, there is an elevated concentration of growth hormone in the blood. Thus, it is likely that the rate of growth can be accelerated by physical training during puberty, when the individual is sensitive to the action of growth hormone. It is felt that as a result of exercise, static dimensions such as lung volume, heart volume, and height will increase more than expected. These resultant changes would have a positive effect on the overall development of the physiological upper limits. Eriksson (1972) reported an accelerated rate of increase in body height with age for children involved in training programs when compared with children who were inactive. Further research in this area is needed to clarify the relationship between activity, growth, and functional capacity in young performers.

There is abundant research evidence to suggest that physical activity is essential for the harmonious development of children. Will strenuous physical training have any deleterious effects on the growing child? One longitudinal study investigated the effects of intense physical training on static dimensions (i.e., heart and lung volume) of 30 top girl swimmers ages 12–16 years (Astrand et al., 1963). Positive changes were reported in the oxygen transport system. That is, not only did max $\dot{V}O_2$ increase, but vital capacity, total Hb and heart volume also increased. From the data reported, there was no indication that hard physical training had caused any negative effects on the growth of the organs involved in the oxygen transport system. The authors noted, however, that any one of the preceding measures taken by itself could be construed as abnormal development (i.e., an enlarged heart). The 30 young girl swimmers were studied for a total of 10 years. By the end of the investigation, all girls had stopped their regular training and had adopted a sedentary lifestyle. Due to this inactivity, the girls showed a pronounced decrease in their aerobic power (29%); but the dimensions of the lungs and heart were relatively unchanged.

Other studies also reported larger heart volumes in retired top athletes who formerly participated in endurance type sports (Holmgren & Strandell, 1959; Saltin & Grimby, 1968). Thus, at present, it appears that no deleterious effects of strenuous activity have been demonstrated on certain static dimensions for adults who participated in athletic competition at younger ages.

In summary, physical training, beginning as early as 10 years of age for girls and boys, may enhance static dimensions and functional capacities. Occasional negative results were reported from high-stress programs. Cardiovascular function was enhanced consistently. Mild to moderate physical training during childhood was not found to produce detrimental structural or functional effects during adulthood, but a paucity of literature exists concerning the effects of intense physical training on children. More research is needed to substantiate findings of earlier studies, especially on children younger than 10 years of age. Additionally, more research is needed to assess the beneficial and detrimental effects of early physical training on growth and development and to determine whether there is a differential association between stressful activity programs during childhood and functional capacity in adulthood.

Psychosocial Effects

Physical activities of a competitive nature have long been regarded as an effective medium for psychosocial development. This belief becomes readily apparent as one examines the testimony of parents, physical educators, coaches, and administrators concerning the potential value of competitive sports. Among the psychosocial values espoused by proponents of competitive sports are the development of character, social adjustment, desirable personality traits, emotional control, positive attitudes, sportsmanship, leadership, consideration for others, responsibility, cooperation, self-discipline, self-confidence, initiative, courage, loyalty, and self-expression (Hale, 1959; Larson, D. L., Spreitzer, & Snyder, 1976; Larson, R. L., & McMahan, 1966).

There are few who would dispute the potential contribution of athletic competition to the psychosocial development of individuals. There is considerable disagreement about the *effectiveness* of participation in competitive situations in promoting such development. In addition, there is a lack of consensus concerning the *time* and *conditions* under which age group athletics should be introduced into the lives of growing boys and girls. Are competitive sports wholesome for children of elementary school age? If not, at what age or developmental level are they appropriate? Do sports programs for children produce the outcomes claimed by their proponents? The purpose of this section is to review the evidence concerning the psychological and social effects of athletic competition on children and youth.

Interest in the influence of competitive sports on the growth and development of youth has been commensurate with the expansion of program offerings by private agencies. Extensive reviews of the literature, both scientific and popular, were conducted by Hale (1959), Dowell (1971), Rarick (1973), and Burke and Kleiber (1976). An examination of these reviews and other available literature reveals that little systematic study has been undertaken to determine the psychological and emotional impacts of competitive youth sports on its participants. In addition, virtually no investigations have considered the psychological effects on those who wished to participate, but were excluded from activity programs for various reasons.

Several criticisms leveled against competitive sports programs are related to the psychological and social development of children. It is argued that there is too much emphasis on winning in these programs, that distorted value systems are fostered, that inadequate adult leadership results in undue pressure and emotional strain on the children, that little instruction in skills takes place, that early specialization is encouraged, and that the operation of a selective process inevitably results in the exclusion of children from these programs (Burke & Kleiber, 1976; Dowell, 1971; Mackler, 1976; McCarthy, 1963).

Some experimental evidence suggests that excessive emphasis on winning can result in unhealthy competitive behavior. In an extended investigation known as the Robbers Cave experiment, Sherif (1956) demonstrated that adult-imposed competition among normal 11-year-old boys resulted in mistrust and interpersonal hostility within the peer group of participants.

Attempts to determine the emotional impact of competitive sports on children have been thwarted by the lack of precise evaluative instruments. Consequently, investigators have resorted to questionnaires for global responses, or to specific instruments that yield limited information. Hanson (1967) and Skubic (1955) used the latter approach and attempted to measure the physiological basis of emotion in Little League participants through the use of telemetered heart rates and galvanic skin responses, respectively. Hanson found extreme stress responses were of short duration, seldom lasting more than a few minutes. Skubic concluded that the emotional responses produced by participation in Little League baseball were of no greater magnitude than those resulting from competition in physical education games. Rarick (1973) cited a report indicating that 97% of 1,300 physician-fathers whose sons were Little League players did not consider the emotional aspects of playing detrimental to the health of their sons. On the other hand, Johnson (1956) found that excessive motivation can produce nausea in some boys during severe physiological stress. In addition, Skubic (1956) determined that one-third of the parents surveyed in her study indicated that their sons were too excited after winning or too depressed after losing a league game to eat a normal meal. In some instances, this excitement was of sufficient duration to interfere with the ability of the boys to sleep at their usual bedtime. Hale (1959) reported a study by Vovas in which the emotional responses of junior high boys were tested in selected team sports. It was found that basketball elicited the greatest emotional responses, followed by football and then baseball. It was not indicated whether these responses were of sufficient magnitude or duration to be detrimental. Thus, current evidence does not permit the formation of definite conclusions concerning the emotional impact of competitive youth sports on those who participate in them.

There is ample evidence to suggest that boys who participate in competitive sports enjoy greater social status and demonstrate more favorable personal qualities than do their nonparticipating peers. Teachers asked to rate players of Little League and Middle League teams considered them to be more physically skilled, better academically oriented, and more emotionally adjusted than boys not participating on the teams. Using a sociometric technique with seventh-, eighth-, and ninth-grade boys, McCraw and Tolbert (1953) obtained a moderately high relationship between the athletic ability of the boys and their sociometric status. H. H. Clarke (1968, 1973) also reported that successful elementary school athletes enjoyed greater peer status than did substitutes on teams or boys with no interscholastic experience. Seymour (1956) found that the Little League participants in his study enjoyed greater social acceptance than did the nonparticipants.

Results from numerous investigations demonstrate that differences exist among the personality traits of athletes and nonathletes. Slusher (1964) administered the Minnesota Multiphasic Personality Inventory (MMPI) to selected groups of high school athletes (baseball, basketball, football, swimming, and wrestling) and nonathletes. Each athletic group scored significantly lower on the femininity scale and in intelligence when compared with a nonathletic group. Except for the swimmers, however, the athletes were significantly higher in hypochondriasis than the nonathletes. The Little League boys investigated by Seymour (1956) were significantly superior to nonparticipants in leadership qualities. Similar results were obtained by Salz with boys and by Lareau with girls, as reported by Hale (1959). Salz found boys involved in competitive athletics to be superior to nonparticipants in the traits of cooperation, friendliness, integrity, leadership, and critical thinking. The eighth- and ninth-grade female athletes in Lareau's study were more popular and displayed higher leadership qualities than the nonathletes. Schendel (1965), who studied the personality traits of ninth- and 12th-grade males, determined that the athletes in these grades possess more desirable personal-social characteristics than nonparticipants from the same grades. In a review of 25 studies, Cooper (1969) characterized athletes as being more outgoing, self-confident, and socially adjusted than nonathletes. There is an inherent danger in drawing conclusions from the results of comparative studies such as those just described. Although the results reported in the literature generally ascribe favorable attributes to those who participate in competitive athletics, care must be taken not to interpret the outcomes as reflecting causal relationships. It is entirely possible that a selection process operates within competitive sports to attract people with certain personality characteristics.

Evidence that competitive youth sports produce early specialization in those who participate is inconclusive. In the study by Salz mentioned previously, boys with competitive athletic experience displayed broader interests in academic subjects, home arts, and in active and quiet play. The athletic girls in Lareau's study were more active in clubs and organizations than were their nonathletic peers. On the other hand, 81 of 97 Little League and Middle League players in Skubic's (1956) study reported that at least one-half of their leisure time was spent on baseball.

Concern for the type of leadership provided in agency-sponsored competitive programs is growing. The first National Youth Sports Directors' Conference was held in Chicago, Illinois, in November 1975. A major concern of the conferees focused on the characteristics of those children who engage in youth sports and the psychological effect of sports participation on their lives. In addition, the effects of coaching behaviors on child participants is being systematically investigated in Washington (see Smith, Smoll, & Curtis, this volume). There is general agreement that the quality of leadership provided to the youth in these programs is the key to their success or failure as vehicles for wholesome psychological growth and development.

OVERVIEW OF THE MICHIGAN YOUTH SPORTS STUDY

The study of competitive athletics for children in the state of Michigan was designed to provide comprehensive and detailed information on a variety of sports, across 13 age groups. This was accomplished by dividing the objectives into three phases, each dependent on the information that was obtained in the previous year. The general objectives of the three phases were as follows:

Phase I: To determine the scope of youth sports programs available and the degree of children's involvement in them. Activities of interest included those played during recreational or free-play periods, intramural and interscholastic offerings, and those sponsored by agencies other than the schools. The sample for Phase I consisted of 109,625 students between the ages of 5 and 17 years, randomly selected to represent the state of

Michigan by geographical area, population density, race, sex, school type, and community type. The data collection for Phase I was completed in June 1976.

Phase II: To be completed by June 30, 1977, is an in-depth analysis of agency-sponsored sports programs as viewed by participants, nonpartici-pants, parents, coaches, officials, and league administrators. The sample for Phase II consisted of 7,151 participants and 2,600 nonparticipants between the ages of 6 and 18 years and an equal number of parents. The sample of coaches and officials is comprised of 500 individuals in each category, and the sample of administrators numbers 100. Phase II will provide information on training procedures, coaching practices, extent and severity of injuries, and opinions concerning the psychosocial ramifica-tions of youth sports programs.

Phase III: Beginning on July 1, 1977, designed to implement the recommen-dations that resulted from Phases I and II. Although it is premature to state the specific content of those recommendations, our present information suggests that they will address the topics of developmental abilities of young athletes, desirable training practices, coaching techniques, prevention and treatment of injuries, team selection, and public relations in the community. These recommendations will be accompanied by materials that are accessible to volunteer coaches through workshops, classes, and clinics. The dissemination of information will take place in communities throughout the state. Classes in adult education and university extension services will be used to carry the message to those involved with youth sport programs.

The absence of available data on Michigan's youth sports programs from which to generate hypotheses had a significant influence on the 3-year research design. The need for basic data indicated that the initial years would be devoted to a descriptive account of current status.

Direction for the first 2 years of study was provided by the following questions:

1. What types of competitive athletic programs are available to Michigan's boys and girls?
2. How frequent is the participation, and what numbers of girls and boys participate in these programs?
3. What criteria do programs use to select their performers (age, sex, skill level)? Are there various teams by skill-ability levels at various ages?
4. Who sponsors the various competitive athletic programs?
5. Who supports the various leagues and private contests?
6. Who are the sponsors, promoters, coaches, and officials that control these competitive activities?

7. What are the qualifications of the coaches and officials in the areas of psychology, physiology, growth and development, and first aid procedures?
8. What procedures are followed in training and playing during the course of the season?
9. What is the nature and severity of the physical injuries that are incurred as a direct involvement with the sport or activity?
10. What are the opinions and attitudes of the athlete participants, parents, officials, and administrators regarding the beneficial and detrimental effects of athletic competition for various age groups?
11. What effect does competitive athletics have on the family as a social unit? As an economic unit?
12. In what recreational activities does the family engage, in addition to their involvement in age-group competition?
13. What is the retention and dropout rate of the various sports programs as the competitors advance in age or as the intensity of competition increases?

The following sections present an account of the first phase of the Youth Sports Study.

PHASE I METHOD

Construction of the Survey Instrument

Although the charge to the Universities Study Committee focused on agency-sponsored sports, it was apparent to the committee members that a more comprehensive attempt to study sports participation could be made with little additional expenditure of effort in the procurement of the raw data. Therefore, the Phase I questionnaire requested the respondents to indicate their frequency of involvement in four activity areas: (a) recreational or free play, (b) intramural activities, (c) interscholastic sports, and (d) agency-sponsored sports. The following are descriptions of each of these activity areas as they appeared on the questionnaries:

1. Free-play activities are sports often played on a recreational basis. This means that there are no official teams, organized leagues, or tournaments. These activities could be played in backyards, in the neighborhood, at the local playground, in a YMCA building, on the beach, and other similar places. Recreational play may take place alone, with friends, or with parents. It *does not* include school-sponsored sport programs or community-sponsored competitive programs such as Babe Ruth Baseball.
2. Intramural activities include all school-sponsored sports of a competitive or recreational nature that *do not* involve competition with other schools.

Examples include flag football competition between the homerooms of your school, or a special interest group such as gymnastics that meets on a regular basis. Activities played during physical education classes and unsupervised play periods *are not* intramural activities.

3. Interscholastic activities are those sports involving competition between teams from different schools. An example is the football team of your school playing the football team from another school.

4. Agency-sponsored activities involve competition between individuals, teams, clubs, or groups that *are not* sponsored by the school. Contests are played according to an approved set of rules under the supervision of officials, such as referees, umpires, timers, and judges. Often, these sport clubs or teams are organized into leagues with a specified schedule of games to be played. Examples of agency-sponsored sport programs are Little League baseball and A.A.U. swimming. Also included are community-sponsored sport events such as golf and tennis tournaments.

The respondents indicated their frequency of participation in sports listed for the activity areas ("never," if they did not play the sport during the past 12 months; "sometimes," if they played the sport one to three times during the past 12 months; "often," if they played the sport four times or more during the past 12 months). Provisions were made for respondents to add to the list of sports in each activity area, but the response was small and the suggestions so diffuse that no additions to the list were necessary on the basis of the statewide return.

The Phase I questionnaire evolved as a result of extensive pilot testing in six school districts that were not included in the sample. Various methods of administration were attempted, involving team members, parents, and teachers on an individual, small-group, or classroom basis. Revisions were made to reduce the length of administrative time, clarify directions, reduce the ambiguity of questions, increase the reliability of responses, and change the order of questions. To conform to the principle that response time was not to exceed 15 min for students, a detailed set of instructions was prepared for teachers, with the view that familiarity with the questionnaire would facilitate their administration of it. Because the reading rate of children below the sixth grade did not allow them to complete the questionnaire in the 15-min time span, the questionnaires for children in the kindergarten through fifth-grade levels were completed within the home by their parents. Students in grades 6 through 11 completed the questionnaires in their schools.

Sampling Procedures

The selection of a sample to represent the state of Michigan posed a formidable problem. No prototypes were available to guide the committee in its selection of sports to be included, percent return to be expected, or feasibility of conducting the study within the school setting. The sampling procedure is described in detail.

The state of Michigan is divided into 582 public school districts. For the purposes of this study, each private school was considered to be a geographic part of the public school district within which it is located. A total of 2,313,477 students were enrolled in Michigan's public and private schools during the 1974-1975 academic year as determined from the Michigan Department of Education and the Michigan Education Directory and Buyer's Guide, 1974-1975. This figure was slightly lower than the actual enrollment because data were not available for certain private schools. The actual number of students unaccounted for by this reference was estimated to be quite small and did not affect the sampling procedures. Although the total number of students (2,313,477) included kindergarten through 12th graders (K-12), it should be noted that the Youth Sports Study sample was comprised of children from kindergarten through 11th grades. Since the state enrollment figures combined grades 10, 11, and 12 as one value, the sum of grades kindergarten through 12th grades was used as the basis for determining the sample size. Thus, the sample drawn for the Youth Sports Study was presumably greater than a 5% representation of the school-aged children in Michigan during the 1974-1975 academic year.

A sample of .1% of all school-age children in Michigan was calculated to be statistically necessary and sufficient for the purposes of the Youth Sports Study. This small sample, however, raised the possibility that not all sports would be adequately represented, due to the small enrollment in some of them. Thus, the statewide sample size was arbitrarily increased. Practical considerations concerning time, money, personnel, and data analysis limited the study to a 5% sample of the school population (approximately 115,200 students). In effect, this sample size was determined to be both adequate and feasible for Phase I of the study.

The state of Michigan was divided into 10 regions according to geographic location and population density. Figure 1 identifies these regions, the school population, and the percent of the total population within each region.

Since the primary purpose of the study was to investigate agency sponsored sports for ages 5-17, it was determined that only grades K-11 would be included in the sample. Using these age limitations, two classrooms per grade level yielded a basic sample unit of 24 classrooms. With approximately 24 students per classroom, each basic sample unit represented 576 children (24 children X 24 classrooms). Since the total sample was to consist of 115,200 children, approximately 200 basic units were required (115,200/576 = 200) to reach the desired 5% representative sample. The allocation of basic sample units to geographic regions is shown in the first five columns of Table 1. Note that 201 units were actually formed, to achieve proportional representation across all regions.

School districts within each region were ordered by size from the largest

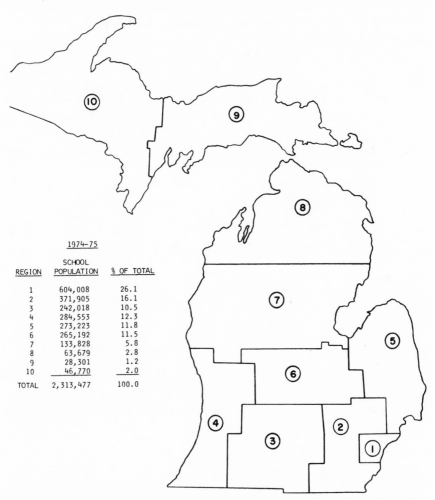

FIGURE 1 Regions, school populations, and percentage of total population in each region.

to the smallest. Within each region, the districts were grouped by approximate multiples of 11,570 students. This figure represents the approximate number of students from which each basic unit would be drawn (2,313,477/200 = 11,570). The following arbitrary decisions were made, to reduce the number of school districts to a reasonable number for study: (a) School districts from regions 1-7 (i.e., regions having a total school population greater than 100,000) would be grouped so as to permit the assignment of a minimum of *two* basic sample units to each district selected, and (b) school districts from regions 8-10 (i.e., regions having total school populations of less than 100,000) would be grouped so as to permit the assignment of a minimum of *one* basic sample unit to each district selected.

TABLE 1 Allocation of basic sample units by school population, according to region

Region	School population	% of total	% X 200 units	Assigned no. of units	No. of districts used
1	604,008	26.1	52.2	52	13
2	371,905	16.1	32.2	32	16
3	242,018	10.5	21.0	21	10
4	284,553	12.3	24.6	25	11
5	273,223	11.8	23.6	24	11
6	265,192	11.5	23.0	23	10
7	133,828	5.8	11.6	12	6
8	63,679	2.8	5.6	6	6
9	28,301	1.2	2.4	2	2
10	46,770	2.0	4.0	4	4
Total	2,313,477	100.1	200.2	201	89

It was determined that one or more school districts might form a group, and therefore, basic sample units were assigned to groups as follows:

Groups from regions 1-7 with combined populations of	Groups from regions 8-10 with combined populations of	No. of basic units
—	11,570	1
23,140		2
34,710		3
46,280		4
etc.		etc.

Whenever it was necessary to combine two or more school districts to achieve a student population with multiples of 11,570, one district was selected randomly from the group as the district to be included in the Youth Sports Study. A total of 89 school districts was selected for study by this procedure (Table 1).

A procedure was outlined for the replacement of a school district that declined to participate in the study. This procedure involved choosing a substitute district from the same geographic region as the district that was selected originally. The district with a student population most nearly equal to that of the original district was designated as a potential replacement. Of the originally selected districts, nine declined an invitation to become involved with the study and were therefore replaced in the manner described previously.

The selection of representative schools within each district was done on a subjective basis in cooperation with the superintendent or a designated representative. Schools were selected to reflect the matriculation of a particular group of students from elementary school to high school and to be representative of the district according to the following criteria: (a) socioeconomic levels, (b) ethnic groups, and (c) geographical areas within the district. The number of classrooms needed per grade per school was dependent on the number of basic units assigned to a district. For example, a two-unit district would need four classrooms per grade. Therefore, a common breakdown of a two-unit district, including schools and classrooms per grade, was as follows: (a) one senior high school—four classrooms per grade, (b) two junior high schools—two classrooms per grade per school, and (c) four elementary schools—one classroom per grade per school. The questionnaires were distributed to the selected schools by the superintendent or a designee. The principals of selected schools then arbitrarily selected classrooms that were representative of each grade (i.e., freshman English or junior history) for participation in the study.

Approximately 7% of the total sample units were designated for private schools (14 units). These private schools were chosen on the basis of geographical location and population density. The procedures for disseminating the questionnaires to the private schools were the same as previously described for the public school districts.

Administration of the Questionnaires

Superintendents of school districts were contacted by telephone to arrange a meeting within their districts for the purpose of distributing the questionnaires and selecting the participating schools. Steps were taken to ensure that the appropriate numbers of questionnaires were packaged and labeled by grade before the initial on-site visit.

The study team met with the superintendent or the designated representative to explain the purpose of the study and the objectives of Phase I. Each superintendent was informed of the school district's role in obtaining data for the study. The procedures for administration of the K-5 (parent-completed) and 6-12 (student-completed) questionnaires were discussed with regard to the teachers' role in the administration of the survey instrument. Special emphasis was placed on the following: (a) Elementary teachers should follow up on delinquent questionnaires and provide a second questionnaire if the first one was not returned within 5 days, and (b) all teachers should indicate the race of the child on each of the questionnaires. Schools were selected as outlined previously and recorded for future reference on the demographic data sheet. It was determined that all questionnaires were returned to the superintendents within 3 weeks of their distribution, and arrangements for their retrieval were made by the study team.

Processing the Data

After the data were retrieved from the school districts, each questionnaire was checked for missing information. The nature of the missing data was recorded on a separate form for each school, and an additional visit or telephone call was made to the district in an attempt to obtain the necessary information. Once the missing data were received, they were recorded on the corresponding questionnaires.

The number of returns and percent of responses were calculated by counting the usable returns within each district, by school and grade, and relating those values to the number of questionnaires that were distributed. This process facilitated the determination of the percentage of response by class, grade, school and district, and statewide by grade, school type, and community type.

All data were analyzed via the Statistical Package for the Social Sciences (SPSS) system on the Control Data Corporation (CDC) 6500 computer at Michigan State University. The specific program used for the study was CROSSTABS, a joint frequency count percentage distribution of cases according to classificatory variables, which provided a separate table for each sport within each stratification. Each table included a cell within the stratified variable (i.e., "never," "sometimes," and "often"). Three items were recorded in each cell: (1) the number of students at that level, (2) a row percent that indicated the percentage of participating students at that level, and (3) a column percent that designated the percentage of students at that age or grade who participated at that level. Total counts, row percents, and column percents were provided at the bottom and side of each table. Overall strata included:

1. Statewide totals—1 set of tables.
2. Sex—2 sets of tables (male, female).
3. Community type—3 sets of tables (urban, suburban, rural).
4. School Type—2 sets of tables (public, private).
5. Race—6 sets of tables (black, Chicano, native American, Oriental, white, other).

Thus, the reporting format was initially organized across sports, followed by analyses of four categories within sports.

RESULTS AND INTERPRETATION

Response to the Questionnaire

The purpose of this section is twofold: (1) to provide information on the number and percentage of questionnaires returned in relation to the number distributed to parents and students of the randomly drawn sample, and (2) to discuss the degree to which the data are representative of children enrolled in grades K-11 in Michigan. Information concerning the questionnaire returns is presented on a statewide basis, by school type (public vs. private) and by the type of community in which schools were located (urban, suburban, and rural).

The percentage of returns for various grade levels was influenced to some extent by the manner in which the questionnaires were administered. For all children in grades K-4 and for most of those in grades 5 and 6, the questionnaires were sent to the home, via the schools, to be completed by the parents. The figures reported for this portion of the sample include the actual number of questionnaires distributed and returned. Questionnaires were administered directly to the remainder of the students in grades 5 and 6 and to those enrolled in grades 7-11. This assured a 100% return on all the questionnaires administered in this manner, but it did not account for the students who were absent on the day of administration.

Few school districts maintained accurate records of daily attendance. Therefore, it was impossible to compute accurate figures concerning the rate of absenteeism at the middle school and high school levels. Figures obtained from some of the districts, however, along with estimates provided by school officials in others, indicate that the rate of daily absenteeism was approximately 8%. Undoubtedly, a corresponding percentage of the students selected in the statewide 5% sample were among those absent when the questionnaires were administered. The potential effect of their lack of responses on the total results cannot be estimated. It must be stated, however, that although no attempt was made to obtain data from those students enrolled in grades 6-11 who were absent when the data were gathered, there is no reason at present to assume a relationship between school attendance and participation in agency-sponsored sports.

The total number of questionnaires actually distributed was 109,625, or 4.74% of all students enrolled during the 1974-1975 school year. Several factors accounted for the discrepancy (5,575) between the sample figure drawn and the number of questionnaires administered. First, the sampling technique employed assumed that a typical classroom would contain 24 children. In reality, the average classroom size was slightly less than this figure. Second, in three instances not all the questionnaires were distributed. Two school districts failed to distribute any questionnaires, and were dropped from the study at a time when replacement was impossible; and a third district neglected to administer the questionnaires to its senior high students. The third reason for the discrepancy between the 5% sample and the 4.7% to whom the questionnaire was administered was the routine absenteeism cited previously.

Statewide returns

Figures concerning the statewide distribution and return of the questionnaires are presented in Table 2. The cooperation of school officials, teachers, and parents is reflected in the high rate of response. Overall, 74.8% of the parents returned questionnaires that were usable. Note that the percentage of returns by the parents increased steadily from kindergarten to grade 6. Except for absentees, the student return was 100%. Thus, the statewide return was 93,993 questionnaires, or 85.7%. With the inclusion of an estimated absentee rate of 8%, the statewide return was 82.6%. Because this return was regarded as representative of the state, no additional sampling of the nonrespondents was deemed necessary.

Public-private school returns

The return of questionnaires for public and private schools is reported in Table 3. In all, 83,336 questionnaires were returned by the public schools, and 10,657 were received from private schools. Note that the percentages of responses were similar for public and private schools at each grade level and for the overall returns. Clearly, the cooperation of public and private school

TABLE 2   Overall statewide return of questionnaires

Grade	Number distributed	Number returned	%
Parent questionnaires			
Kindergarten	8,294	5,520	66.6
1	9,217	6,572	71.3
2	9,476	6,811	71.9
3	9,631	7,309	75.9
4	9,990	7,646	76.5
5	9,689	7,584	78.3
6	5,626	4,849	86.2
Total	61,923	46,291	74.8
Student questionnaires			
5	154	154	100.0
6	3,558	3,558	100.0
7	9,529	9,529	100.0
8	9,529	9,529	100.0
9	8,711	8,711	100.0
10	8,421	8,421	100.0
11	7,800	7,800	100.0
Total	47,702	47,702	100.0
Grand total	109,625	93,993	85.7

TABLE 3 Public-private school returns of questionnaires

Grade	Public school			Private school		
	Distributed	Returned	%	Distributed	Returned	%
Parent questionnaires						
Kindergarten	7,661	5,099	66.6	633	421	66.5
1	8,109	5,782	71.3	1,108	790	71.3
2	8,340	6,018	72.2	1,136	793	69.8
3	8,510	6,445	75.7	1,121	864	77.1
4	8,800	6,745	76.6	1,190	901	75.7
5	8,509	6,619	77.8	1,180	965	81.8
6	5,235	4,480	85.6	391	369	94.4
Total	55,164	41,188	74.7	6,759	5,103	75.5
Student questionnaires						
5	154	154	100.0	–	–	–
6	2,802	2,802	100.0	756	756	100.0
7	8,398	8,398	100.0	1,131	1,131	100.0
8	8,328	8,328	100.0	1,201	1,201	100.0
9	7,839	7,839	100.0	872	872	100.0
10	7,621	7,621	100.0	800	800	100.0
11	7,006	7,006	100.0	794	794	100.0
Total	42,148	42,148	100.0	5,554	5,554	100.0
Grand total	97,321	83,336	85.6	12,313	10,657	86.6

administrators, teachers, and parents was evident from the high percent of response from both school types.

Urban, suburban, and rural school returns

The number of questionnaires distributed and returned by urban, suburban, and rural schools is presented in Table 4. Differences exist in the percentage of questionnaires returned by the parents according to the type of community in which the schools were located. The respective parental returns for urban, suburban, and rural schools were 70.3%, 74.4%, and 79.2%. The urban return rate was affected by the limited responses from several central city schools. This problem had been anticipated due to the known difficulties in obtaining parental responses in the central-city setting. This condition, however, did not exist across all central city schools. In fact, the cooperation of parents, school administrators, and teachers in urban settings was better than expected.

TABLE 4 Urban, suburban, and rural school returns of questionnaires

Grade	Urban			Suburban			Rural		
	Distributed	Returned	%	Distributed	Returned	%	Distributed	Returned	%
Parent questionnaires									
Kindergarten	2,055	1,370	66.7	3,414	2,098	61.5	2,825	2,052	72.6
1	2,566	1,749	68.2	3,614	2,603	72.0	3,037	2,220	73.1
2	2,804	1,872	66.8	3,736	2,630	70.4	2,936	2,309	78.6
3	2,968	2,005	67.6	3,874	2,972	77.3	2,816	2,332	82.8
4	3,050	2,111	69.2	3,943	3,132	79.4	2,997	2,403	80.2
5	2,919	2,234	76.5	3,706	2,374	77.5	3,064	2,476	80.8
6	1,399	1,146	81.9	1,861	1,624	87.3	2,366	2,079	87.9
Total	17,761	12,481	70.3	24,121	17,933	74.4	20,041	15,871	79.2
Student questionnaires									
5	–	–	–	154	154	100.0	–	–	–
6	1,137	1,137	100.0	1,856	1,856	100.0	565	565	100.0
7	2,992	2,992	100.0	3,671	3,671	100.0	2,866	2,866	100.0
8	3,052	3,052	100.0	3,740	3,740	100.0	2,737	2,737	100.0
9	2,453	2,453	100.0	3,470	3,470	100.0	2,788	2,788	100.0
10	2,328	2,328	100.0	3,404	3,404	100.0	2,689	2,689	100.0
11	2,252	2,252	100.0	3,096	3,096	100.0	2,452	2,452	100.0
Total	14,214	14,214	100.0	19,391	19,391	100.0	14,097	14,097	100.0
Grand total	31,975	26,701	83.5	43,512	37,324	85.8	34,138	29,968	87.8

Although representation from the central city schools is not equal to that from other urban schools, the returns for this study were relatively high. Perhaps this was due to the type of information requested on the questionnaire. It is highly questionable whether further effort would yield much additional information. Furthermore, as subsequent data will show, the returns from the urban areas are sufficiently high to yield the information desired in this study.

Differences in the rate of returns from the suburban and rural schools were somewhat surprising. The highest rate of return had been anticipated from the suburban schools. Table 4 shows that the rate of response from parents in rural schools was higher than that of parents in suburban schools across all grade levels. Total response figures indicate that returns from rural schools exceeded those of suburban schools by nearly 5%.

Total Participation in Agency-sponsored Sports

Numerical totals for the combined males and females who participated in various agency-sponsored sports during the year 1975-1976 are shown in Figure 2. Since the sample was randomly drawn from the state of Michigan, the extent of participation is assumed to be representative of the entire state. Therefore, on Figures 2 and 3 a second ordinate has been included on the right of each graph to show the projected total number of children in the state participating in each of the sports.[1] The part of each bar in the graph with oblique lines indicates the portion of the total sample that participated "often" in that sport. The term "often" indicates that an entire season of the sport was completed. The clear part of the bar represents the portion of the sample that participated "sometimes" in the sport. The term "sometimes" indicates that individuals competed and were attached to a team or group, but did not complete an entire season. The two figures shown inside each bar indicate the actual number of children who participated either "often" or "sometimes." The values of the left ordinate represent the percent of the sample of 93,090 students that participated in a particular sport. The total sample varies slightly from sport to sport due to missing values. Note that the total of the values across sports will yield an inflationary sum of youth sports participants due to the multiple-sports involvement of many children.

The 15 most popular agency-sponsored sports are listed according to extent of participation in Table 5. The number of students from the sample involved in each sport and the percentage of participation represented by these values appear in the first and second columns, respectively. Inferences to

---

[1] Preliminary evidence from Phase II indicates that the projected totals of statewide participation are inflated due to the confusion of some respondents between the categories of "agency sponsored" and "recreational activities." An accurate estimate of statewide sports participation will be available after the completion of Phase II.

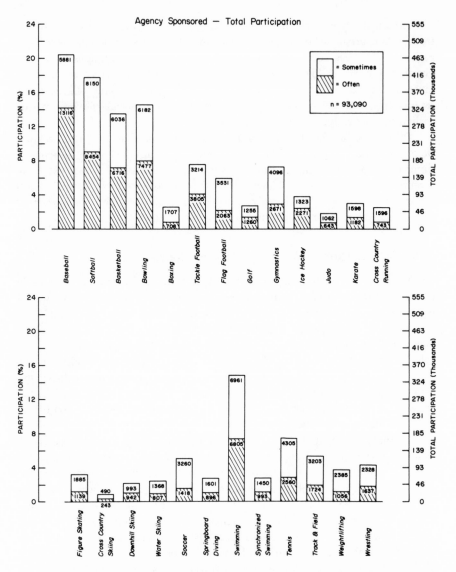

FIGURE 2 Statewide total participation: independent of age and sex.

the total student population in the state between the ages of 5 and 17 are made in the final column. Even though the sample was random, some error will result in drawing inferences to the total population. The total numbers of youngsters projected to be participating in the various agency-sponsored sports across the state are therefore rounded to the nearest thousand. Minor error is of little consequence since the numbers are large and, for the most part, the differences are quite distinct.

The numbers of youngsters participating in agency-sponsored sports are much higher than anticipated. Over 300,000 youngsters across the state participate in each of the sports of baseball, softball, swimming, bowling, and basketball. The agency-sponsored contact sports, including tackle football, wrestling, and ice hockey, also have wide participation. Projected figures for these sports are 176,000, 99,000, and 88,000, respectively. Clearly, the extent of participation in these activities is much greater than is generally acknowledged.

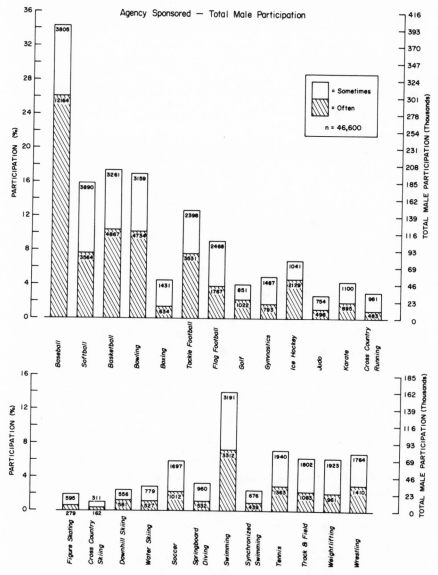

FIGURE 3 Statewide total male participation: independent of age.

TABLE 5 The 15 most popular agency-sponsored sports: Independent of age and sex

Sport	No. of participants in sample	% participation	Total no. in state (in thousands, rounded to nearest thousand)[a]
Baseball	18,197	20.4	472
Softball	16,604	17.9	414
Swimming	13,766	14.8	342
Bowling	13,659	14.6	338
Basketball	12,752	13.7	317
Tackle football	7,019	7.6	176
Tennis	6,895	7.4	171
Gymnastics	6,767	7.3	169
Flag (touch) football	5,594	6.0	139
Track and field	4,927	5.3	123
Soccer	4,678	5.0	116
Wrestling	3,965	4.3	99
Ice hockey	3,594	3.8	88
Weight lifting	3,441	3.7	86
Figure skating	3,024	3.2	7.4
Total no. = 93,090			

[a]Based on a total enrollment of 2,313,477.

Sports Participation by Males

The frequency of male participation in agency-sponsored sports is shown in Figure 3. The total number of males who completed questionnaires was 46,600, or nearly one-half the total sample of 93,090. The inferences drawn to the entire state are based on an estimated total male population of 1,156,738 between the ages of 5 and 17. This figure is one-half the total student population reported earlier in this report.

The most popular agency-sponsored sports for males are presented in Table 6. Baseball is clearly the most popular sport among males between the ages of 5 and 17 years. An estimated 397,000 males participated in this sport, with over 301,000 completing an entire season. This indicates that more than one out of every three boys participated in baseball and that 25% of the boys in the state completed the entire season.

Participation in basketball, bowling, and softball was approximately one-half that of baseball. The extent of participation in these three sports was still high, with estimated values of 202,000 (basketball), 197,000 (bowling), and 184,000 (softball). Approximately one out of every six boys participated in each of these sports with approximately one boy in seven participating in an agency-sponsored swimming program.

Participation was also quite extensive in the contact sports of tackle football, wrestling, ice hockey, boxing, and karate. Approximately 1 out of every 8 males between the ages of 5 and 17 participated in tackle football (147,000). Nearly 1 of every 15 competed in agency-sponsored wrestling (79,000) and ice hockey (79,000). An estimated 1 in 22 boys engaged in boxing (52,000), and one in 23 boys was involved in karate (50,000). Participation was also high in touch football and soccer with approximately 1 of every 10 males competing in flag or touch football (105,000) and 1 in 17 involved in agency-sponsored soccer (67,000).

It is obvious, from the percent of the males involved in the various sports, that some boys participated in several agency-sponsored sports. For example, the total percentage of the first six sports in Table 6 is 111.2. At this point in this investigation, however, neither the multiple agency-sponsored sport participants nor those boys who participated in no sport activities have been

TABLE 6   The most popular agency-sponsored sports participated in by males: Independent of age

Sport	No. of participants in sample	% participation	Total no. in state (in thousands, rounded to nearest thousand)[a]
Baseball	15,969	34.3	397
Basketball	8,128	17.4	202
Bowling	7,893	17.0	197
Softball	7,454	15.9	184
Swimming	6,503	13.9	161
Tackle football	5,929	12.7	147
Flag (touch) football	4,235	9.1	105
Tennis	3,303	7.1	82
Wrestling	3,174	6.8	79
Ice hockey	3,170	6.8	79
Track and field	2,885	6.2	72
Weight lifting	2,884	6.2	72
Soccer	2,709	5.8	67
Gymnastics	2,280	4.9	57
Boxing	2,065	4.5	52
Karate	1,995	4.3	50
Golf	1,873	4.0	46
Total no. males = 46,600			

[a]Based on an enrollment of 1,156,738.

identified. These variables will be studied in a subsequent phase of the investigation.

Male participation by age

Examples of male participation, by age, in the various agency-sponsored sports is presented in Figures 4-6. There are some obvious differences in the patterns of participation across the various sports. This is true with regard to both the age of highest incidence of participation and the relative numbers participating "sometimes" and "often." Attention will focus on the different types of patterns that emerged, but available data do not permit an interpretation of these patterns.

Most of the sports show a progressive increase in incidence of participation up to 11, 12, or 13 years of age. This is followed by a general but progressive decline through age 17. Sports displaying patterns of this type include baseball, basketball, bowling, boxing, tackle football, flag football, gymnastics, ice hockey, judo, cross-country running, figure skating, soccer, springboard diving, swimming, synchronized swimming, tennis, track and field, and wrestling. Involvement in other sports does not peak at ages 11-13, but rather the incidence of participation continues to rise through age 17 or reaches its summit at an earlier age with little subsequent decline in incidence of participation. Softball, golf, karate, cross-country skiing, downhill skiing, water skiing, and weight lifting have this latter type of pattern across the age span studied.

In some sports, the number of boys who indicated that they participated "often" clearly outnumbered those who said they participated "sometimes." The sports in which this occurred are baseball, basketball, bowling, tackle football, and ice hockey. In other sports, those who participated "sometimes" far exceeded those who participated "often." Activities in this category include boxing, flag football, gymnastics, judo, cross-country running, figure skating, cross-country skiing, water skiing, soccer, springboard diving, synchronized swimming, tennis, track and field, weight lifting, and wrestling. For the remainder of the sports, no discernible differences existed between the incidence of those who participated "often" and those who participated "sometimes."

Some of the sports show a relatively high incidence of participation among the boys who were 5, 6, and 7 years of age. In other sports, participation during these early years was virtually absent. Those sports in which more than 2% of the 5-, 6-, and 7-year-old boys participated include baseball, softball, bowling, gymnastics, ice hockey, and swimming. Less than 2% of these young males participated in basketball, boxing, tackle football, flag football, golf, judo, karate, cross-country running, figure skating, cross-country skiing, downhill skiing, water skiing, soccer, springboard diving, synchronized swimming, tennis, track and field, weight lifting, and wrestling.

The peak years for male participation in agency-sponsored sports range from ages 11 to 14 years. More 11-year-old boys were involved in gymnastics than boys of any other age. Sports in which peak participation occurs at 12

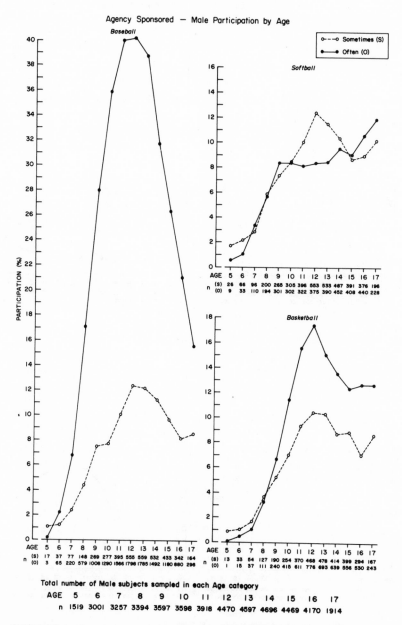

FIGURE 4 Statewide male participation by age: baseball, softball, and basketball.

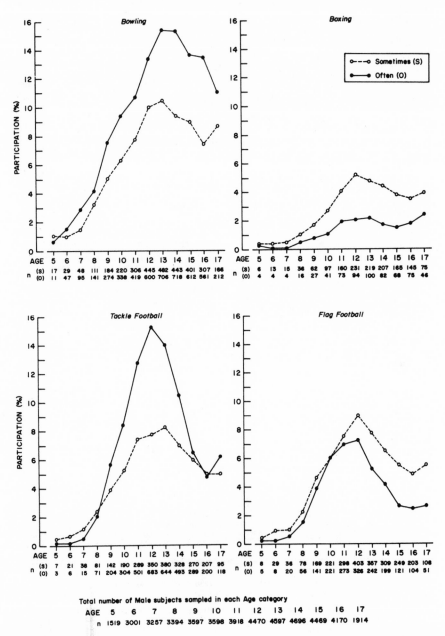

FIGURE 5 Statewide male participation by age: bowling, boxing, tackle football, and flag football.

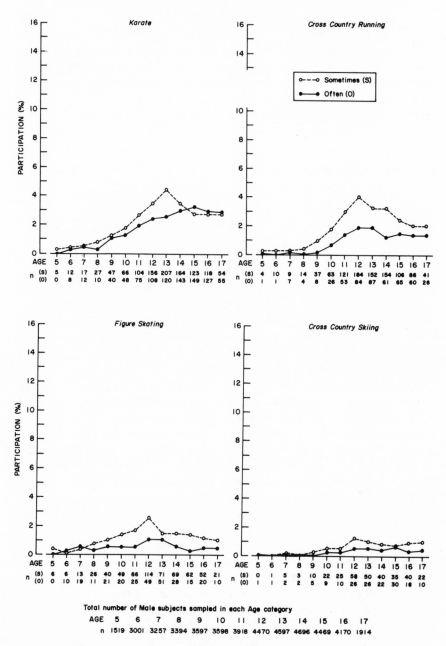

FIGURE 6   Statewide male participation by age: karate, cross-country running, figure skating, and cross-country skiing.

years of age include baseball, softball, basketball, boxing, tackle football, flag football, ice hockey, judo, cross-country running, figure skating, cross-country and downhill skiing, soccer, springboard diving, swimming, synchronized swimming, tennis, and track and field. Those sports in which extent of participation was greatest among 13-year-old boys were bowling, judo (tied with age 12), karate, weight lifting, and wrestling. The peak year for golf and water skiing occurred at age 14. Several sports showed a second peak at 17 years. Sports in which the incidence of participation nearly equalled or exceeded the peak that occurred at an earlier age were softball, downhill skiing, water skiing, and weight lifting.

Sports Participation by Females

The frequency of female participation, independent of age, in agency-sponsored sports during 1975-1976 is shown in Figure 7. The inferences to the population of females aged 5-17 years in the state of Michigan were developed in the same manner as those for males, described in the previous section. The sports most preferred by females as determined by extent of participation are shown in Table 7. Also included is the estimated number of females, 5-17 years of age, who were active in the various sports across the state.

Softball was the most popular agency-sponsored sport for females, with 228,000 statewide participants. Approximately 1 out of every 5 girls participated in this sport. Furthermore, 1 out of 10 females completed a season of softball competition in 1974-1975.

Approximately 180,000 (one of six) girls were involved in agency-sponsored swimming programs across the state, and approximately one out of every eight girls participated in bowling (143,000 participants). Nearly 10% of the girls participated in basketball (116,000) and in gymnastics (111,000).

The number of girls involved in baseball (75,000), soccer (50,000), flag football (34,000), and tackle football (28,000) was surprising. Inspection of Figure 7 shows that females were also participating, to a limited degree, in wrestling (1.7%), weight lifting (1.2%), karate (1.7%), judo (1.0%), ice hockey (.9%), and boxing (.8%). Available data do not provide sufficient information to interpret these findings at this time. The incidence of participation by females in the sports indicated was much higher than anticipated.

A comparison of Tables 6 and 7 shows that the extent of participation on the part of females in agency sports programs is lower than that of males, but sports participation in general by girls was much higher than anticipated. Due to the increased interest in women's athletics, it would appear that the present data provide only a transitory measure at a time of relatively rapid change. Without adequate data for comparison, it is impossible to draw any inferences regarding trends of participation among females.

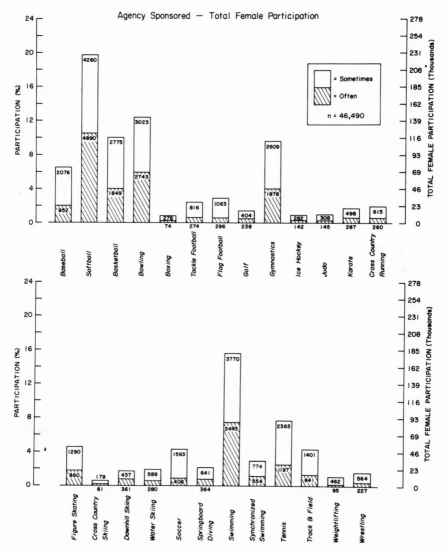

FIGURE 7   Statewide total female participation: independent of age.

Female participation by age

Examples of the incidence of participation by age for females in various agency-sponsored sports is presented in Figures 8-10. The patterns depicting incidence of participation across ages for the females are not as distinct as those for the males. Most sports show peak incidences at 12 or 13 years of age, with progressive increases preceding these years and rather steady declines following the peak years. With the possible exceptions of downhill skiing and water skiing, however, there were no sports in which progressive increases in participation occurred across the span of ages 5-17 years, as was observed for the males.

TABLE 7 Most popular agency-sponsored sports participated in
by females: Independent of age

Sport	No. of participants in sample	% participation	Total no. in state (in thousands, rounded to nearest thousand)[a]
Softball	9,150	19.7	228
Swimming	7,263	15.6	180
Bowling	5,766	12.4	143
Basketball	4,624	10.0	116
Gymnastics	4,487	9.6	111
Tennis	3,562	7.7	89
Baseball	3,028	6.5	75
Figure skating	2,150	4.6	53
Track and field	2,042	4.4	51
Soccer	1,959	4.3	50
Flag (touch) football	1,356	2.9	34
Synchronized swimming	1,329	2.9	34
Tackle football	1,090	2.4	28
Springboard diving	1,005	2.2	25
Cross country running	875	1.9	22
Total no. females = 46,490			

[a]Based on an enrollment of 1,156,738.

The patterns of those who participated "often" or "sometimes" are also not as readily apparent in the data of the females. Nearly all sports showed a higher incidence of "sometimes" than of "often" participation across the ages, as noted in baseball, gymnastics, and basketball. The exceptions are in softball, where those who participated "often" exceeded those who participated "sometimes," and in bowling and swimming where the incidence of "often" and "sometimes" was about the same. It is possible that female participation in agency-sponsored sports is currently in such a state of flux that clear patterns have not yet evolved. In a number of sports, including golf, ice hockey, judo, karate, cross-country skiing, and weight lifting, the extent of participation was too low to permit judgments to be made concerning patterns of response across the age span studied.

The similarity in the years of peak incidence in sports participation for males and females was unexpected. Since females mature earlier than males, with declining levels of participation following puberty, they were expected to reach their peak incidences at earlier ages. The greatest incidence of participation at 12 years of age occurred in baseball, basketball, flag football, gymnastics, ice hockey, judo (tied with age 13), cross-country running, figure skating, soccer, springboard diving, swimming, synchronized swimming, track

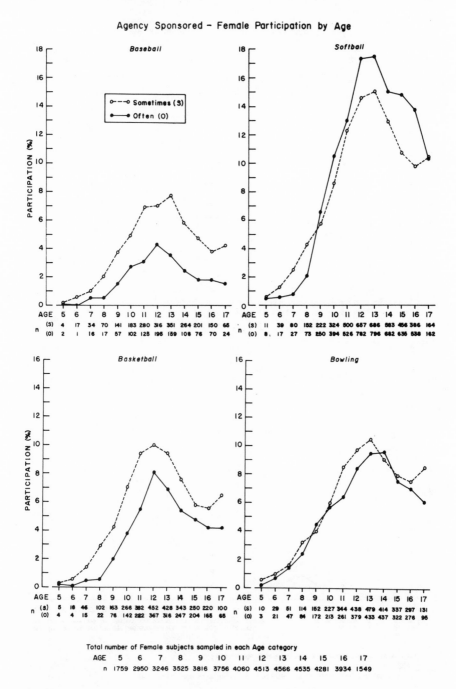

FIGURE 8 Statewide female participation by age: baseball, softball, basketball, and bowling.

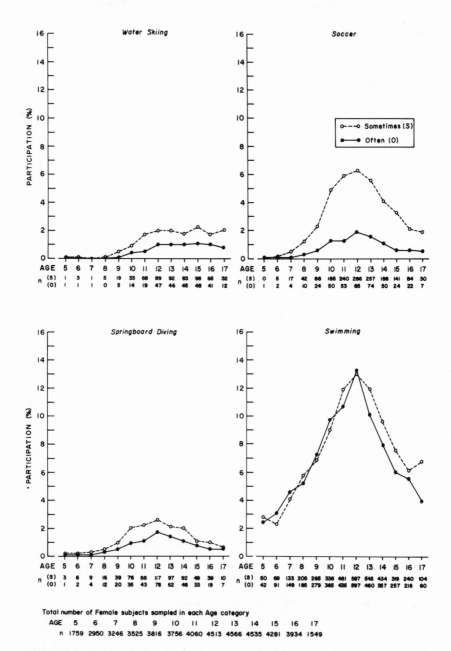

FIGURE 9 Statewide female participation by age: water skiing, soccer, springboard diving, and swimming.

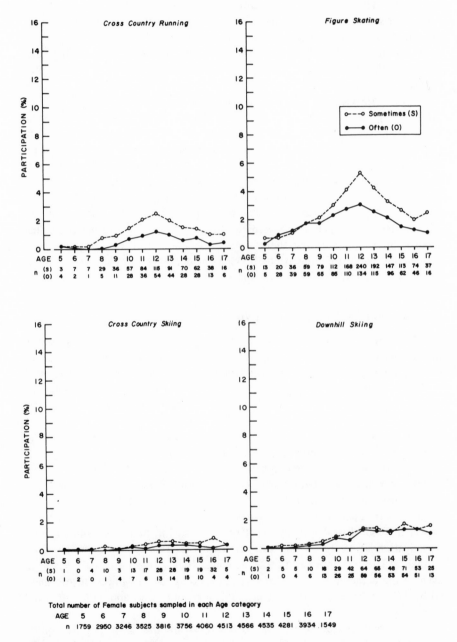

FIGURE 10 Statewide female participation by age: cross-country running, figure skating, cross-country skiing, and downhill skiing.

and field, weight lifting, and wrestling. Age 13 was the year of greatest involvement in the sports of softball, bowling, tackle football, golf, karate, and tennis. The peak age for downhill skiing and water skiing was age 15. In some sports, namely softball, tackle football, gymnastics and tennis, the peak participation for the females occurred later than for the males. Conversely, in such activities as golf, water skiing, downhill skiing, weight lifting, and wrestling, the highest rate of participation occurred earlier for females than for males.

These data indicate that females, in greater numbers than anticipated, are participating in contact and combative sports and in sports that were traditionally considered to be male oriented. The highest incidences of participation occurred around 12 years of age, which would be prepubertal for some girls. The criterion of prepuberty is not significant, however, because incidences of peak participation are still relatively high in some sports at 14 years of age and older. Tackle football is just one example of this. Explanations or inferences for these phenomena cannot be drawn from the present data. Information concerning the nature of the organizations that sponsor these programs and the kinds of program control that are provided in conjunction with the unexpectedly high incidences of participation will be obtained in Phase II of the Youth Sports Study.

Participation by Community Type

To assess the possible variances between community types, each school in the sample was classified into one of the following general descriptions: urban (metropolitan city areas), suburban (surrounding residential areas), and rural (isolated communities without ready access to urban areas). The following is a narrative interpretation of data that were stratified according to community type.

As shown in Figure 11, community participation in sports was highest in baseball, softball, basketball, swimming, and bowling. The percentages of urban participation for these sports were 22.0%, 21.8%, 19.2%, 18.7%, and 15.9%, respectively. The order of the top sports in total suburban participation is baseball, softball, bowling, swimming, and basketball. The range of participation in these sports is from 20.3% to 13.0%. As might be expected, baseball was also the most popular sport in rural communities, with participation at 19.2% of the total respondents. This sport was followed by softball, 15.1%; swimming, 11.9%; bowling, 10.9%; and basketball, 9.8%. In each of the community types, cross-country skiing had the lowest involvement with .9% participation for urban, .7% for suburban, and .8% for rural communities.

The trend suggested by the percentages of the most popular sports throughout the data showing the greatest participation, in both the "sometimes" and "often" categories, occurred in the urban areas, with the

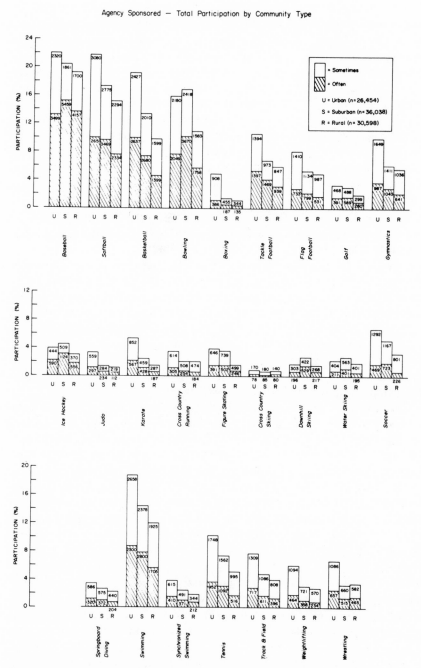

FIGURE 11 Total participation by community type (urban, suburban, and rural): independent of age and sex.

lowest involvement in the rural areas. The percent of participation in the suburbs was generally between that of urban and rural communities. This observation is further supported in that the suburban participation generally followed the statewide total participation, whereas urban ranked above and rural below. Exceptions to this trend were shown in bowling, ice hockey, downhill skiing, and water skiing, where percentages of the suburban areas surpassed those of the urban areas. Though the total participation followed the trend described, for three sports (baseball, flag football, and soccer) the urban groups were composed of relatively more students who participated "sometimes," rather than the usual higher percents of those who participated "often." This observation could be attributed to either increased attrition in the urban areas or to more sustained involvement in these sports in the suburban and rural areas.

The comparative number of urban participants in approximately 80% of the sports sampled was greater than the suburban and rural participants at practically every age level for both sexes. There were exceptions to this trend, however, and they were generally in sports (i.e., bowling, golf, downhill skiing, and water skiing) that require expensive equipment, special facilities, and a more sophisticated level of coaching. In these situations, the suburban percentages of participation approached or surpassed the urban participant percentages at some ages. In more established sports, such as softball, basketball, and football, the urban involvement exceeded that in the suburban areas for practically every age. Throughout the sports, the rural areas maintained their relative position of lower participation at most ages when compared with those of the urban and suburban sections.

As mentioned earlier, peak involvement in youth sports occurred around the ages of 12–13 years. Essentially, the three community types followed this pattern with no discernible differences between the urban, suburban, and rural areas. A few activities (bowling, golf, downhill skiing, and water skiing) tended either to have peak participation at slightly later ages (13–15 years) or to maintain a somewhat constant level of participation throughout approximately the latter half of the ages sampled. Golf, in the suburban schools, and water skiing, in the rural schools, illustrate these patterns. Both sports have peak youth involvement at age 15 years, after which participation in golf declines, while involvement in water skiing remains approximately the same from age 12 through 17 years.

The reasons for abrupt reductions in sports participation after the peak age of involvement are of considerable interest to physical educators. Several possible explanations could be that (a) participants begin specializing in a single sport after this age, (b) other interests begin to encroach on the time that was once devoted to sports, and (c) agencies provide fewer opportunities for the older age groups to become involved in organized sports. These questions may be answered as a result of the Phase II data analysis by identifying and soliciting information pertaining to the potential reasons for declining participation.

Participation by School Type

The percent of participation in the various sports was relatively independent of school type. The distribution of participation in public and private schools was similar across sport categories. Some general trends in the data, however, were evident. Participants from private schools favored noncontact individual or dual sports requiring special equipment, facilities, and instruction (i.e., swimming, tennis, golf, and skiing). On the other hand, students from the public school systems were more inclined to select the dual combative sports (i.e., wrestling, boxing, karate, judo, and weight lifting). No explanation for this trend in the data is warranted at this time, but the possibility exists that this is a socioeconomically related phenomenon.

It is also of interest that in all sport categories other than the dual combative sports, weight lifting, and bowling, the incidence of participation in the "often" category is higher for participants who attended the private schools. This observation may be related to an increased opportunity for private school children to maintain their sport participation throughout their school-age years.

Male participation by age levels

Participation by males showed no distinct differences in sport preference between the school types. In addition, the general pattern of male participation by age for each sport is also similar in the public and private schools. Ages of peak participation, plateaus, and patterns in attrition are strikingly similar within each sport between school types. The incidence of participation in individual sports is generally higher, especially at the age levels of peak participation, for males from the private schools. In addition, the cross-sectional decrease in participation in the private school sector diminished at a faster rate than did the public sector. This pattern is depicted in swimming, but is also obvious for tennis, bowling, and golf. It would be of interest to determine if this trend continued for these three lifetime sports.

Female participation by age levels

Participation levels in team sports were generally higher for the public school females than for the private school girls. The distribution patterns for participation across age levels for the most popular team sports were quite similar for females in the public and private schools. Age of peak participation and attrition trends were usually coincidental between school types for each activity.

There was consistent preference of private school girls for participation in individual sports requiring the use of special equipment. Girls from private schools had higher percentages for both the "total" and "often" categories for all the individual sports except bowling. This trend was found across most age levels and applied to tennis, figure skating, downhill skiing, springboard diving, swimming, synchronized swimming, and golf.

Sports Participation According to Race

A major concern of the Youth Sports Survey was the extent to which race influenced the frequency of participation in agency-sponsored sports for children between the ages of 5 and 17 years. This section provides information on the incidence and percentage of participation in 25 sports as indicated by a sample of Michigan's school-age population. The category of race is subdivided as follows: Black, Chicano, Indian (Native American), Oriental, White, and Other.

The determination of "race" as a category was the single most sensitive issue during the acquisition of information during the Youth Sports Survey. Pilot studies indicated that some students were reluctant to provide their sports history if they had previously been asked to indicate their race on the sheet containing demographic information. This potential problem was resolved by requesting the classroom teachers to identify their students by race. Therefore, the veracity of the racial designation is dependent on the knowledge or judgment of the teachers concerning the racial heritage of their students. Numerous contact with teachers concerning this question revealed that they were confident that their knowledge of the racial identity of their students was accurate.

The designation of race as a category for the statewide analysis resulted in a lower number of respondents than in the previous analyses for the categories of age, sex, school type, and community type. This situation resulted from the following: (a) Some of the teachers failed to indicate the race of their students on the demographic data section of each questionnaire. Despite attempts by the survey team to obtain this information, complete retrieval of the data pertaining to the race of each subject was impossible. (b) Some school districts had a policy that prohibited their personnel from providing information on race to external sources. Therefore, this analysis included only those questionnaires for which the racial designation had been provided. Of the 93,090 usable questionnaires in this portion of the statewide survey, 76,938 (82.6%) contained information on race and were included in this analysis.

The number and percentage of statewide participants, according to race, is shown in Table 8. Note that 72.8% of the respondents were white, with the five other categories of race comprising the remaining 26.2% of the sample. The reader should be mindful of the differences between races in terms of the numbers who participated in a specific sport. For example, the percentage of

TABLE 8 Participation in agency-sponsored sports on the basis of race and sex

Sex	Black		Chicano		American Indian		Oriental		White		Other	
	N	%	N	%	N	%	N	%	N	%	N	%
Female	3,810	8.2	478	1.0	187	0.4	125	0.3	88,672	72.4	103	0.2
Male	3,558	7.6	480	1.0	205	0.4	133	0.3	34,057	73.1	130	0.3
Total	7,368	7.9	958	1.0	392	0.4	258	0.3	67,729	72.8	233	0.25

Note. Grand total = 76,938 (82.6% of the statewide returns).

participation in a given sport may be similar for two races, but for one race that figure may represent several thousand participants, while for the other it may involve only 10 individuals. Because the statewide sample was randomly drawn by geographical area and population density, the writers have proceeded on the assumption that the data are representative of the six categories of race across the state of Michigan. In an attempt to carry out the randomization process, sampling within each school district was conducted to reflect its racial and socioeconomic composition as determined by the district's school superintendent.

The assumption of proportionate sampling by race was upheld where the return from a school district was high and the percentage of returns was similar across socioeconomic strata. The lower return of questionnaires from the Detroit Public School System was the only notable bias that may have been introduced into the analysis of participation in specific sports, by race. The 63.4% return from the Detroit Public School District suggested that the black race may not have been represented in proportion to their total school enrollment. Such a suggestion is purely speculative, since there was no feasible way to determine the race of those students in the sample who did not return their questionnaires. State demographic data from the 1970 census were not used to verify the composition of the school-age population, by race. These data were 5 years old by the time the statewide sample was drawn. Hence, they would have added little to the information that was already in our possession.

The data on agency-sponsored sports participation by race reveal several interesting features:

1. Team sports generally attracted more interest than did individual sports. This was true for baseball, softball, basketball, and tackle football. Several individual-type activities, however, had moderate participation values: bowling, swimming, tennis, wrestling, and gymnastics.

2. All sports with low percentage-of-participation values were of an individual nature. Included in this list were golf, cross-country running, figure skating, cross-country skiing, downhill skiing, water skiing, springboard diving, and synchronized swimming.

3. Black respondents had the highest percentage-of-participation figures in 18 of the 25 sports. This was true for all team sports except soccer and ice hockey. In the dual and individual sports, black respondents led in percentage of participation for all sports, with the exception of golf, downhill skiing, water skiing, tennis, and figure skating.

4. Black respondents generally had a higher proportion of their total percent of response made up of those who participated at the "often" level than any of the other races. This indicates that not only were black participants involved to a greater extent in agency-sponsored sports, but that they also tended to be more intensely involved than were respondents of other races. One stereotype of sports participation by race that was not corroborated by these data was the involvement of Oriental respondents in judo or karate. The percentage of participation in judo and karate by black and Chicano participants was greater than that of Oriental respondents.

SUMMARY OF PHASE I, YOUTH SPORTS STUDY

The Youth Sports Study was initiated in January 1975 with the introduction of Joint Resolution No. 39 to the Legislature of the state of Michigan. Approval of Resolution No. 39 led to the formation of a Joint Legislative Study Committee on Youth Sports, comprised of three senators and three representatives of the Michigan Legislature. In March 1975, a Consortium of Universities was formed to assist the Joint Legislative Study Committee in its charge to study the structure and conduct of youth sports in the state of Michigan. The Consortium consisted of personnel from Michigan State University, Northern Michigan University, University of Michigan, and Wayne State University. Personnel from each university selected a coordinator to represent them at meetings of the Consortium. The four coordinators selected one of their number to act as project coordinator and serve as the liaison between the Universities Consortium and the Joint Legislative Study Committee on Youth Sports.

The Legislative charge to the University Consortium was detailed in a proposal submitted to and approved by the Joint Legislative Study Committee on Youth Sports in May 1975. The Study of Youth Sports was divided into three phases, with each phase requiring approximately one school year for its completion. Phase I, which is the essence of this report, involved a comprehensive study concerning the incidence and frequency of participation in youth sports for children between the ages of 5 and 17 years in the state of Michigan. Through a process of stratification random sampling, 89 school districts were identified as the areas to be studied in Phase I.

The process of distributing and retrieving questionnaires relating to the incidence and frequency of participation in youth sports began in January and terminated in May 1976. A sample of approximately 5% of Michigan's school-age children was chosen as the basic study unit. The state of Michigan was divided into 10 regional districts. Each district was then assigned to one of the four universities comprising the Consortium. School districts within each region were selected for inclusion in the sample on the basis of size, community type, geographical location, and socioeconomic composition.

The data pertaining to the incidence and frequency of sports participation were obtained through the cooperation of the administrators and teachers of the schools chosen in the sample. A total of 109,625 questionnaires were distributed to the 89 school districts, to be further distributed to the parents of the children in kindergarten through fifth grade or to be completed within the school by the children in grades 6-11. A total of 93,993 questionnaires, or 85.7% of the total distributed, were completed and returned to the regional university through this process. A more conservative appraisal of the percentage of return takes into consideration an estimated 8% daily statewide absenteeism in grades 6-11, where questionnaires were administered to 100% of the children present. This resulted in an overall adjusted return of 82.6%. A response rate of this magnitude, in conjunction with the random sampling procedures used, can be considered to be representative of the youngsters in grades K-11 in the state of Michigan.

The questionnaires were processed and checked for missing information at each university. Attempts were then made to acquire information for those questionnaires with missing data by telephone or through an additional visit to the school district. After manual coding of information to complete the student profiles, the data were keypunched on Hollerith cards directly from the questionnaires. Before submitting the data to computer analysis at Michigan State University, the basic information was subjected to vigorous scrutiny. Errors were corrected, and the data were again verified for accuracy. These procedures resulted in a data base for recreational, intramural, interscholastic, and agency-sponsored activities. The data were so voluminous that only the information pertaining to agency-sponsored activities is contained in this report. This seems appropriate, since the major emphasis of the investigation was to determine the influence of agency-sponsored athletic participation on children.

The incidence and frequency of participation in agency-sponsored sports are presented by sex and age. Information is provided on statewide participation by sport, with subcategories of this information presented by community type, school type, and race. Several consistent findings were observed as a result of these analyses.

1. The extent of participation was far greater than anticipated. For example, 1 out of every 3 boys in the state participated in baseball (a total of 397,000), and 1 in 4 completed the season. Approximately 1 in every 8

males participated in agency-sponsored tackle football (147,000); moreover, 1 in 15 participated in the other recognized contact sports of wrestling (79,000) and ice hockey (79,000). Female participation, although not as prevalent as for males, was also much greater than expected. One in five girls participated in softball (228,000), 1 in 7 in swimming (180,000), and 1 in 10 in basketball (116,000).

2. Differences in patterns of participation in the sports across age were observed. Most of the sports such as baseball, basketball, and ice hockey showed a progressive increase in incidence of participation up to a peak at 11, 12, or 13 years of age, followed by a progressive decline. In others, such as softball (for males only), golf, and downhill skiing, the incidence of participation by age varied in the different sports. A sport may have two peak ages, whereas another may peak at age 12 years and then maintain a consistent level of participation. In some sports with high rates of participation, such as baseball (males), softball (females), basketball (males), tackle football (males), and ice hockey (males), the number of students participating "often" exceeded those participating "sometimes." Interestingly, the peak years of participation in the sports for males and females were identical. The known earlier maturation of the female did not appear to affect the peak age of participation.

3. The percentage of participation in the agency-sponsored sports was relatively independent of school type. The distribution of participation in public and private schools was similar across sport categories. The discernible trends were twofold: (1) participants from private schools were more active than their public school counterparts in noncontact individual or dual sports such as swimming, tennis, golf, and skiing; and (2) participants from the public schools tended to be more involved in weight lifting and the dual combative sports such as wrestling, boxing, karate, and judo than were the students of private schools.

4. The incidence of participation across sports, in general, was highest in the urban areas, next highest in the suburban, and lowest in the rural. This finding was not anticipated. The incidence of highest participation had been expected for the suburban areas. Only in bowling, ice hockey, downhill skiing, and water skiing were the percentage-of-participation values higher in the suburban than in the urban areas. There was also a trend for greater relative participation at the "often" level in selected sports such as baseball and soccer in the suburban and rural areas. The overall trend was evident in approximately 80% of the sports sampled. Participation in the urban areas was comparatively greater than that of the suburban and rural areas at practically every age level for both sexes.

5. The incidence of participation by race was the most difficult to obtain and may have some minor limitations. Black respondents had the highest percentage-of-participation figures in 18 of 25 sports studied. This was true for all team sports except soccer and ice hockey. In dual and

individual sports, their participation was highest for all except golf, downhill skiing, water skiing, tennis, and figure skating. Moreover, they generally had a higher proportion of their total percentage of response made up of those who participated "often" than did the other races. Black participants, then, were not only involved to a greater extent in agency-sponsored sports, but also tended to be more intensely involved as well. The reader is cautioned to keep in mind that the percentages in this report are proportions of respective groups. That is, although percentages of participation may be identical or similar for two groups, the actual number of participants may vary substantially.

6. Across sports, the incidence of participation for males and females generally followed the stereotypes of female-oriented and male-oriented sports, particularly in the activities with the greatest incidence of participation. The results are striking, however, because relatively large numbers of females, particularly under the age of 14 years, are participating in agency-sponsored sports such as baseball, tackle football, karate, and wrestling, which traditionally have been male-oriented. More in-depth information concerning male/female participation and agency policies pertinent to the sexes will emanate from Phase II of the Youth Sports Study.

REFERENCES

Adams, J. E. Injury to the throwing arm. *California Medicine*, 1965, *102*, 127–132.

Adams, J. E. Little League shoulder. *California Medicine*, 1966, *105*, 22–25.

Astrand, P-O. The child in sport and physical activity—physiology. In J. G. Albinson & G. M. Andrew (Eds.), *Child in sport and physical activity*. Baltimore: University Park Press, 1976.

Astrand, P-O., Engstrom, L., Eriksson, B. O., Karlberg, P., Nylander, I., Saltin, B., & Thoren, C. Girl swimmers. *Acta Paediatrica*, 1963, *147*, 1–79 (Supplement 147).

Beznak, M. The role of anterior pituitary hormones in controlling size, work and strength of the heart. *Journal of Physiology*, 1960, *150*, 251–265.

Brown, C. H., Harrower, J. R., & Deeter, M. F. The effects of cross-country running on pre-adolescent girls. *Medicine and Science in Sports*, 1972, *4*, 1–5.

Burke, E. J., & Kleiber, E. Psychological and physical implications of highly competitive sports for children. *The Physical Educator*, 1976, *33*, 63–70.

Clarke, H. H. Characteristics of the young athlete: A longitudinal look. In *Kinesiology review*. Washington, D.C.: AAHPER, 1968.

Clarke, H. H. (Ed.) Characteristics of athletes. *Physical fitness research digest* (Series 3, No. 2), Washington, D.C.: President's Council on Physical Fitness and Sports, 1973.

Clarke, K. C. Predicting certified weight of young wrestlers: A field study of the Tcheng-Tipton method. *Medicine and Science in Sports,* 1974, *6,* 52-57.

Cooper, L. Athletics, activity and personality: A review of the literature. *Research Quarterly,* 1969, *40,* 17-22.

Cumming, G. R., Garand, T., & Borysky, L. Correlation of performance in track and field events with bone age. *Journal of Pediatrics,* 1972, *80,* 970-973.

Dowell, L. J. Environmental factors of childhood competitive athletics. *The Physical Educator,* 1971, *28,* 17-21.

Ekblom, B. Effect of physical training in adolescent boys. *Journal of Applied Physiology,* 1969, *27,* 350-355.

Emerson, R. S. Sports report. *Medical Tribune,* 1964, *5,* 36-37.

Eriksson, B. O. Physical training, oxygen supply and muscle metabolism in 11-13 year old boys. *Acta Physiologica Scandinavica,* 1972, *384,* 1-48 (Supplement 384).

Eriksson, B. O., Gollnick, P. D., & Saltin, B. Muscle metabolism and enzyme activities after training in boys 11-13 years old. *Acta Physiologica Scandinavica,* 1973, *87,* 485-497.

Eriksson, B. O., Gollnick, P. D., & Saltin, B. The effect of physical training on muscle enzyme activities and fiber composition in 11-year old boys. *Acta Paediatrica Belgica,* 1974, *28,* 245-252.

Espenschade, A. S. The contributions of physical activity to growth. *Research Quarterly,* 1960, *31,* 351-364.

Fait, H. *An analytical study of the effects of competitive athletics upon junior high school boys.* Unpublished doctoral dissertation, University of Iowa, 1951.

Hale, C. J. Physiological maturity of Little League baseball players. *Research Quarterly,* 1956, *27,* 276-284.

Hale, C. J. What research says about athletics for pre-high school age children. *Journal of Health, Physical Education and Recreation,* 1959, *30,* 19-21, 43.

Hale, C. J. Injuries among 771,810 Little League baseball players. *Journal of Sports Medicine and Physical Fitness,* 1961, *1,* 3-7.

Hanson, D. L. Cardiac response to participation in Little League baseball competition as determined by telemetry. *Research Quarterly,* 1967, *38,* 384-388.

Holmgren, A., & Strandell, T. The relationship between heart volume, total hemoglobin and physical working capacity in former athletes. *Acta Medica Scandinavica,* 1959, *163,* 149-160.

Johnson, B. L. Influence of puberal development on responses to motivated exercise. *Research Quarterly,* 1956, *27,* 182-193.

Krogman, W. M. Maturation age of 55 boys in the Little League World Series. *Research Quarterly,* 1959, *30,* 54-56.

Larson, D. L., Spreitzer, E., & Snyder, E. E. An analysis of organized sports for children. *The Physical Educator,* 1976, *33,* 59-62.

Larson, R. L., & McMahan, R. O. The epiphyses of the childhood athlete. *Journal of the American Medical Association,* 1966, *196,* 607-612.

Mackler, B. Taking the fun out of children's sports. *The Physician and Sports-medicine*, 1976, *4*, 102–104.

Malina, R. M. Exercise as an influence upon growth. *Clinical Pediatrics*, 1969, *8*, 16–26.

McCarthy, J. J. Little League lunacy. *The National Elementary Principal*, 1963, *43*, 80–83.

McCraw, L. W., & Tolbert, J. W. Sociometric status and athletic ability of junior high school boys. *Research Quarterly*, 1953, *24*, 72–80.

Parizkova, J. Longitudinal study on the influence of physical activity on body build and composition in boys from 11 to 15 years. *Teorie a Praxe Tělesné Výchovy*, 1968, *16*, 31–34 (Supplement to No. 6).

Rarick, G. L. Competitive sports in childhood and early adolescence. In G. L. Rarick (Ed.), *Physical activity: Human growth and development*. New York: Academic Press, 1973.

Rochelle, R. H., Kelliher, M. S., & Thornton, R. Relationships of maturation age to incidence of injury in tackle football. *Research Quarterly*, 1961, *32*, 78–82.

Rowe, F. A. Growth comparisons of athletes and non-athletes. *Research Quarterly*, 1933, *4*, 108–116.

Saltin, B., & Grimby, G. Physiological analysis of middle-age and former athletes: Comparison with still active athletes of same age. *Circulation*, 1968, *38*, 1104–1115.

Schendel, J. Psychological differences between athletes and nonparticipants in athletics at three educational levels. *Research Quarterly*, 1965, *36*, 52–67.

Schmucker, B., & Hollmann, W. The aerobic capacity of trained athletes from 6 to 7 years of age on. *Acta Paediatrica Belgica*, 1974, *28*, 92–101.

Seymour, E. W. Comparative study of certain behavior characteristics of participant and non-participant boys in Little League baseball. *Research Quarterly*, 1956, *27*, 338–346.

Sherif, M. Experiments in group conflict. *Scientific American*, 1956, *195*, 54–58.

Shuck, G. R. Effects of athletic competition on the growth and development of junior high school boys. *Research Quarterly*, 1962, *33*, 288–298.

Sigmond, H. The adolescent and athletics: Orthopedic aspects. *Pediatric Clinics of North America*, 1960, *7*, 165–172.

Skubic, E. Emotional responses of boys to Little League and Middle League competitive baseball. *Research Quarterly*, 1955, *26*, 342–352.

Skubic, E. Studies of Little League and Middle League baseball. *Research Quarterly*, 1956, *27*, 97–110.

Slusher, H. S. Personality and intelligence characteristics of selected high school athletes and nonathletes. *Research Quarterly*, 1964, *35*, 539–545.

Steinhaus, A. H. Chronic effects of exercise. *Physiological Reviews*, 1933, *13*, 103–147.

Tipton, C. M., & Tcheng, T-K. Iowa wrestling study: Weight loss in high school students. *Journal of the American Medical Association*, 1970, *214*, 1269–1274.

3

AGE AT MENARCHE AND FAMILY CHARACTERISTICS OF HIGH SCHOOL ATHLETES AND NONATHLETES

Robert M. Malina and Karan A. H. Moss

With heightened participation of females in competitive sports, there is considerable interest in the physical characteristics, maturity status, psychosocial profiles, and familial backgrounds of female athletes (see, e.g., Gerber, Felshin, Berlin, & Wyrick, 1974; Harris, 1972; Malina, 1978). Further, the influence of Title IX legislation undoubtedly resulted in an increase in the number of younger females, especially adolescents, participating in sport. For example, the number of high schools in Texas offering competitive sports for girls increased considerably over the last decade. The number of schools in Texas offering interscholastic competition in basketball increased to the degree that a new division for larger high schools was formed. A similar increase characterized interscholastic volleyball in Texas, participation in large high schools increasing from 32% in 1970-1971 to 84% of all schools in 1975-1976. Demand for participation by girls in golf, gymnastics, swimming, and track and field was sufficiently great in the mid-1970s to justify competition at the state level.

Although participation of adolescent females in competitive sports is increasing, information on the young female athlete is generally limited. Physical and physiological characteristics have been considered to some extent (see Malina, 1978), but demographic, psychosocial, and familial characteristics of the young female athlete have not been considered that often (e.g., Berlin, 1974; Snyder & Spreitzer, 1976). The present study was undertaken to describe and compare the timing of menarche and selected familial characteristics of varsity athletes and nonathletes at the high school level.

METHOD

School

The girls comprising the study population were enrolled in one of the nine high schools which make up the Austin Independent School District. The school is located in southeast Austin. This area consists primarily of lower middle-income families of largely white (Anglo) and Mexican-American ethnic backgrounds. Some black children, also from lower middle-income backgrounds, are bused into the school from east Austin.

The ethnic composition of the school population for the 1975–1976 academic year was 50% white, 42% Mexican-American (Spanish surname), and 8% black. Except for some of the black children, who were bused to the school, all girls lived in the residential community immediately surrounding the school.

Participants

A total of 52 young women, who were athletes in interscholastic varsity sports, were the participants. They represented all female varsity athletes at the school during the 1975–1976 academic year. One athlete, a 16-year-old black girl, had not yet attained menarche and was deleted from the analysis, thus resulting in a sample of 51 athletes, all of whom had attained menarche.

The ethnic composition of the varsity sample differed from the general school population (number of students in parentheses): 44% (23) white, 35% (18) Mexican-American, and 21% (10) black. The higher percentage of black girls on the varsity teams reflects a general trend observed in the nine high schools comprising the school district. The ethnic distribution of athletes by sport is shown in Table 1.

TABLE 1   Ethnic distribution of female athletes by sport

Sport	Black	Mexican-American	White	Total
Basketball	6	4	1	11
Golf	–	1	–	1
Gymnastics	–	–	4	4
Tennis	1	2	4	7
Track and field	1	4	6	11
Volleyball	2	7	8	17

In addition to competing in interscholastic sports, all athletes had received a letter award. Those who lettered in more than one sport were required to select a single sport for classification purposes. The athletes thus represented six sports (number of athletes in parentheses): basketball (11), golf (1), gymnastics (4), tennis (7), track and field (11), and volleyball (17). Of these, the track and field participants are perhaps least representative. The four top track and field athletes selected basketball or volleyball as their preferred sport, and are thus not included in the track and field sample. Further, the track and field program had a new coach, who was late in organizing the team. As a result, the coach could not be as selective as she would have preferred. On the other hand, the volleyball team had been the district champions.

An equal number of nonathletes were selected from health and government classes. Nonathletes were defined as students who had not participated in competitive sports at any school level (e.g., elementary and junior high school), except for physical education participation. A total of 51 nonathletes were randomly chosen from the available pool comprising the classes in the same ethnic proportions as the athletic sample, i.e., 23 whites, 18 Mexican-Americans, and 10 blacks. All girls had already attained menarche.

Interview

After obtaining essential administrative and parental permission, all girls were interviewed individually by one of the authors (Moss). The girls were familiar with the interviewer, who was a physical education teacher, as well as a coach at the school. The interview procedure was based on a questionnaire designed by R. M. Malina and W. W. Spirduso of the University of Texas for a study of college and Olympic female athletes (Malina, Spirduso, Tate, & Baylor, 1977).

The interview was designed to obtain information on the age at menarche (to the nearest month); family size, i.e., the number of children in the student's family; the ordinal position (birth order) of the girl among her siblings; in the case of girls with an older sibling, the sex of the older sibling; occupation of the head of the household; and education of the head of the household. The educational level and occupation of the head of the household were used to determine social class via the Hollingshead (1963) two-factor index.

Menarche was estimated to the nearest month. Although retrospective menarche information is influenced by error of recall, evidence indicates that most girls and women can recall this developmental landmark within a range of 2-3 months (Bergsten-Brucefors, 1976; Damon & Bajema, 1974; Damon, Damon, Reed, & Valadian, 1969). This level of accuracy is sufficient for surveys involving group comparisons.

RESULTS

Variation by Sport

The distribution of athletes by sport, and means and standard deviations for chronological age at the time of interview and the age at menarche, are shown in Table 2. Distributions of family size and birth order by sport are shown in Table 3. There is no clear distributional pattern associated with the small samples in each sport. It is perhaps interesting that none of the athletes is an only child. Approximately 29% of the athletes are from families with six or more children. On the other hand, about 45% of the athletes are either first- or second-born children, in contrast to 18% who are fifth or later born.

The social class distribution of high school athletes by sport is shown in Table 4. Only one athlete was classified in the lowest social class, while the majority of athletes (59%) were from families classified as middle class.

A summary of the analyses of variance associated with sport type is shown in Table 5. The athletes in different sports did not differ significantly in chronological age, social class, family size, and ordinal position. The athletes in different sports, however, differed significantly in the mean age at menarche ($p < .05$). The subsequent test of independence among the means (Kramer, 1956) indicated that the basketball players attained menarche, on the average, significantly later than did the track and field ($p < .01$) and volleyball athletes ($p < .05$) (see Table 2). They did not differ significantly from the athletes in other sports. Further, the track and field, volleyball, gymnastics, and tennis athletes did not differ significantly among themselves in the mean age at menarche.

Comparisons of Athletes and Nonathletes

Because differences among the athletes in specific sports are small and generally not statistically significant, the 51 athletes were treated as a group

TABLE 2 Means and standard deviations for chronological age and age at menarche for high school athletes in different sports

Sport	N	Chronological age		Age at menarche	
		M	SD	M	SD
Basketball	11	16.89	1.21	14.09	1.03
Golf	1	15.42	–	13.92	–
Gymnastics	4	16.48	1.13	13.06	1.21
Tennis	7	16.90	1.17	13.10	.83
Track and field	11	16.53	.88	12.48	.89
Volleyball	17	16.91	.97	12.89	1.24

TABLE 3 Distribution of family size and birth order by sport in high school female athletes

Sport	Family size: Number of children					
	1	2	3	4	5	6+
Basketball	–	3	2	–	1	5
Golf	–	–	1	–	–	–
Gymnastics	–	1	1	1	–	1
Tennis	–	–	2	3	1	1
Track and field	–	2	3	2	2	2
Volleyball	–	2	–	5	4	6

Sport	Birth order				
	1	2	3	4	5+
Basketball	3	3	2	–	3
Golf	1	–	–	–	–
Gymnastics	1	1	2	–	–
Tennis	1	1	2	3	–
Track and field	1	4	2	2	2
Volleyball	3	4	3	3	4

for comparisons with nonathletes. Means and standard deviations for chronological age at the time of the survey and age at menarche for athletes and nonathletes, and for each category grouped by ethnicity are shown in Table 6. Mean chronological ages and standard deviations are virtually the same in the athletes and nonathletes. Mean age differences between and within ethnic groups are small.

Age at menarche is only slightly later in athletes (13.12 ± 0.16 years) compared with nonathletes (12.89 ± 0.18 years). The athletes of the three

TABLE 4 Distribution of social class (Hollingshead two-factor index) by sport in high school female athletes

Sport	Social class				
	I (high)	II	III	IV	V (low)
Basketball	–	1	8	2	–
Golf	1	–	–	–	–
Gymnastics	–	–	3	1	–
Tennis	1	–	3	2	1
Track and field	1	2	7	1	–
Volleyball	1	2	9	5	–

TABLE 5 Summary of analyses of variance associated with
sport type in high school female athletes

Variable	df	MS	F	p
Chronological age				
Between (B)	5	87.6	.56	NS
Within (W)	45	155.3		
Age at menarche				
B	5	480	2.91	.05
W	45	165.1		
Social class				
B	5	201.2	1.34	NS
W	45	150.4		
Family size				
B	5	2.7	.60	NS
W	45	4.5		
Ordinal position				
B	5	1.3	.51	NS
W	45	2.6		

ethnic groups are almost identical in mean age at menarche among the black
girls (12.52 ± 0.58 years) to the white girls (12.86 ± 0.23 years) to the
Mexican-American girls (13.12 ± 0.29 years). None of the differences in the
age at menarche associated with athletic status (i.e., athlete and nonathlete),
with ethnicity (i.e., black, Mexican-American, and white), or with the interaction
of athletic status and ethnicity are statistically significant (Table 7).

TABLE 6 Means and standard deviations for chronological age and age at
menarche in high school athletes and nonathletes

Group	N	Chronological age		Age at menarche	
		M	SD	M	SD
Athletes	51	16.75	1.03	13.12	1.17
Black	10	16.80	.98	13.19	.93
Mexican-American	18	16.70	1.21	13.11	1.44
White	23	16.77	.93	13.11	1.07
Nonathletes	51	16.72	1.00	12.89	1.31
Black	10	17.01	.84	12.52	1.84
Mexican-American	18	16.83	.65	13.12	1.25
White	23	16.51	1.24	12.86	1.09

TABLE 7 Summary of analyses of variance associated with athletic status and ethnicity in female athletes

Variable	df	MS	F	p
Age at menarche				
Athletic status (A)	1	264.3	1.16	NS
Ethnicity (E)	2	61.2	.27	NS
A X E	2	131	.58	NS
Error	96	227.1		
Family size				
A	1	12.4	.08	NS
E	2	48.8	.33	NS
A X E	2	91.1	.61	NS
Error	96	148.6		
Ordinal position				
A	1	14.3	3.54	.06
E	2	15.3	3.77	.03
A X E	2	5.1	1.27	NS
Error	96	4.1		
Social class				
A	1	1.03	4.91	.03
E	2	.06	.29	NS
A X E	2	.04	.20	NS
Error	96	.21		

Although differences between the athletes and nonathletes in menarche are not significant, the relative distributions of reported ages at menarche for both groups are shown in Figure 1. The distribution for the two groups are similar. About 60% of the athletes and nonathletes attain menarche during the 12th and 13th years. The peak distribution for the nonathletes occurs in the 12th year (35%), whereas that for the athletes occurs in the 13th year (33%). The athletes also have a slightly greater concentration of later maturers, 25% attaining menarche during or later than the 14th year compared with 18% of the nonathletes.

The distribution of family size, i.e., number of children, for athletes and nonathletes is shown in Figure 2. The distribution is somewhat skewed toward a smaller number of children in the family. Note that these data are limited in that the sibships of some of the athletes and nonathletes are probably not yet complete in terms of total number of offspring. None of the athletes is from an only-child family, and only three nonathletes are an only child. Athletes are from slightly larger families than nonathletes (Table 8). Analysis of variance in family size associated with athletic status and ethnicity, as well as their interaction, indicated no statistically significant

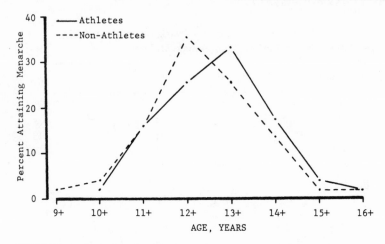

FIGURE 1   Relative distribution of reported ages at menarche in high school athletes and nonathletes.

differences (see Table 7). The median test of differences, however, between median family size of athletes and nonathletes was significant ($\chi^2 = 3.94$, $p < .05$).

The distribution of birth order in athletes and nonathletes is shown in Figure 3. Twice as many nonathletes (39%) as athletes (20%) are first born, so that athletes tend to have, on the average, later birth orders (Table 8). The difference in birth order between athletes and nonathletes was just short of significant at the 0.05 level by either analysis of variance ($p = .06$, Table 7) or the median test ($\chi^2 = 3.67$, $p < .10 > .05$). The analysis of variance indicated a significant ethnic effect on birth order ($p = .03$), but the interaction of athletic status and ethnicity was not significant (Table 7).

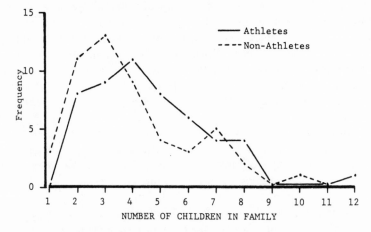

FIGURE 2   Distribution of family size, i.e., number of children in the family, for high school female athletes and nonathletes.

TABLE 8 Medians, means, and standard deviations for family size and birth order in female athletes and nonathletes

Group	Family size			Birth order		
	MD	*M*	*SD*	*MD*	*M*	*SD*
Athletes	4.3	4.6	2.1	2.7	3	1.6
Nonathletes	3.4	3.9	2.1	2.1	2.3	1.4

Because family size is related to the age at menarche, i.e., girls in smaller families attain menarche earlier than those in larger families (Jenicek & Demirjian, 1974; Piasecki & Waliszko, 1975; Roberts, Rozner, & Swan, 1971; Singh, 1972), we grouped the athletes and nonathletes by family size into small (1 and 2 children), medium (3 and 4 children), and large (5 or more children). In addition, we also grouped the athletes and nonathletes by birth order, since girls born later in a sibship tend to mature earlier (Roberts & Dann, 1967). Results of this analysis are shown in Table 9. The sample sizes per category are small, and there are no significant differences between mean ages at menarche of the family size and birth-order categories in Table 9. Among both athletes and nonathletes, however, there is a tendency for girls in smaller families to attain menarche, on the average, earlier than those in larger

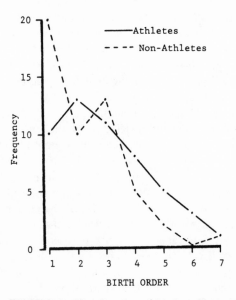

FIGURE 3 Distribution of birth order in high school female athletes and nonathletes.

TABLE 9 Age at menarche in athletes and nonathletes grouped by family size and birth order

	Athletes			Nonathletes		
Variable	*N*	*M*	*SD*	*N*	*M*	*SD*
Family size						
1–2	8	12.56	1.01	14	12.48	1.38
3–4	20	13.45	1.02	22	12.86	1.30
5+	23	13.04	1.29	15	13.31	1.18
Birth order						
1	10	13.17	1.33	20	12.62	1.46
2	13	13.14	.94	10	12.50	1.34
3	11	13.15	1.16	13	13.46	1.16
4+	17	13.06	1.33	8	13.11	.85

families. Within the nonathletes, there is a gradient of increasing age at menarche associated with increasing family size. No such tendency is evident in the athletes.

Mean ages at menarche are essentially the same across all birth-order positions for the sample of athletes. Among nonathletes, first- and second-born girls tend to have earlier mean ages at menarche.

As indicated previously, twice as many nonathletes (20) were first-born than were athletes (10). For the 41 later-born athletes and 31 later-born nonathletes, we looked at the sex of the immediately preceding (i.e., older) sibling. Of the 41 later-born female athletes, 26 (63%) had a brother as the next oldest sibling, whereas only 14 (45%) of the 31 later-born female nonathletes had a brother as the immediately preceding sibling. Thus, the later-born female athletes have a greater percentage of brothers as their next oldest sibling than have later-born nonathletes.

The relative distribution of social class of the heads of the households of the athletes and nonathletes is illustrated in Figure 4, and mean social class indexes and standard deviations are shown in Table 10. The differences between the index of social position of athletes and nonathletes is statistically significant ($p = .03$, Table 7), although both fall within the middle class. The mean index for the heads of the households of the athletes tends towards the midportion of the range for class III on Hollingshead's scale, whereas that for the nonathletes tends towards the upper portion (i.e., lower social class) of the range for class III. Thus, the families of the athletes are in a slightly, but significantly, better socioeconomic position than those of the nonathletes. This is clearly evident in the relative distribution of social classes in Figure 4. About 76% of the athletes are in classes I, II, and III, compared with 61% of the nonathletes. In contrast, about 39% of the nonathletes are from families in lower social classes, IV and V, compared with about 24% of the athletes.

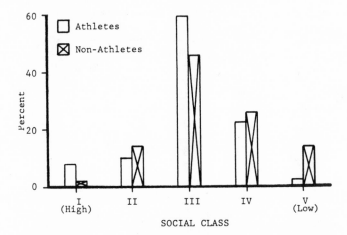

FIGURE 4 Relative distribution of social class of the heads of households of high school female athletes and nonathletes.

Although the analysis of variance of social class differences did not indicate a significant ethnic effect or an athletic status-ethnic interaction (Table 7), the distribution of ethnic- and athletic status-specific indexes of social position and class (Tables 11 and 12) suggests that the overall significant difference between athletes and nonathletes is due to the lower social class background of Mexican-American nonathletes. Thus, the Mexican-American athletes are from families that are better off socio-economically than families of nonathletes. A similar trend, though slight, is evident for the families of black athletes.

DISCUSSION

The mean age at menarche in our mixed racial sample of high school athletes (13.12 ± 0.16 years) is almost identical with that for college students who had

TABLE 10 Means and standard deviations for indexes of social class of the heads of the households of female athletes and nonathletes

Group	Index of social position		Class equivalent and range[a]
	M	SD	
Athletes	39.6	12.5	III (32–47)
Nonathletes	45.4	14.4	III (32–47)

[a]The range as reported by Hollingshead (1963).

TABLE 11 Distribution of ethnic-specific social classes for female athletes and nonathletes

Social class	White A[a]	White NA[b]	Mexican-American A	Mexican-American NA	Black A	Black NA	Total A	Total NA
I (high)	2	1	2	–	–	–	4	1
II	3	5	–	1	2	1	5	7
III	10	14	13	4	7	5	30	23
IV	7	3	3	6	1	4	11	13
V (low)	1	–	–	7	–	–	1	7

[a]A = athletes.
[b]NA = nonathletes.

competed in interscholastic varsity sports at the high school level (13.02 ± 0.16 years) and college athletes in a variety of sports (13.05 ± 0.18 years) (Malina et al., 1977). These college athletes were surveyed from 1974 through 1976 when intercollegiate athletics for women at the University of Texas were relatively recent. Hence, the athletes were perhaps not at the level one would expect with increased recruiting, emphasis on sports, and competition among colleges and universities for top class or national-caliber athletes.

The average ages at menarche for these three samples, however, are earlier than those for Hungarian national athletes (13.6 years; Erdelyi, 1962), for Finnish athletes (14.0 years, Ingman as cited by Erdelyi, 1976), and

TABLE 12 Means and standard deviations for indexes of social position of the heads of households of black, Mexican-American, and white female athletes and nonathletes

Group	Index of social position N	Index of social position M	Index of social position SD	Class equivalent and range[a]
Black athletes	10	38.2	10.7	III (32–47)
Black nonathletes	10	43.9	11.5	III
Mexican-American athletes	18	40.7	12	III
Mexican-American nonathletes	18	55.2	13.8	IV (48–63)
White athletes	23	39.3	13.9	III
White nonathletes	23	38.5	11.9	III

[a]The ranges as reported by Hollingshead (1963).

participants at the Montreal Olympic Games (13.66 ± 0.11 years; Malina et al., 1977). Further, the mean value for Hungarian athletes is equivalent to the average age at menarche for the Hungarian population as a whole. On the other hand, the mean age at menarche for participants at the Montreal Olympics is significantly later than that for a probability sample of U.S. white women, 20-24 years of age (12.77 ± 0.06 years; National Center for Health Statistics, 1973). The retrospective estimates of the age at menarche in athletes comprising several sports at different competitive levels thus suggest a relationship between age at menarche and competitive level. Later menarche, on the average, occurs in national- and international-caliber athletes, i.e., and association between delayed menarche and more advanced competitive levels.

The preceding considered athletes grouped across several sports. Some evidence suggests variability in the timing of menarche associated with specific sports. For example, Astrand, Engstrom, Eriksson, Karlberg, Nylander, Saltin, and Thoren (1963) reported a mean age at menarche of 12.88 years for 29 Swedish girl swimmers, 11.9 to 16.4 years of age, of national- and international caliber. This average was lower than the mean value for Swedish reference data (13.59 years). Other observations on young swimmers 10 to 12 years of age showed advanced breast and pubic hair development (both of which are related to the age at menarche) in finalists of a national age-group competition, compared with semifinalists (Bar-Or, 1975). In contrast, participants at a national intercollegiate track and field competition had an average age at menarche of 13.58 ± 0.16 years, which was significantly later than that of nonathlete college women (Malina, Harper, Avent, & Campbell, 1973). Data from candidates for the U.S. Olympic volleyball team in 1976 had a mean age at menarche of 14.12 ± 0.22 years, and were thus significantly delayed relative to nonathletes (Malina et al., 1977). These observations of national-caliber athletes might thus suggest different maturity relationships for different sports.

Small samples in each of the sports represented in our high school athletes makes it difficult to compare menarche for participants in different sports. Nevertheless, menarche in our high school athletes grouped by sport are compared with similar data for athletes from the University of Texas at Austin (Table 13). Mean age at menarche in high school basketball players is slightly more than a year later than in college players. High school volleyball athletes are also slightly later in menarche than the small sample of college players. In contrast, the college tennis players are somewhat delayed in menarche compared with the high school players. The average age at menarche in Olympic volleyball players and national level track and field athletes cited earlier are considerably delayed in comparison to that of the high school and college athletes in these respective sports. This would perhaps suggest different maturity relationships for different competitive levels within a given sport. Sampling variation, however, must not be overlooked.

The mean age at menarche in our sample of nonathletes, 12.89 ± 0.18

TABLE 13 Mean ages at menarche and standard deviations for high school
and college athletes grouped by sport

Sport	High school[a]			College[b]		
	N	M	SD	N	M	SD
Basketball	11	14.09	1.03	16	12.89	1.16
Golf	1	13.92	–	4	12.50	.93
Gymnastics	4	13.06	1.21	3	13.17	–
Tennis	7	13.10	.83	13	13.73	1.31
Track and field	11	12.48	.89	3	13.25	–
Volleyball	17	12.89	1.24	7	12.54	1.12
All athletes	51	13.12	1.17	53	13.05	1.28

[a]Present study.
[b]Malina, Spirduso, Tate, and Baylor, 1977.

years, is similar to the median age at menarche of 12.77 years, for a
probability sample of girls in the U.S. Health Examination Survey,
1963–1970. The mean ages at menarche for our black and white
nonathletes—12.52 ± 0.58 and 12.86 ± 0.22 years, respectively—are nearly the
same as the median ages for black and white girls in the U.S. Health
Examination Survey—12.52 and 12.80 years, respectively (National Center for
Health Statistics, 1973). Comparative data for Mexican-American girls are not
available. The mean age at menarche for our Mexican-American nonathletes
was 13.12 ± 0.29 years, slightly later than that for girls in the U.S. Health
Examination Survey. This might reflect the lower social class background of
the Mexican-American nonathletes (Table 12). Although later menarches are
usually reported for girls living in lower social strata (e.g., Laska-Mierzejewska,
1970; Piasecki & Waliszko, 1975; Tanner, 1962; Tanner & Evelth, 1975),
other evidence suggests no significant differences in the time of menarche
among girls in different social strata (Jenicek & Demirjian, 1974; Roberts &
Dann, 1967; Roberts et al., 1971).

Age at menarche is influenced by a number of factors, including
nutritional status, physique, and family size. Undernourished girls characteristically are delayed in menarche (Tanner, 1966; Tanner & Eveleth, 1975).
Girls with more linear physiques generally experience latter menarche (Jenicek
& Demirjian, 1974; Roberts & Dann, 1967; Widholm & Kantero, 1971). Girls
and women who excel in athletics tend to have more linear physiques than do
the nonathletic population (Malina, 1978); therefore, linearity of physique
may be related, in part, to the later menarche commonly observed in samples
of athletes.

Regarding family size, menarche generally occurs later in children from
larger families, even when socioeconomic factors are controlled (Jenicek &

Demirjian, 1974; Piasecki & Waliszko, 1975; Roberts et al., 1971; Singh, 1972). The estimated family size effect in British data, for example, is 0.18 years per additional sibship (Roberts et al., 1971). Our analysis of family size and menarche (Table 9) indicated a tendency toward later menarche with increasing family size only in nonathletes. Athletes from small families had an earlier average age at menarche than those from medium and larger sized families, but menarche in our small samples occurred later in athletes from medium sized families than from larger families.

Girls born later in a sibship generally attain menarche earlier than those born earlier (Roberts & Dann, 1967). No such trend is evident in our data (Table 9). Among nonathletes, the earlier born (first and second) girls attain menarche, on the average, earlier than the later born. Among athletes, average ages at menarche are virtually the same across the birth-order categories.

Our mixed racial sample of the athletes were from slightly larger families, i.e., larger number of children in the family than the nonathletes (Table 8). The median family size for athletes was 4.3 children, compared with 3.4 for the nonathletes. Comparative family size data for athletes is limited. The average family size for 18 candidates for the U.S. Olympic volleyball team in 1976 was 4.3 (Malina & Spirduso, 1977). The average family size for our 17 high school volleyball players was 5.0. Preliminary observations for a sample of women participants in the Montreal Olympic Games give a mean family size of 3.6 children (Malina et al., 1977). The average family size of the young Swedish swimmers reported by Astrand et al. (1963) was 2.3 children, which was almost identical for that characteristic of Stockholm (2.4 children). It should be noted that the young Swedish swimmers were from families in the upper two social strata for Stockholm, i.e., employers and salaried employees. In contrast, our athletes (Table 10) as well as the U.S. Olympic volleyball aspirants (Malina & Spirduso, 1977) were from the middle class (III) on the Hollingshead (1963) two-factor index of social position. There may thus be social class differences in sport preference and opportunity for participation in a given sport. The sport-specific social class distributions (Table 4), however, show no clear pattern for the small groups of athletes.

Birth order of the athletes within their particular sibships is slightly later (3.0) than for the nonathletes (2.3) in the present study (Table 8). No athlete was an only child, and twice as many of the nonathletes (39%) were first born than the athletes (20%). As in the case of family size, birth order data for female athletes are limited. Seven of the 30 swimmers studied by Astrand et al. (1963) were only children. In contrast, none of the 18 U.S. Olympic volleyball aspirants studied in 1976 was an only child, and only 3 of the 18 were first born. The average birth order of the volleyball players was 2.7 (Malina & Spirduso, 1977). Three of the 17 volleyball players in our sample were first born (Table 3), and none was an only child. The average birth order of the 17 high school players was 3.1, which is similar to that for the Olympic aspirants.

Preliminary results for female participants at the Montreal Olympic Games give an average birth order of 2.2, with about 35% of the athletes being first born (excluding only children) and 29% being second born (Malina et al., 1977). Only 6% of the women athletes were only children. On the other hand, the small sample of U.S. Olympic volleyball candidates were 17% first born and 39% second born. A combined sample of male and female athletes at the Mexico City Olympic Games in 1968 had 8.5% only children, with 23% and 32% of the athletes being first and second born, respectively (DeGaray, Levine, & Carter, 1974). A combined sample of male (135) and female (37) Czechoslovakian Olympic representatives had 38% first- and 44% second-born children (Řehoř, 1976). Thus, the Mexico City Olympic participants, the Czechoslovakian Olympic athletes, and the U.S. Olympic volleyball aspirants had an apparent excess of second births. The Montreal data, on the other hand, had a slight excess of first born. Our data for 51 high school athletes also indicate a slight excess of second-born children (26%), whereas 20% were first and third born, respectively. There was no clear pattern of birth order distributions for specific sports in our sample of high school athletes.

There is the possibility, however, or sport-specific variation in birth order. Data for males suggest a relationship between birth order and participation in dangerous sports (Casher, 1977; Nisbett, 1968; Yiannakis, 1976). Later-born males tended to participate more often in dangerous sports, whereas first borns tended to avoid dangerous sports. None of the sports represented in our female athletes, except perhaps gymnastics, could be characterized as dangerous, as in the studies of males. In fact, many fall into the "low harm" category used by Casher (1977), e.g., tennis, swimming, and golf.

It is interesting that our second- and later-born female athletes more often had a brother as the next oldest sibling (63%). In contrast, fewer (45%) second- and later-born nonathletes had a brother as the immediately preceding sibling. The significance of an older brother in influencing the sports participation of a younger sister, however, is unclear. Evaluating the hypothesis that females with sisters in contrast to females with brothers would be underrepresented in a group of physical education majors (i.e., individuals generally committed to sport), Landers and Lüschen (1970) found an underrepresentation of only females with younger sisters and not females with older sisters. Sutton-Smith and Rosenberg (1970) also reported lesser sports participation among females with younger sisters. Among a group of education majors (i.e., those less committed to sport), Landers (no date) noted that females with younger brothers, rather than those with older brothers, reported more participation in masculine sports. The college women with younger brothers also scored lower in feminity scores.

The preceding discussion, though limited (see Berlin, 1974, for a more detailed discussion of the antecedents of competitive sport involvement by adult women), indicates a lack of consistent findings regarding family size, ordinal position, and sibling sex status in relation to sports participation.

Studies of family relationships, including parents, as well as peer interactions, are obviously necessary for a more complete understanding of the determinants of sports preference and participation. Too often the role of parents' sport experience is overlooked. For example, in 28 of the 30 families of the young Swedish swimmers studied by Astrand et al. (1963), one or both parents had been active in competitive (21 families) or noncompetitive (7 families) sports. In addition, 29 of the 38 siblings of the 30 swimmers had been active athletes.

SUMMARY

Age at menarche and selected family characteristics were considered in a triracial sample of 51 high school varsity athletes and an equivalent number of nonathletes. The athletes were distributed across several sports, and familial data included family size, ordinal position, and socioeconomic status. All data were based on individual interviews. Varsity athletes did not differ significantly in the age at menarche compared with nonathletes. Athletes came from slightly larger families and more often were later-born children. Participants in interscholastic sports more frequently had a brother as the next-oldest sibling, in contrast to nonparticipants, who more often were first born. Both the athletes and nonathletes fell within level III (middle class) on the Hollingshead two-factor socioeconomic index, but the athletes had a slightly higher socioeconomic score within the category. These data are also compared with other information for female athletes at the high school level as well as at higher competitive levels.

REFERENCES

Astrand, P-O., Engstrom, L., Eriksson, B. O., Karlberg, P., Nylander, I., Saltin, B., & Thoren, C. Girl swimmers. *Acta Paediatrica*, 1963, *147*, 1–79 (Supplement 147).

Bar-Or, O. Predicting athletic performance. *The Physician and Sportsmedicine*, 1975, *3*, 80–85.

Bergsten-Brucefors, A. A note on the accuracy of recalled age at menarche. *Annals of Human Biology*, 1976, *3*, 71–73.

Berlin, P. The woman athlete. In E. W. Gerber, J. Felshin, P. Berlin, & W. Wyrick (Eds.), *The American woman in sport*. Reading, Mass.: Addison-Wesley, 1974.

Casher, B. B. Relationship between birth order and participation in dangerous sports. *Research Quarterly*, 1977, *48*, 33–40.

Damon, A., & Bajema, C. J. Age at menarche: Accuracy of recall after thirty-nine years. *Human Biology*, 1974, *46*, 381–384.

Damon, A., Damon, S. T., Reed, R. B., & Valadian, I. Age at menarche of mothers and daughters, with a note on accuracy of recall. *Human Biology*, 1969, *41*, 161–175.

DeGaray, A. L., Levine, L., & Carter, J. E. L. *Genetic and anthropological studies of Olympic athletes.* New York: Academic Press, 1974.

Erdelyi, G. J. Gynecological survey of female athletes. *Journal of Sports Medicine and Physical Fitness,* 1962, *2,* 174–179.

Erdelyi, G. J. Effects of exercise on the menstrual cycle. *The Physician and Sportsmedicine,* 1976, *4,* 79–81.

Gerber, E. W., Felshin, J., Berlin, P., & Wyrick, W. *The American woman in sport.* Reading, Mass.: Addison-Wesley, 1974.

Harris, D. V. (Ed.). *Women and Sport: A National Research Conference.* Pennsylvania State University, HPER Series, No. 2, 1972.

Hollingshead, A. B. *Two-factor index of social position.* New Haven, Conn.: Yale University, 1963. (mimeographed)

Jenicek, M. & Demirjian, A. Age at menarche in French Canadian urban girls. *Annals of Human Biology,* 1974, *1,* 339–346.

Kramer, C. Y. Extension of multiple range tests to group means with unequal numbers of replications. *Biometrics,* 1956, *12,* 307–310.

Landers, D. M. *Sibling-sex-status and ordinal position effects on females' sport participation and interests.* Children's Research Center, University of Illinois at Urbana-Champaign, no date. (mimeographed)

Landers, D. M., & Lüschen, G. Sibling sex-status and ordinal position effects on the sport participation of females. In G. S. Kenyon (Ed.), *Contemporary psychology of sport.* Chicago: Athletic Institute, 1970.

Laska-Mierzejewska, T. Effect of ecological and socio-economic factors on the age at menarche, body height and weight of rural girls in Poland. *Human Biology,* 1970, *42,* 284–292.

Malina, R. M. Physical growth and maturity characteristics of young athletes. In R. A. Magill, M. J. Ash, & F. L. Smoll (Eds.), *Children and youth in sport: A contemporary anthology.* Champaign, Ill.: Human Kinetics Publishers, 1978.

Malina, R. M., Harper, A. B., Avent, H. H., & Campbell, D. E. Age at menarche in athletes and non-athletes. *Medicine and Science in Sports,* 1973, *5,* 11–13.

Malina, R. M., & Spirduso, W. W. *Family backgrounds of female Olympic volleyball players.* Manuscript in preparation, 1977.

Malina, R. M., Spirduso, W. W., Tate, C., & Baylor, A. M. *Age at menarche in athletes at different competitive levels and in different sports.* Manuscript submitted for publication, 1977.

National Center for Health Statistics. Age at menarche. *Vital and Health Statistics,* Series 11, Number 133. Washington, D.C.: U.S. Government Printing Office, 1973.

Nisbett, R. E. Birth order and participation in dangerous sports. *Journal of Personality and Social Psychology,* 1968, *8,* 351–353.

Piasecki, E., & Waliszko, A. Zmienność wieku menarchy dziewczat wrocławskich w uzależnieniu od wielkości rodziny. *Materialy i Prace Antropologiczne,* 1975, *89,* 103–116.

Rehoř, E. Analýza niektorých rodinných znakov Československých olym-pionikov. *Acta Facultatis Educationis Physicae Universitatis Comenianae, Publicatio XV,* Bratislava: Slovenské Pedagogické Nakladatel'stvo, 1976.

Roberts, D. F., & Dann, T. C. Influences on menarcheal age in girls in a Welsh college. *British Journal of Preventive and Social Medicine*, 1967, *21*, 170–176.

Roberts, D. F., Rozner, L. M., & Swan, A. V. Age at menarche, physique and environment in industrial north east England. *Acta Paediatrica Scandinavica*, 1971, *60*, 158–164.

Singh, H. D. Family size and age of menarche. *American Journal of Obstetrics and Gynecology*, 1972, *114*, 837–838.

Synder, E. E., & Spreitzer, E. Correlates of sport participation among adolescent girls. *Research Quarterly*, 1976, *47*, 804–809.

Sutton-Smith, B., & Rosenberg, B. G. *The sibling*. New York: Holt, Rinehart, & Winston, 1970.

Tanner, J. M. *Growth at adolescence* (2nd ed.). Oxford: Blackwell Scientific Publications, 1962.

Tanner, J. M. The secular trend towards earlier physical maturation. *Tydschrift voor Sociale Geneeskunde*, 1966, *44*, 524–539.

Tanner, J. M., & Eveleth, P. B. Variability between populations in growth and development at puberty. In S. R. Berenberg (Ed.), *Puberty, biologic and psychosocial components*. Leiden: Stenfert Kroese, 1975.

Wildholm, O., & Kantero, R-L. A statistical analysis of the menstrual patterns of 8,000 Finnish girls and their mothers. *Acta Obstetrica et Gynecologica Scandinavica*, 1971 (Supplement 14).

Yiannakis, A. Birth order and preference for dangerous sports among males. *Research Quarterly*, 1976, *47*, 62–67.

IMPACT OF SPORTS ON PSYCHOSOCIAL DEVELOPMENT

4

SOCIAL LEARNING OF VIOLENCE IN MINOR HOCKEY

Michael D. Smith

Violence and Canadian hockey have been synonymous since at least 1907, when a player was killed in a fight during a major league game. A court case resulted in that instance, but the accused was acquitted because it could not be proved that it was he, and not others, who had struck the fatal blow (Brent, 1975). In the following decades, violence came to be accepted as a legitimate part of the game (save for an occasional dissenting, generally unheeded voice). *Violence*—insofar as it refers to one person physically assaulting another in a manner proscribed by the official rules of hockey—has been, literally, *nonviolence*. Most of today's players, professional and amateur, thoroughly socialized, do not consider fighting with fists violent; professionals claim that their games are generally not violent. This highly charged term is reserved for only the most extreme and injurious of acts.[1]

Even the staunchest defenders of traditional hockey, however, agree when pressed that fighting and all sorts of other illegal assaults are sufficiently commonplace in both professional and professionalized leagues as to be normal. But, they argue, this behavior is a natural and inevitable by-product of (a) the speed, (b) the body contact, and (c) the frustration inherent in the game. Besides, if fighting were not allowed, there would be more *stick-work* (that aggressiveness has to come out somehow). In any case, the argument

This research was funded by Canada Council grant S-74-1693.

[1] Subjective meanings imputed to the term vary widely, of course (e.g., Blumenthal, Khan, Andrews, & Head, 1972, pp. 72-95). The statements regarding players' usage were derived from interviews with approximately 100 National Hockey League (NHL) performers and dozens of amateurs conducted during a field-work phase of the present research.

goes, hockey is not for the faint of heart. It's a "man's game." The transcript of the recent Ontario government inquiry into violence in amateur hockey is replete with such testimony for the defense (McMurtry, 1974).

But beginning in the late 1960s, against a backdrop of public concern about violence in general, a series of dramatic events pushed hockey violence onto the front stage, making visible what for so long had been taken for granted.

1969—The Green-Maki Fight. Boston's "terrible" Ted Green and Wayne Maki of St. Louis engage in a stick duel during an exhibition game in Ottawa. Green is struck on the head by a full-swinging blow. His skull fractured, he almost dies. Both men are charged with assault causing bodily harm (the first prosecutions in Ontario since 1907); both are acquitted on grounds of self-defense. Later, naturally, Green writes a book about his experience.

1972—The First Canada-Russia Hockey Series. Amid accusations and counter-accusations of dirty play, Canada's truculent Bobby Clarke eliminates the Russian star, Kharmalov, from the remainder of the series with a blatant two-handed stick-swipe across the ankle. Canada had exported hockey violence for years but never before quite so many millions of television viewers. Reaction in the mass media is mixed: some commentators glorify Clarke for his insatiable "desire"; others express embarrassment; a handful, shame.

1972—The Paul Smithers Case. Smithers, a 17-year-old hockey player, engages an opposing player in a scuffle outside a Toronto arena following a raucous midget hockey game. Kicked in the groin, the other boy collapses, chokes on his own vomit, dies. Smithers is convicted of manslaughter and sentenced to six months in jail, a decision causing bitter and prolonged public controversy.

1974—The Hamilton-Bramalea Game. Players, officials, and spectators brawl throughout this Ontario Junior B playoff game in which 189 penalty minutes are assessed and five players and one team official are injured. Fourteen policemen finally quell the fighting. The Bramalea team withdraws from the playoffs and is promptly suspended by the Ontario Hockey Association, which finds no justification for the team's refusal to play "because the game was not as violent as many others in recent years" (McMurtry, 1974, p. 17).

1974—The Ontario Government Inquiry and Investigation into Violence in Amateur Hockey. Toronto lawyer Bill McMurtry is commissioned by the province to inquire into the Hamilton-Bramalea debacle. In an extensive investigation, culminating in five days of public hearings and producing a 1,256 page transcript, McMurtry concludes that professional hockey is the number one cause of amateur hockey violence. His report is widely circulated and hotly debated.

1975—The Forbes-Boucha Case. Boston's Dave Forbes and Minnesota's Henry Boucha engage in a minor altercation for which both are penalized. Forbes threatens Boucha from the penalty box; then, leaving the box, lunges at Boucha, striking him near the right eye with the butt-end of his stick. Boucha falls to his knees, hands over face; Forbes jumps on his back, punching, until pulled off by another player. Boucha is taken to the hospital, where he receives 25 stitches and the first of what turns out to be several eye operations. Forbes is indicted for aggravated assault in Minnesota, but a hung jury results in his acquittal.

1975—The Maloney-Glennie Fight. Toronto Maple Leaf, Brian Glennie, bodychecks a Detroit player. In retaliation, Detroit's quick-fisted Dan Maloney knocks Glennie down with a forearm blow, punches him repeatedly, and allegedly bounces his head on the ice. Glennie goes to the hospital with a concussion and other injuries. Maloney is charged with assault causing bodily harm. Hung jury, charges dropped.

1976—The Jozdio-Tardiff Beating. In a World Hockey Association playoff game, Calgary Cowboys' Rick Jozdio administers a devastating beating to top scorer Marc Tadiff of the Quebec Nordique. Both benches empty, and a wild, half-hour melee ensues. Tardiff, unconscious, with a severe concussion and other injuries, is finished for the season. Quebec threatens to withdraw from the series unless (a) Jozdio is suspended for life, (b) the Calgary coach is suspended for the rest of the playoffs, (c) the League President (the official observer at this game) is fired or resigns. The demands are met in part, and the series continues. Jozdio is charged in Quebec with assault with intent to injure.

1976—The Philadelphia-Toronto Playoff. In a brawl-filled playoff contest in Toronto (resulting in a new Philadelphia penalty record) Toronto's Borje Salming, a Swedish nonfighter, is badly beaten by Philadelphia's Mel Bridgeman. Further brouhahas involving players, fans, and a policeman result in three Philadelphia players being charged—on orders of Ontario's Attorney General Roy McMurtry—with criminal offenses, from possession of a dangerous weapon (a hockey stick) to assaulting a police officer. The hockey establishment, insisting it can look after its own affairs, accuses McMurtry of headline-seeking, but considerable support for his actions is registered from other quarters.

A myriad of other less sensational happenings have combined with the foregoing to keep hockey violence in the public consciousness: criminal indictments and convictions—of players, coaches, and fans—at the minor level; refusals of teams to play against certain other teams for fear of serious injuries; revelation that professional organizations have deliberately mer-chandised violence; denunciations by a few highly respected players and coaches (Bobby Hull, Jacques Lapierriere) of what has come to be known as *goon* hockey. Even a member of Parliament has urged the Canadian Government to condemn the NHL's "encouragement of excessive violence"

(*Toronto Star*, 1976, Dec. 17:c3). Rule changes in professional and amateur hockey have occurred.

Yet reduction in overall levels of violence are not apparent, claims to the contrary notwithstanding. And despite increasingly perceptive and responsible commentary in the mass media, professional hockey's "cheerleaders" continue to fawn over the fighters and tough guys. The ethos of the professional game, the nullification of skill and ability by physical intimidation, remains entrenched from at least the midget level (age 15) up (Smith, 1977).

An issue generating much popular attention is whether violence in sport has increased, decreased, or remained constant over the decades. Certainly it is not a recent phenomenon. There were public outcries and official reform actions in boxing, wrestling, football, and hockey early in the century. The question becomes somewhat irrelevant, however, in light of two consider-ations. First, the transformation of sport to industry and its attendant exposure via the electronic media gives rise to different implications for the different eras (Hallowell & Meshbesher, 1976). Second, the emergent character of social problems renders comparative data on incidence spurious (even if such data were available); social problems are what people say and think they are at any given point in time; indeed, they tend to have a three-stage career, as Hubbard, DeFleur, and DeFleur (1975, p. 23) point out. Initially, there is an *emergent* stage. Persons or groups perceiving a social condition as problematic lobby for attention and support from politicians, agencies, the media, and others. Public awareness grows, and shared definitions about the condition begin to emerge. Judgments are made that corrective steps should be taken; ameliorative action is urged. Given enough recognition, the problem becomes legitimized. During the *legitimization* stage, widespread consensus is reached that people ought to be concerned about the condition. If official social machinery comes into being for long-term alleviation of the problem, then the *institutionalization* stage has been reached. At this point, bureaucratic interests, whose careers depend upon continuance of the problem, may generate information that it is indeed still present. In this way, social problems become more or less embedded in a culture.

Professional hockey's influence on youth hockey seems to operate in two main ways.

The first has to do with the structure of the system. The 50 or so professional teams in North America depend on junior leagues for a steady outflow of *talent*. Most of the ablest amateur players are strongly motivated to advance through minor hockey to junior professional and thence to professional ranks. But en route, the number of available positions progressively diminishes, and competition for spots becomes increasingly intense. Professional standards determine who moves up and who does not. These standards include the willingness and ability to employ, and withstand, illegal physical coercion. Some performers with marginal playing skills are upwardly mobile, even as young as 14 years, primarily because they meet this criterion. For sociological studies of violence in professional hockey see Faulkner (1973, 1974); on minor hockey, Smith (1974 a,b, 1975, 1977), Vaz (1976), and Vaz and Thomas (1974).

Second, North Americans have been socialized into acceptance of professional hockey's values, chiefly through the communications media. Small wonder that minor hockey is the professional game in miniature when consumption of the latter has for decades been nothing short of voracious. Violence has been purveyed by an almost bewildering variety of means, blatantly, artfully, often no doubt unconsciously: attention-getting pictures of fights (sometimes without accompanying stories); radio and television *hot stove league* commentary (chuckles about Gordie Howe's legendary elbows or the hundreds of stitches in Ted Lindsay's face, a breathless report that a new penalty record has been set); the sheer amount of attention given *enforcers* and tough guys (Dave Schultz was a virtual media star in his Philadelphia heyday); newspaper and magazine pieces ("Detroit's Murderer's Row," "Hit Man"). In North American cities, full-page newspaper advertisements show Neanderthal-like, cartoon characters belaboring one another with hockey sticks. "Crunching No Nos are slashing, hooking, charging and high-sticking," one legend informs, "Don't let this happen to you; buy a season ticket to the Robins' 74–75 season. Watch it happen to others." The Atlanta Flames' yearbook cover of a few years ago, sold in NHL arenas everywhere, featured an eye-catching scene of a multiplayer brawl. Highway billboards: San Diego's "Mad, Mean, Menacing, Major League Mariners." At least two feature movies whose major themes turn on hockey violence are currently in the making. *Blades and Brass,* the award-winning National Film Board of Canada short film, highlights body thumping and bloody faces. The Better T Shirt Company manufactures shirts emblazoned with pictures of cartoon players gleefully engaging in various types of dirty work ("Hooking" and "Charging," the captions read). Even the Topps Chewing Gum people are in the violence business. Consider this not atypical bubble gum card biography: "André is one of the roughest players in the NHL. Opponents have learned to keep their heads up when he is on the ice. André won't score many goals, but he's a handy guy to have around when the going gets tough." Whatever their form, the media messages are clear: violence and hockey go together.

Young performers, too, may learn specific behaviors from professional hockey, directly and through the mass media. The conditions for observational learning and modeling (i.e., Bandura's social learning theory) via TV are almost laboratory perfect: models who get money and attention for aggressive acts, observers' expectations of rewards for the same behavior, close similarity between the social situations portrayed on the screen and subsequently encountered by observers.

Reviews of this theory and the research it has generated can be found in Bandura (1973), Bandura and Walters (1964), and in the Surgeon General's Report (*Television and Growing Up,* 1972; especially vol. 2). In an unpublished critique, Ellis (1977) argued that this and the other principal social psychological paradigms of the effects of media violence on violence in society are of limited utility because they are designed to explain impulsive, rather than instrumental violence; and it is the latter that citizens are likely to experience. More than this, the dominance of these paradigms has diverted attention from the connection between media violence and instrumental violence in society.

It appears that most hockey violence is of the instrumental type (Smith, 1974b). It can be accommodated within the observational learning paradigm, however, by shifting the latter's emphasis from learning to performing. That learning of aggressive acts from live or media-mediated models occurs appears solidly established. What remains unclear are the variables that determine whether aggressive behavior in the observer follows. Bandura (1973) stated that this varies with the observer's perceptions of the rewards and punishments given to the model and likely to be given his own matching behavior, but then paid little attention to these response consequences for the observer. Ellis (1977) maintained that the *pay-off structure* for the observer is crucial in coming to understand instrumental aggression: "What happens to us after we behave aggressively is a critical influence on the likelihood that we will behave aggressively in the future" (p. 12). The present research does not deal directly with this notion, but previous work reveals the existence in hockey of a social climate in which violence is rewarded increasingly as boys get older and in select leagues as opposed to house leagues (Smith, 1975; Vaz, 1976). The point is: observational learning theory is capable of handling some kinds of instrumental aggression.

The theory becomes sociological when it includes what DeFleur and Ball-Rokeach (1975, pp. 226–227) called the social-categories and social-relations perspectives. The latter might consider, for instance, the extent to which observers encounter real interactional situations similar to those presented on TV (thereby increasing the likelihood that they will behave aggressively). The social categories perspective might, for example, focus on why boys behave more aggressively than girls, even though girls learn as much aggression from watching violent TV programs. This would be explained by reference to sex differences in conduct norms (see also Goranson, 1969, pp. 395–413).

The association between violence in sport as portrayed by the communications industry and violence in youth sport has gone virtually unexamined by researchers. It receives, to my knowledge, no mention in the voluminous outpourings of the Violence and Media Task Force Report of the National Commission on the Causes and Prevention of Violence (Baker & Ball, 1969) or in the Surgeon General's Report on Television and Social Behavior (*Television and Growing Up,* 1972). The Ontario Royal Commission on Violence in the Communications Industry (LaMarsh, Beaulieu, & Young, 1976, p. 16) manages a seven-line statement on the current state of knowledge—and a plea for research.

In the remainder of this chapter, mainly descriptive data are presented on the relationship between professional and minor hockey violence, particularly as mediated by television. The theoretical perspective is that of observational learning. Young players and nonplayers are compared on the extent of their consumption of the professional game and the amount and kinds of violence they claim to have learned—and for the players, practiced. Attitudes regarding the role of violence in professional hockey are examined.

METHOD

These data are from a 1976 survey study of amateur hockey violence. Participants were chosen from three populations of Toronto males, aged 12-21 years: (a) *select* or *allstar* hockey players, (b) house-league hockey players, (c) nonhockey players. From the first two populations, eight hockey organizations were selected (six select and two house league); the organizations were then stratified by age-graded playing division. Including the nonplayers, who were not subdivided, 34 strata were thus constructed.

The sampling frame consisted of all registered players in the organizations. Using simple random sampling without replacement, 740 selections were made, proportionately from each strata. Selection probabilities ranged from .33 to .45. Removing nonrespondents and foreign elements (goaltenders, players released, traded, injured, or for some other reason not playing at least half a season) resulted in a response rate of 88%; the actual number of players successfully interviewed was 551, a 74% completion rate. Weighting, to correct for unequal selection probabilities, resulted in a final weighted sample of 604. A total of 180 nonplayers, from six schools, were sampled with certainty, yielding response and completion rates of 96% and 84% and 153 interviews.

Following a pretest in late 1975, the survey was carried out during April 1976, immediately after the hockey season. Professionals employed by York University's Survey Research Centre conducted the interviews, which averaged 1 hr in length and took place, in most cases, in the participants' homes.

The findings reported here are primarily in the form of cross-tabulations, in percentages of players' and nonplayers' responses to primarily closed-ended questions. Chi-square values are presented. Inspection of the between-rows variation, in percentage, provides on indication of the magnitude of relationships.

RESULTS

Tables 1-4 provide data on players' and nonplayers' consumption of professional hockey, directly and via the mass media. Tickets to major professional hockey in Toronto are both scarce and expensive; and therefore, the majority of players (64.4%) and nonplayers (88.5%) saw games live only two or three times a year, at best (Table 1). Professional hockey is consumed chiefly

TABLE 1 How often do you attend professional hockey games?

	Frequency (%)					
Respondents	Once a week	2–3 times a month	Once a month	2–3 times a year	Once a year	Never
Players	3.0	12.5	20.1	43.1	16.6	4.7
Nonplayers	0	2.6	7.9	37.5	30.9	21.1
Total						
%	2.4	10.5	17.7	42.0	19.5	8.0
N	18	79	133	316	147	60

Note. $\chi^2 = 80.55, p < .001$.

TABLE 2 How often do you read about professional hockey in the newspaper?

	Frequency (%)						
Respondents	Daily	2–3 times a week	Once a week	2–3 times a month	Once a month	2–3 times a year	Never
Players	53.4	18.5	11.6	5.7	4.5	1.7	4.7
Nonplayers	39.5	17.8	13.8	6.6	5.9	3.3	13.2
Total							
%	50.6	18.3	12.1	5.8	4.8	2	6.4
N	381	138	91	44	36	15	48

Note. $\chi^2 = 21.21, p = .002$.

TABLE 3 How often do you watch professional hockey on TV?

	Frequency (%)					
Respondents	2–3 times a week	Once a week	2–3 times a month	Once a month	2–3 times a year	Never
Players	39.6	30.6	17.5	7.2	3.3	1.8
Nonplayers	43.4	17.1	17.1	12.5	7.9	2
Total						
%	40.4	27.9	17.4	8.2	4.2	1.9
N	304	210	131	62	32	14

Note. $\chi^2 = 18.57, p = .002$.

TABLE 4 How often do you read about professional hockey in magazines or books?

	Frequency (%)					
Respondents	2–3 times a week	Once a week	2–3 times a month	Once a month	2–3 times a year	Never
Players	10	18.5	14.6	27.6	15.8	13.5
Nonplayers	2.6	7.9	7.2	30.3	20.4	31.6
Total						
%	8.5	16.3	13.1	28.2	16.7	17.1
N	64	123	99	212	126	129

Note. $\chi^2 = 46.11$, $p < .001$.

through the newspaper, it seems. Approximately 53% of the players and 39% of the nonplayers did so on a daily basis; and over 80% and 70% at least once a week (Table 2). Table 3 reveals that TV was the next most popular medium, with almost 70% of the players and 60% of the nonplayers watching once a week or more. Magazines and books ranked third (Table 4). In each case, players clearly out-consumed their nonplaying counterparts. Consumption also increased slightly in the player sample among older and select (as opposed to house league) boys (data not shown).

Tables 5–9 show the effects of watching hockey on learning and acquired behaviors. When respondents were asked if they had ever learned anything from watching professional hockey, almost 90% of the players and almost

TABLE 5 Have you ever learned anything from watching professional hockey?

	Learned anything (%)		
Respondents	Yes	No	Not sure
Players	89.5	8.8	1.7
Nonplayers	78.8	20.5	.7
Total			
%	87.4	11.2	1.5
N	656	84	11

Note. $\chi^2 = 17.17$, $p < .001$. Missing observations = 2.

TABLE 6 About how many times this season have you learned
something from watching professional hockey?

	Number of times learned (%)			
Respondents	5 or more	3–4	1–2	Never
Players	28.2	20.1	37.8	13.9
Nonplayers	19.2	13.3	37.5	30
Total				
%	26.5	18.9	37.8	16.8
N	177	126	252	112

Note. $\chi^2 = 20.59$, $p < .001$. Missing observations = 86.

80% of the nonplayers replied affirmatively (Table 5). Table 6 gives an
indication of the amount of learning that took place, undoubtedly partly a
function of viewing frequency, greater among players than nonplayers. As for
the learning of violence, specifically, over half of each group responded "Yes"
to the question: Have you ever learned how to hit another player illegally in
any way from watching professional hockey (Table 7)? A selection of
descriptions of what was learned appears in Table 8. But learning is not
necessarily doing. Table 9 shows frequency of performance, among players, of
the illegal tactics acquired.

To what degree do consumers accept the "goon," or "enforcer," in
professional hockey (Tables 10–12)? Table 10 indicates that the great majority
of players (76.1%) and nonplayers (88.1%) felt that such a player did not
deserve his high salary. At least two reasons could account for this:

TABLE 7 Have you ever learned how to hit
another player illegally in any way from
watching professional hockey?

	Learned how to hit illegally (%)		
Respondents	Yes	No	Not sure
Players	56.9	42.1	1
Nonplayers	55.3	44.1	.7
Total			
%	56.6	42.5	.9
N	426	320	7

Note. $\chi^2 = .32$, $p = .852$.

TABLE 8 Descriptions of illegal hitting learned from watching
professional hockey

I learned spearing and butt-ending.

You sort of go on your side like turning a corner and trip him with a skate.

Charging. You skate towards another guy who doesn't have the puck and
knock him down. Or coming up from behind and knocking him down.

Sneaky elbows, little choppy slashes Bobby Clarke style.

Hitting at weak points with the stick, say at the back of the legs.

Getting a guy from behind. Getting a guy in the corner and giving him an elbow.

Coming up from behind and using your stick to hit the back of his skates and
trip him.

Butt-end, spearing, slashing, high sticking, elbow in the head.

Put the elbow just a bit up and get him in the gut with your stick.

Wrap your arms over his shoulder from the back and tear his arms and stick.
Step forward and stick your foot in front of his foot.

Along the boards, if a player is coming along you angle him off by starting
with your shoulder then bringing up your elbow.

I learned how to butt-end from the Soviet team.

The way you "bug" in front of the net.

Clipping. Taking the guy's feet out by sliding underneath.

Sticking the stick between their legs. Tripping as they go into the boards.

I've seen it and use it: when you check a guy, elbow him. If you get in a
corner you can hook or spear him without getting caught.

Giving him a shot in the face as he is coming up to you. The ref can't
see the butt-ends.

Dirty tricks—butt-ending, spearing—without the referee seeing them.

How to trip properly.

Like Gordie Howe, butt-ends when the ref isn't looking.

---

respondents' disapproval of the role on moral, aesthetic, or similar grounds
and their belief that it is more hindrance than help in a team's ultimate goal:
winning games. Data (not shown) suggests the former reason probably figured
strongly; almost half the respondents stated that a player of this type
probably does help his team to win.

The majority view aside, a significant number of players (close to one
fifth) expressed support for so-called goon hockey (Table 10). Data in Tables
11 and 12 reveal that these advocates tend to be found at the older and select
levels, where boys are probably more completely socialized into the culture of
the game.

TABLE 9 How many times this season have you actually hit another player in this way?

5 or more		3–4		1–2		Never		Don't know		Inappropriate	
%	N	%	N	%	N	%	N	%	N	%	N
15	90	6	36	15.9	96	20.5	124	.21	1	42.5	257

TABLE 10 One professional player has said, "I get paid to beat up the other guys." In your opinion, does he deserve or not deserve the high salary he gets for this?

	Deserve or not deserve high salary (%)		
Respondents	Deserves	Does not deserve	Depends
Players	17.9	76.1	6
Nonplayers	7.9	88.1	4
Total			
%	15.9	78.5	5.6
N	119	589	42

Note. $\chi^2 = 10.56$, $p = .005$. Missing observations = 3.

TABLE 11 One professional player has said, "I get paid to beat up the other guys." In your opinion, does he deserve or not deserve the high salary he gets for this?

	Deserve or not deserve salary (%)			Total	
Respondents' age (in years)	Deserves	Does not deserve	Depends	%	N
12–13	10.1	86.1	3.8	27.7	208
14–15	12.1	83.1	4.8	30.8	231
16–17	21.7	73.9	4.4	24.4	180
18–21	23.7	64.9	11.5	17.5	131
Total					
%	15.9	78.5	5.6	100	
N	119	589	42		750

Note. $\chi^2 = 30.83$, $p < .001$. Missing observations = 3. Gamma = −.14.

TABLE 12 One professional player has said, "I get paid to beat up the other guys." In your opinion, does he deserve or not deserve the high salary he gets for this?

Respondents	Deserve or not deserve salary (%)			Total	
	Deserves	Does not deserve	Depends	%	N
House league	12.3	84	3.7	54.4	326
Select	24.5	66.7	8.8	45.6	273
Total					
%	17.9	76.1	6	100	
N	107	456	36		599

Note. $\chi^2 = 24.88, p < .001$. Missing observations = 5.

Tables 13-15 present data on the general issue of fighting in professional hockey. Most respondents wanted less (Table 13); yet 36.1% of the players wanted about the same amount (which is to say, a lot). Again, this support varied positively with age (Table 14) and select hockey background (Table 15).

SUMMARY AND CONCLUSION

1. A majority of the 704 youth interviewed consumed professional hockey once a week or more through newspaper and TV. Live attendance and consumption via books and magazines was considerably less frequent. Players were generally greater consumers than nonplayers.

TABLE 13 Regarding the amount of fighting in professional hockey this year, would you like to see more, about the same amount, or less fighting?

Respondents	Amount of fighting (%)		
	More	About the same	Less
Players	2.9	36.1	61
Nonplayers	.7	8.2	86.8
Total			
%	2.4	31.3	66.3
N	18	233	493

Note. $\chi^2 = 35.65, p < .001$. Missing observations = 9.

TABLE 14 Regarding the amount of fighting in professional hockey this year, would you like to see more, about the same amount, or less fighting?

Respondents' age (in years)	Amount of fighting (%)			Total	
	More	About the same	Less	%	N
12–13	2.4	23.8	73.8	27.7	206
14–15	.9	29.3	69.8	31.2	232
16–17	5.6	37.6	56.7	23.9	178
18–21	.8	38.3	60.9	17.2	128
Total					
%	2.4	31.3	66.3	100	
N	18	233	493		744

Note. $\chi^2 = 24.74$, $p < .001$. Missing observations = 9. Gamma = $-.19$.

TABLE 15 Regarding the amount of fighting in professional hockey this year, would you like to see more, about the same amount, or less fighting?

Players	Amount of fighting (%)			Total	
	More	About the same	Less	%	N
House league	4.3	28.6	67.1	54.3	322
Select	1.1	45	53.9	45.7	271
Total					
%	2.9	36.1	61	100	
N	17	214	362		593

Note. $\chi^2 = 20.63$, $p < .001$. Missing observations = 11.

2. Most respondents reported learning various skills and orientations from viewing professional hockey, including methods of illegal hitting, some of which were described in colorful detail. A greater percentage of players than nonplayers reported general learning; approximately equal percentages learned illegal hitting. No differences by age or level of competition were found in the player samples.

3. Among players who learned illegal tactics, over 60% stated that they had used one or more of the tactics at least once or twice during the season.

4. Only a small minority of respondents (but more players than nonplayers) apparently supported the enforcer role in professional hockey, being of the opinion that those who filled it deserved their high salaries.

5. A larger minority of both groups (but, again, more players than nonplayers) wanted about the same amount or more fighting in the professional game.
6. Affirmation of the enforcer role and of fighting in general was strongest among older and select team players.

I have argued that mass media portrayals of violence in professional hockey have contributed to the spread of a social climate in youth hockey conducive to violence. The findings indicate also that specific acts of assault are learned via observation of professional hockey, and subsequently performed. Survey research methods, of course, do not unravel causality, and the present data can be taken as supportive of more than one explanation of media effects; but the data seem to make most sense in the light of observational learning theory. My guess is that media presentations of professional hockey provide observers with blueprints for violent behavior in their own games.

REFERENCES

Baker, R., & Ball, S. J. (Eds.). *Violence and the media.* Washington, D.C.: U.S. Government Printing Office, 1969.

Bandura, A. *Aggression: A social learning analysis.* Englewood Cliffs, N.J.: Prentice-Hall, 1973.

Bandura, A., & Walters, R. M. *Social learning and personality development.* New York: Holt, Rinehart, & Winston, 1964.

Blumenthal, M. D., Kahn, R. L., Andrews, F. M., & Head, K. B. *Justifying violence: Attitudes of American men.* Ann Arbor: University of Michigan Institute for Social Research, 1972.

Brent, A. S. The criminal code governs the hockey rink too! *Crown's Newsletter,* June 1975, pp. 8–13.

DeFleur, M. L., & Ball-Rokeach, S. J. *Theories of mass communication.* New York: David McKay, 1975.

Ellis, D. *Mass media effects on violence in society.* Unpublished manuscript, Department of Sociology, York University, 1977.

Faulkner, R. R. On respect and retribution: Toward an ethnography of violence. *Sociological Symposium,* 1973, *9,* 19–36.

Faulkner, R. R. Making violence by doing work: Selves, situations, and the world of professional hockey. *Sociology of Work and Occupations,* 1974, *1,* 288–312.

Goranson, R. A review of the recent literature. In R. Baker & S. J. Ball (Eds.), *Violence and the media.* Washington, D.C.: U.S. Government Printing Office, 1969.

Hallowell, L., & Meshbesher, R. I. *Sport violence and the criminal law: A socio-legal viewpoint.* Unpublished manuscript, Department of Sociology, University of Minnesota, 1976.

Hubbard, J. C., DeFleur, M. L., & DeFleur, L. B. Mass media influences on public conceptions of social problems. *Social Problems,* 1975, *23,* 23–24.

La Marsh, J., Beaulieu, L., & Young, S. *Interim report of the Royal Commission of Violence in the Communications Industry.* Toronto: Ontario Government Printing Office, 1976.

McMurtry, W. R. *Inquiry and investigation into violence in amateur hockey.* (Report to the Honourable R. Brunell, Ontario Minister of Community and Social Services). Toronto: Ontario Government Bookstore, 1974.

Smith, M. D. Significant others' influence on the assaultive behavior of young hockey players. *International Review of Sport Sociology,* 1974, *3–4,* 45–56. (a)

Smith, M. D. Violence in sport: A sociological perspective. *Sportwissenschaft,* 1974, *4,* 164–173. (b)

Smith, M. D. The legitimation of violence: Hockey players' perceptions of their reference groups' sanctions for assault. *Canadian Review of Sociology and Anthropology,* 1975, *12,* 72–80.

Smith, M. D. *Hockey violence: A test of the subculture of violence thesis.* Paper presented at the annual meeting of the Southern Sociological Association, Atlanta, March 1977.

Television and growing up: The impact of televised violence. (Report to the Surgeon General, United States Public Health Service, from the Surgeon-General's Scientific Advisory Committee on Television and Social Behavior). Washington, D.C.: U.S. Government Printing Office, 1972.

Vaz, E. The culture of young hockey players: Some initial observations. In A. Yiannakis, T. D. McIntyre, M. J. Melnick, & D. P. Hart, (Eds.), *Sport sociology: Contemporary themes.* Dubuque, Iowa: Kendall-Hunt, 1976.

Vaz, E., & Thomas, D. What price victory? An analysis of minor hockey league players' attitudes towards winning. *International Review of Sport Sociology,* 1974, *2,* 33–53.

5

ANXIETY-INDUCING FACTORS IN COMPETITIVE YOUTH SPORTS

Tara K. Scanlan and Michael W. Passer

The growth evidenced in organized competitive youth sports participation over the past decade is staggering. Recent estimates indicate that 20 million children between 6 and 16 years of age are involved in competitive sport programs (Parker, 1975). Paralleling the growth has been increasing concern over the psychological and social effects of the competitive sport experience on children. The concern is warranted not because sport competition is inherently good or bad, but because any social process involving so many children should be clearly understood. Currently, little empirical evidence exists on which to derive this necessary understanding; and many relevant questions remain unanswered. Fortunately, an increasing number of researchers are becoming involved in investigating the competitive youth sport experience. The project presented in this chapter represents one of these research efforts.

The primary purpose of this discussion is to examine factors that induce anxiety in children participating in competitive youth sports. The findings that are presented, however, represent only a small facet of a much larger field study entitled "The Psychosocial Effects of Competition on Young Boys." Therefore, to place the anxiety data into the larger context of the work being conducted at the University of California at Los Angeles (UCLA), a brief overview of the entire project is presented before focusing more specifically on the topic of anxiety.

This research was supported by grant MH 27750–01 from the National Institute of Mental Health and grant 3188 from the University of California, Los Angeles. We gratefully acknowledge the cooperation of the American Youth Soccer Organization and its participants.

PROJECT OVERVIEW

The project was conducted with the enthusiastic cooperation of the American Youth Soccer Organization (AYSO). The participants were players and coaches from 16 soccer teams, representing two complete AYSO divisions from Torrance, California. In total, 205 boys 11-12 years of age and 16 coaches were tested throughout the 1975-1976 soccer season, which extended from September through February.

The decision to conduct the study in the field setting was made for three major reasons. The first was to determine the external validity or generalizability of previous laboratory findings (Martens & Gill, 1976; Scanlan, 1975, 1977). The second was to obtain data regarding relationships or patterns among several naturallly occurring variables that are operative during the complex process of competition. The third was to profit from the discovery potential of the natural environment. Considering the dearth of extant literature on children and competition, the realistic arena of competitive youth sports was the most appropriate starting place for a fruitful line of inquiry.

The underlying rationale to the entire project was that sport competition is an important social process to most young boys and, therefore, can have a considerable impact on them (Scanlan, 1978). Sport competition is important because it provides the arena in which boys' athletic or motor ability is publicly demonstrated and extensively evaluated by people who are significant to them, such as parents, coaches, and peers. Further, participation frequently occurs during the elementary school years when athletic prowess is a central and prized ability of young boys (Sherif, 1976; Veroff, 1969). It is also during this age period that social evaluation is a particularly important and intensely engaged-in process (Cook & Stingle, 1974; Masters, 1971; Scanlan, 1978; Veroff, 1969). In sum, sport competition is important to boys because motor ability is being evaluated by significant persons when the children are at an age when their motor ability and the social evaluation process are both highly critical. (For greater elaboration see Scanlan, 1978.)

The general purpose of the field study, therefore, was to examine the impact of this important social process on children. Our first objective was to determine the effects of various intrapersonal and situational factors on children's perceptions of the competitive sport situation. Our second objective was to determine intrapersonal consequences of participation in competitive youth sports. The more specific concerns addressed in each aspect of the project are briefly presented in the ensuing paragraphs.

Factors Influencing the Perception of the Competitive Sport Situation

The first major concern of this portion of the investigation was to determine intrapersonal and situational factors that are related to the child's perceiving the competitive situation as personally threatening. The primary indicant of perceived threat was children's anxiety reactions both when anticipating a pending competition and after the outcome of the competitive game was known. A more detailed treatment of this facet of the project and the resulting data are presented in the latter portion of this chapter.

The second major concern related to the perception of the competitive sport situation was to determine the causes to which competition outcomes were attributed by children evidencing differential levels of perceived threat. Levels of threat were induced by game win-loss experiences and were assessed by anxiety reactions. The results of several investigations (Chaikin, 1971; Fitch, 1970; Weiner & Kukla, 1970; Wolosin, Sherman, & Till, 1973) indicated that people experiencing success usually credit that outcome to themselves by making attributions to personal ability or effort. People experiencing failure, however, tend to attribute causality to external factors such as task difficulty or luck. These external attributions tend to minimize personal responsibility for failure outcomes and, thereby, can potentially reduce the perceived threat to self. In sum, the findings seem to indicate that people protect self-esteem by taking credit for successful outcomes and by assuming less responsibility or blame for failure outcomes.[1]

It should be noted, however, that the majority of the attributional studies indicating this finding were conducted in relatively norm-free laboratory settings. In contrast, a laboratory experiment was conducted by Scanlan (1977) specifically to simulate a high evaluative, realistic competitive situation. The results from this study contradicted the typical attribution findings even though differential levels of perceived threat were clearly evidenced by postcompetition anxiety responses. Boys experiencing failure made internal attributions. It is possible that these attributions indicated compliance to norms of conduct that are operative in the competitive sport situation and that are well known by children through their own participation in sports and their constant exposure to sport models.

One competitive norm that is frequently observed and strongly reinforced could be termed the *good winner* norm. According to this norm, appropriate behavior includes extending credit and praise to the defeated opponent and placing temporal and situational limits on one's own successful performance. For example, comments similar to the following are often heard: "They are a great team; things just went better for us, today." Another competitive norm frequently evidenced is the *good loser* norm. Here, the appropriate behavior includes accepting responsibility for defeat and extending praise to the victor,

---

[1] It is not clear, however, whether these differential attributional patterns of succeeding and failing individuals are a result of self-serving biases and cognitive distortions or are simply the result of more rational information-processing mechanisms. For a discussion of the current debate in the literature see Ajzen and Fishbein (1975) and Miller and Ross (1975). The present investigation is the only study that has assessed perceived threat just before causal ascriptions were made; therefore, the results potentially provide some insight into the issue.

as exemplified by comments such as "They just outplayed us, we just didn't play well, today."

Although the normative interpretation provides a plausible explanation for the atypical attributions made by children in the previous competition study, this explanation is strictly ex post facto and requires further investigation. To examine this interpretation, attribution data were collected immediately following a competitive game, and assessments of competitive norms were made at the end of the season to determine how children characteristically attribute the cause of their game win or loss in the realistic setting of competitive youth sports. The major question of concern was:

> Are typical attributional patterns evidenced after a win or loss or are there norms peculiar to the naturalistic competitive situation that result in causal ascriptions that are contrary to those evidenced in the relatively "norm free" laboratory environment?

Consequences of Participation in Competitive Youth Sports

The second major objective of this investigation was to examine some of the intrapersonal consequences of participation in competitive youth sports. The focus was on factors determining self-esteem and mediating self-esteem change during the course of the soccer season. Self-esteem was defined by Coopersmith (1967) as "the evaluation which an individual makes and customarily maintains with regard to himself: it expresses an attitude of approval or disapproval, and indicates the extent to which the individual believes himself to be capable, significant, successful, and worthy" (p. 5).

Evaluation, with the resultant success achieved or failure incurred, is a major determinant of self-esteem and mediator of its change (Coopersmith, 1967; Gergen, 1971; Hartup, 1970). Coopersmith (1967) also specified four general types of experiences that define success: (1) competence—indicating successful or unsuccessful performance at achievement tasks; (2) significance—depicting one's acceptance and popularity; (3) power—referring to a person's ability to influence and control other people; and (4) virtue—involving conformity to ethical principles.

It is contended that experiences of competence, significance, and power are central to the sport competition process in the following ways. Competence relates directly to the level of athletic prowess achieved by the individual participant and perhaps also to team success-failure experiences. Significance is reflected in the child's socially oriented interactions with teammates. Finally, power is indicated by the child's leadership status or influence over teammates in task-oriented interactions.

In the present experiment, data were collected to assess the level of success that each player achieved on these three experiences. Each player's competence, significance, and power were assessed by coach and peer ratings of soccer ability, popularity, and leadership, respectively. Peer ratings were assessed early in the season and again at the end of the season. Team competence was determined by the overall win-loss record for the season. The following exploratory questions were posed.

1. How is a child's absolute level of soccer ability related to self-esteem?
2. What role does improvement in soccer ability play in self-esteem change?
3. How do team success or failure experiences over the season affect self-esteem?
4. What is the relationship between self-esteem and others' ratings of ability, popularity, and leadership?
5. What is the relationship between soccer ability and others' ratings of popularity and leadership? Are the most competent players also the more popular, and do they also enjoy greater leadership status in their groups?

It should be mentioned that experiences of the fourth factor, viture, can also be involved in the competitive sport experience. A person's internalization and demonstration of rules of fair play and good sportsmanship would reflect experiences of virtue. Although such experiences may play an important role in mediating self-esteem change among young athletes, this factor' was not examined in the present investigation.

Outline of Procedures

The two major foci of this investigation have been discussed. They include the examination of factors influencing the perception of the competitive sport situation and the consequences of participation in competitive youth sports. To provide a summary of the variables examined in this study, a brief outline of our testing procedures is presented.

Psychological assessments were administered at five stages during the soccer season including the preseason, midseason, pregame, postgame, and postseason periods. The variables assessed during each testing period are briefly presented as follows.

1. Preseason. Measures of children's competitive trait anxiety, basal state anxiety, and self-esteem were administered during early season practices. In addition, ratings of each player's soccer ability were obtained from league records. These ratings were based on the assessments of five AYSO coaches who evaluated the child's performance on a standard set of soccer drills.
2. Midseason. Sociometric tests were administered to the players during the fifth week of practice. Each player rank ordered his teammates in terms of how much he liked them, as well as on their soccer ability and leadership status. Each coach also rank ordered his players on their popularity among teammates, soccer ability, and leadership status.

3. Pregame. Players' state anxiety was assessed before the eighth game of the season. A questionnaire was also administered to examine players' perceptions regarding the importance of the game and their expectations for personal and team success.
4. Postgame. Players' state anxiety again was assessed immediately following the game. A postgame questionnaire was administered to examine the following factors: (a) players' causal attributions for their own and their team's performance; (b) various affective reactions to the game including, for example, satisfaction; and (c) expectancies of future success against the same opponent.
5. Postseason. Self-esteem and rankings of interpersonal attraction among teammates were reassessed during the final week of regular season play. Another questionnaire was administered to examine the following factors: (a) competitive norms regarding causal attributions for team success-failure; (b) players' evaluation of, and satisfaction with, the ability demonstrated by themselves and their team; and (c) players' evaluation of their coach. Finally, coaches were asked to rate each player on the degree of skill improvement evidenced throughout the season.

ANXIETY-INDUCING FACTORS

The significant impact that competition can have on children was detailed previously. In brief, the competition process quite clearly involves extensive social evaluation of motor ability, which is a particularly prized attribute for young boys. This social evaluation can provide the information necessary for children to establish accurate and complete assessments of their motor ability. Implicit in this appraisal process, however, is the possibility of engendering unfavorable evaluations and negative information about their motoric competence. Consequently, the competitive sport experience can be perceived as personally threatening and, therefore, result in anxiety reactions by the participants. It does seem reasonable to assume, however, that whether competition is perceived as threatening depends on the particular child, the situational circumstances, and the interaction between the two. Therefore, the purpose of this portion of the field study was to determine various intrapersonal and situational factors that relate to the perception of threat just before and immediately following competition. Consideration of intrapersonal factors addresses the question: Are some children more anxious about competition than others? Consideration of situation factors addresses the question: What are some of the events that occur while competing or as a result of competing that induce anxiety?

In the ensuing discussion, the necessary background information to the study is detailed. First, a brief overview of Spielberger's Trait-State Anxiety Theory is presented because it provides the major theoretical framework on which this study was based. Spielberger's theory elucidates the construct of the perception of threat, provides a way to operationalize it, and identifies some factors that induce perceived threat. Second, recently conceptualized anxiety constructs and empirical findings related more specifically to the competitive situation are presented.

Spielberger (1971) and Gaudry and Spielberger (1971) conceptualized the anxiety process as a three-stage temporal sequence of events including stress, threat, and anxiety. These constructs are defined, respectively, in the following manner: (a) "the objective stimulus characteristics of a situation," (b) "the subjective appraisal of the situation," and (c) "the emotional reaction experienced in situations and individual appraises as dangerous or threatening" (Spielberger, 1971, p. 268). Therefore, Spielberger's theory of anxiety is based not on the actual psychological or physical threat that exists in a situation, but rather on the person's perception of the threat. Further, Spielberger developed a way to assess this perception of threat with the construct of state anxiety. The theory assumes that when threat is perceived, state anxiety levels are elevated (Gaudry & Spielberger, 1971). State anxiety (A-State) is defined as "subjective consciously perceived feelings of apprehension and tension, accompanied by or associated with activation or arousal of the autonomic nervous system" (Spielberger, 1966, p. 17). State anxiety represents a transitory or "right now" stress reaction that can be assessed by physiological indicants of autonomic arousal such as palmar sweating, respiration, and pulse rate; by self-report measures such as the Spielberger State Anxiety Inventory (Spielberger, Gorsuch, & Lushene, 1969); or by observational techniques.

Spielberger (1971) indicated that the perception of threat is determined by various intrapersonal factors, including personality dispositions, abilities, skills, and past experiences in similar situations. One intrapersonal factor influencing the perception of threat that is central to his theory is trait anxiety. Trait anxiety (A-Trait) is defined as a "motive or acquired behavioral disposition that predisposes an individual to perceive a wide range of objectively nondangerous circumstances as threatening, and to respond to these with A-State reactions disproportionate in intensity to the magnitude of the objective danger" (Spielberger, 1966, p. 17). Trait anxiety is assessed by the Spielberger Trait Anxiety Inventory (Spielberger et al., 1969).

Trait anxiety is a particularly important construct for purposes of the present investigation because it identifies persons who are threatened by situations that involve personal evaluation in which failure and negative evaluations of performance can be incurred (Spielberger, 1971). Trait anxiety relates specifically to threat to self-esteem, as opposed to threat due to potential physical harm. Findings in the general anxiety literature indicated consistently that high trait-anxious persons perceive self-esteem-threatening situations as more threatening, as indicated by elevations in state anxiety levels, than do low trait-anxious persons (Hodges, 1968; Hodges & Durham, 1972; McAdoo, 1970; Sarason, I. G., 1960, 1968; Spielberger et al., 1969).

Research evolving from Spielberger's theory also indicated that success-failure is a major situational determinant of perceived threat to self-esteem. The findings of several studies evidenced that perceived threat and corresponding state anxiety levels decrease with success experiences and increase with failure experiences (Gaudry & Poole, 1972; Hodges & Durham, 1972; McAdoo, 1970). Further, some findings showed that greater threat and higher state anxiety is evidenced by high trait-anxious people experiencing failure then by low trait-anxious people (Hodges, 1968; McAdoo, 1970).

Spielberger's theory provides the conceptual clarity, the operational definitions, and the assessment tools needed to understand and empirically test the anxiety process. It has had a significant theoretical impact on recent conceptualizations and empirical investigations concerning anxiety in the competitive sport situation. The clear theoretical and operational definitions given to the construct of perceived threat to self-esteem and to the identification of trait anxiety and success-failure as two factors that influence this threat, have certainly had a major impact in guiding the present investigation. Working within Spielberger's general theoretical framework, recent conceptual refinements and empirical findings related specifically to threat perceived in the competitive sport situation are reviewed here.

The major refinement to Spielberger's theory was to increase the situational specificity of the broad and general construct of trait anxiety. The Sarasons and their colleagues (Sarason, I. G., 1960, 1968; Sarason, S. B., Davidson, Lighthall, Waite, & Ruebush, 1960) demonstrated the importance of defining trait anxiety in situationally specific terms with the development of the construct of test anxiety. Test anxiety is defined as the predisposition to respond to test-taking situations with varying levels of state anxiety. Similarly, Martens (1977) increased the situational specifically of trait anxiety to the competitive sport situation. He defined the construct of competitive trait anxiety as "a tendency to perceive competitive situations as threatening and to respond to these situations with feelings of apprehension and tension" (Martens, 1977, p. 21). The Sport Competition Anxiety Test (SCAT) was developed to assess this disposition, and threat was again operationally defined as elevation in state anxiety levels (Martens, 1977).

Recent investigations indicated that competitive trait anxiety is an important intrapersonal determinant of perceived threat when people are anticipating participation in a competitive experience. The results of these studies showed that high competitive-trait-anxious adults and children exhibit higher elevations in state anxiety than do low competitive-trait-anxious persons when facing competition (Martens, 1977; Martens & Gill, 1976; Marten & Simon, 1976; Scanlan, 1975).

Although no research has been conducted concerning the antecedents of competitive trait anxiety, Martens (1977) postulated that individual differences are determined by "accumulated consequences of participation in the competitive process" (p. 32). It appears that high competitive-trait-anxious persons probably have not been successful in their past competitive endeavors;

have incurred negative evaluations; and, therefore, face the competitive situation with the expectation of again falling short of its demands. It is proposed that the opposite is true for people evidencing low competitive trait anxiety.

Consistent with the general anxiety research, the major situational factor found to be related to the perception of threat during and immediately following sport competition is success-failure or game win-loss. Success experiences were shown to reduce threat and to decrease state anxiety levels, whereas failure experiences were found to induce threat and to increase state anxiety levels (Gill, 1976; Martens, 1977; Martens & Gill, 1976; Scanlan, 1977). Furthermore, game win-loss is such a potent situational variable in the perception of threat that it completely overshadows any postgame differences due to competitive trait anxiety.

An early study by Skubic (1956) involving Little League and Middle League players between 8 and 15 years of age provided interesting questionnaire data that also illustrated the importance of success-failure in competition. When asked if winning a game meant a great deal to the child, 83 of 95 boys responded affirmatively. The importance of personally playing well in the game was indicated by a question asking each player if he felt very bad when he played a poor game. A total of 75 of 96 players gave affirmative responses.

The findings in the competition literature clearly indicate that competitive trait anxiety and success-failure are two important determinants of perceived threat. The first factor appears to relate to individual differences in the perception of how successful or unsuccessful an anticipated performance will be and the type of performance evaluation likely to be incurred. The second factor appears to relate to the evaluative information incurred when a person's actual level of competence at the task is clearly evidenced to himself and to others.

One objective of the present investigation was to extend the generalizability of these findings to the realistic field setting of competitive youth sports. A second objective was to determine other factors that influence the perception of threat when anticipating competition and immediately following competition, when the outcomes are known and eminent. To date, there is a paucity of information concerning other determinants of threat.

METHOD

As mentioned earlier, the participatnt in our study were 11- and 12-year-old boys from 16 youth soccer teams. A total of 205 players were tested during the preseason phase of the project. Parental permission was obtained for each player involved in the study.

The preseason assessment period began 1 week before the soccer season, and the members of the teams were tested individually during their weekly practice sessions by trained, male graduate students from UCLA. The majority of the players were tested before the first game of the season. Because of scheduling constraints, however, several absentees and players from two teams were tested a few days after the first game. Analyses were conducted to determine if there were significant differences on any of the preseason measures between players tested before or after the first game, and no significant differences were indicated.

The psychological scales administered during the preseason period included the SCAT (Martens, 1977), Spielberger's State Anxiety Inventory for Children (SAIC, Spielberger, 1973), and the Piers-Harris Children's Self-Concept Test (Piers & Harris, 1969). These scales assessed players' competitive trait anxiety, basal state anxiety, and self-esteem, respectively. In addition, coaches' ratings of each player's soccer ability were obtained from league records.

Pregame and postgame measures were administered during the eighth game of the season. The structure of the AYSO season involves two miniseasons consisting of two complete round-robin tournaments. The eight teams within each of the two AYSO divisions complete the first round-robin tournament, and a division winner is determined. The teams then enter the second round robin with a blank win-loss record, and the entire process is repeated. The eighth game, therefore, was the first game of the second miniseason, or tournament.

A total of 191 players were present for the pregame testing. The SAIC was administered to each player, 30 min before the game, to assess pregame state anxiety. After completing this measure, players were given a questionnaire, which assessed the following factors: (a) their expectancies regarding whether their team would win or lose the game, (b) their expectancies regarding the quality of their individual performance during the game, (c) the importance of winning the game, (d) the importance of playing well individually, (e) how important the players perceived that winning the game was to their coach, and (f) how skilled they perceived the opposing team to be. Two other variables relating to the team's performance during the first miniseason were obtained from AYSO league records. These factors included the team's overall win-loss record and the previous game outcome against their current opponent.

Postgame measures were administered immediately after the game and before the players had the opportunity to interact with parents, teammates, or their coach. The players completed the SAIC to assess postgame state anxiety and were then given a questionnaire, which asked them to rate the following items: (a) how well they and their team had played, (b) their satisfaction with their own and their team's performance, (c) how well they had performed relative to their teammates, and (d) how much fun they experienced during the game.

The game outcome and the closeness of the game were recorded for each team. One of the eight games ended in a tie; consequently, only the responses of the remaining 160 players participating on winning or losing teams were included in the postgame analyses. Game closeness was determined by classifying each game into one of three categories, including very close, moderately close, and not close. This classification was based on the final score of each game and the pattern of scoring during the game. The margin of victory in the very close, moderately close, and not close games was one, two, and three goals, respectively.

RESULTS

Pregame State Anxiety

Players' basal state anxiety and pregame state anxiety scores were compared to determine how their anxiety levels were affected by the pregame setting. The scores on the SAIC range from 20 to 60 points, indicating low and high state anxiety levels, respectively. The respective basal and pregame state anxiety means were 29.17 and 29.86. Although the difference between these means was statistically significant, the magnitude of this difference was exceedingly small. Clearly, the difference does not support the conclusion that players, as a group, were more anxious before the game than they were at the time of their basal state anxiety assessment. Although all players did not evidence high anxiety before the game, many players did find the pregame setting to be anxiety inducing. For example, the pregame state anxiety levels of some players increased as much as 10–20 points over their basal scores, whereas other players showed a decrease in basal to pregame anxiety of as much as 10 points. The important point here is that these differences in players' pregame state anxiety levels were significantly related to several intrapersonal factors.[2]

An examination of the correlations between competitive trait anxiety, basal state anxiety, and pregame state anxiety revealed that all three variables were significantly related to one another. As predicted, players with higher levels of competitive trait anxiety evidenced greater state anxiety before the game than did players with lower levels of competitive trait anxiety. Higher levels of basal state anxiety were also associated with greater pregame state anxiety. Finally, competitive trait anxiety and basal state anxiety were

---

[2]The data from this portion of the study were analyzed via bivariate and multiple-regression techniques. The multiple-regression analyses employed a hierarchical procedure whereby the predictor variables were entered into the regression equation on the basis of their theoretical importance and their temporal order. Within any given inclusion level, the predictors were examined using a stepwise procedure. A more detailed description of these procedures, including the presentation of appropriate significance tests, correlation coefficients, and regression weights, is available from the authors.

positively correlated with one another. A subsequent multiple-regression analysis indicated that, even when competitive trait anxiety and basal state anxiety were controlled for each other, both of these preseason factors remained significant predictors of players' pregame state anxiety. The finding that competitive trait anxiety was a significant predictor of pregame state anxiety is consistent with the results of previous laboratory studies and adds to the generalizability of those findings.

The multiple-regression analysis also revealed that several other intrapersonal factors were significantly related to pregame state anxiety after covarying out the effects of competitive trait anxiety and basal state anxiety. These factors included: (a) self-esteem, with low-self-esteem players evidencing greater pregame anxiety than high-self-esteem players; (b) expectancy of team performance, with players having low expectancies of winning the game demonstrating greater pregame anxiety than players with high expectancies; and (c) expectancy of own performance, with players having low expectancies of playing well, again evidencing greater pregame anxiety than players with high-self-performance expectancies. No other variables were significantly related to pregame state anxiety.

Postgame State Anxiety

Multiple-regression analysis indicated that game win-loss was a powerful predictor of players' postgame anxiety, accounting for 40% of the variance. Losing players ($n = 78$) evidenced substantially greater postgame anxiety than did winning players ($n = 82$), even when controlling for differences in competitive trait anxiety, basal state anxiety, and pregame state anxiety. The adjusted postgame anxiety means for the losing and winning players were 37.44 and 26.54, respectively. Moreover, a comparison of the pregame and postgame anxiety scores revealed that losing players demonstrated a significant increase in pregame to postgame anxiety. Conversely, winning players were significantly less anxious after the game than before the game.

Although no main effect of game closeness was found, there was a significant game win-loss X game closeness interaction. The means of the winning teams at the three levels of game closeness did not significantly differ from one another. Thus, the closeness of the game apparently did not influence the postgame anxiety of winning players. Game closeness, however, significantly affected the postgame anxiety of losing players. Players who lost a very close game were more anxious than players who lost either a moderately close game or a game that was not close. The losers of moderately close and not close games did not differ in their postgame state anxiety. Finally, losers were significantly more anxious than were winners, regardless of game closeness.

Multiple-regression analysis revealed that three intrapersonal factors were significantly associated with postgame state anxiety after controlling for game win-loss and several other covariates. These intrapersonal factors were (a) fun experienced during the game, with players who indicated that they had less fun evidencing greater postgame anxiety than players who indicated they had more fun; (b) basal state anxiety, with higher levels of basal state anxiety associated with greater postgame state anxiety; and (c) perceived importance of the game to the coach, with players who felt that winning was extremely important to their coach showing greater postgame anxiety than players who felt that winning was less important to their coach. Of these three factors, however, only the item assessing fun experienced during the game accounted for more than 5% of the variance in players' postgame state anxiety.

To briefly summarize our results, the major determinants of pregame state anxiety were several intrapersonal factors including competitive trait anxiety, basal state anxiety, self-esteem, and players' expectancies concerning their own and their team's performance. The primary determinants of postgame state anxiety were the situational factors of game win-loss and the win-loss X game closeness interaction. Moreover, with the exception of basal state anxiety, the intrapersonal factors that were found to be significant predictors of pregame state anxiety were not associated with postgame state anxiety to any appreciable degree.

DISCUSSION

The extensive social evaluation that can be incurred regarding motor ability makes sport competition an important social process to most young boys. The findings presented indicate that sport competition can be perceived as a threatening or an anxiety-inducing experience by some children and under some circumstances. Various intrapersonal and situational factors related to threat perception and state anxiety reactions were determined.

Intrapersonal factors that appear to reflect a child's *perceived* capabilities or limitations in meeting the performance demands of the situation are the primary determinants of pregame state anxiety. These intrapersonal factors include the relatively stable personality dispositions of competitive trait anxiety and self-esteem, as well as more game-specific factors, such as self- and team-performance expectancies. Players who were high competitive trait anxious, who had low self-esteem, and who had low performance expectancies perceived greater threat and experienced higher state anxiety when facing a pending competition than did those who were low competitive trait anxious, who had high self-esteem, and who had high performance expectancies.

Postgame anxiety is dramatically influenced by the *actual* capabilities or limitations demonstrated by children in meeting the performance demands of the situation. The situational factors of game win-loss and margin of win clearly indicate the importance of success and failure in evaluative settings with respect to decreases and increases in perceived threat and state anxiety levels. Consistent with past research findings, the success-failure factor was so strong that it overshadowed the effects of the intrapersonal factors that had influenced threat during precompetition.

Another factor related to postgame state anxiety was the amount of fun experienced by the child during the game. It is not particularly surprising to learn, post factum, that children who experienced more fun during the game were less anxious after the game than children who experienced less fun. What is important, however, is that this relationship held true for both winning and losing players. Moreover, for winners and losers, the item pertaining to "fun experienced during the game" exhibited fairly strong correlations with other items assessing perceived satisfaction with individual and team performance. This finding lends support to our intuitive notion that the "fun" item represents a global or summary measure of the child's satisfaction with regard to playing the game. The actual causal nature of the relationship between postgame state anxiety and fun experienced during the game is not clear. For example, it is possible that higher levels of anxiety experienced throughout the game caused the child to perceive himself as having less fun. Conversely, it is possible that less fun experienced throughout the game caused the child to feel anxious. The causal nature of this relationship needs further examination in the laboratory setting. For now, the contention posed for fun, is that a little of it never hurt anyone.

Two limiting factors should be kept in mind when interpreting the results of this investigation. First, only young boys were studied, and it cannot be assumed that the results generalize to girls. In recognition of this problem, we have just completed a similar study to examine anxiety inducing factors in 10- to 12-year-old girls participating in AYSO soccer. Unfortunately, the data have just been collected and have not yet been analyzed.

The second limiting factor is that postcompetition state anxiety was assessed immediately following the game. Therefore, the data do not describe or relate to potential long-term anxiety effects of competition.

In sum, the two goals of this portion of the field investigation were achieved. First, the competitive trait anxiety and success-failure results evidenced in previous experiments were replicated in the present investigation. Thus, the external validity of these results is extended to the natural arena of competitive youth sports. Second, other intrapersonal and situational factors influencing children's perception of threat and their state anxiety were determined. The findings of this investigation provide some of the data that are necessary to gain a greater understanding of the impact that competition has on children.

REFERENCES

Ajzen, I., & Fishbein, M. A Bayesian analysis of attribution processes. *Psychological Bulletin*, 1975, *82*, 261–277.

Chaikin, A. L. The effects of four outcome schedules on persistence, liking for the task, and attributions of causality. *Journal of Personality*, 1971, *39*, 512–526.

Cook, H., & Stingle, S. Cooperative behavior in children. *Psychological Bulletin*, 1974, *81*, 918–933.

Coopersmith, S. *The antecedents of self-esteem*. San Francisco: W. H. Freeman, 1967.

Fitch, G. Effects of self-esteem, perceived performance, and choice on causal attributions. *Journal of Personality and Social Psychology*, 1970, *16*, 311–315.

Gaudry, E., & Poole, C. The effects of an experience of success or failure on state anxiety level. *Journal of Experimental Education*, 1972, *41*, 18–21.

Gaudry, E., & Spielberger, C. D. *Anxiety and educational achievement*. Sydney: Wiley, Australasia Pty. Ltd., 1971.

Gergen, K. J. *The concept of self*. New York: Holt, Rinehart, & Winston, 1971.

Gill, D. L. *The influence of ability composition on group motor performance and intrapersonal variables in competition*. Unpublished doctoral dissertation, University of Illinois at Urbana-Champaign, 1976.

Hartup, W. W. Peer interaction and social organization. In P. H. Mussen (Ed.), *Carmichael's manual of child psychology*. (Vol. 2). New York: Wiley, 1970.

Hodges, W. F. Effects of ego threat and threat of pain on state anxiety. *Journal of Personality and Social Psychology*, 1968, *8*, 364–372.

Hodges, W. F., & Durham, R. L. Anxiety, ability, and digit span performance. *Journal of Personality and Social Psychology*, 1972, *24*, 401–406.

Martens, R. *Sport Competition Anxiety Test*. Champaign, Ill.: Human Kinetics Publishers, 1977.

Martens, R., & Gill, D. L. State anxiety among successful and unsuccessful competitors who differ in competitive trait anxiety. *Research Quarterly*, 1976, *47*, 698–708.

Martens, R., & Simon, J. A. Comparison of three predictors of state anxiety in competitive situations. *Research Quarterly*, 1976, *47*, 381–387.

Masters, J. C. Social comparison by young children. *Young Children*, 1971, *27*, 37–60.

McAdoo, W. G., Jr. *The effects of success, mild failure, and strong failure feedback on A-state for subjects who differ in A-trait*. Unpublished doctoral dissertation, Florida State University, Tallahassee, 1970.

Miller, D. T., & Ross, M. Self-serving biases in the attribution of causality: Fact or fiction? *Psychological Bulletin*, 1975, *82*, 213–225.

Parker, T. *Establishing communication, leadership and motivation in youth sports*. The National Youth Sports Directors' Conference Proceedings Report. Chicago, Ill.: The Athletic Institute, 1975.

Piers, E., & Harris, D. *The Piers-Harris Children's Self Concept Scale*. Nashville, Tenn.: Counselor Recordings and Tests, 1969.

Sarason, I. G. Empirical findings and theoretical problems in the use of anxiety scales. *Psychological Bulletin*, 1960, *57*, 403–415.

Sarason, I. G. Verbal learning, modeling, and juvenile delinquency. *American Psychologist*, 1968, *23*, 254–266.

Sarason, S. B., Davidson, K. S., Lighthall, F. F., Waite, R. R., & Ruebush, B. K. *Anxiety in elementary school children*. New York: Wiley, 1960.

Scanlan, T. K. *The effect of competition trait anxiety and success-failure on the perception of threat in a competitive situation.* Unpublished doctoral dissertation, University of Illinois at Urbana-Champaign, 1975.

Scanlan, T. K. The effect of success-failure on the perception of threat in a competitive situation. *Research Quarterly,* 1977, *48,* 144–153.

Scanlan, T. K. Social evaluation: A key developmental element in the competition press. In R. A. Magill, M. J. Ash, & F. L. Smoll (Eds.), *Children and youth in sport: A contemporary anthology.* Champaign, Ill.: Human Kinetics Publishers, 1978.

Sherif, C. W. The social context of competition. In D. M. Landers (Ed.), *Social problems in athletics.* Urbana: University of Illinois Press, 1976.

Skubic, E. Studies of Little League and Middle League baseball. *Research Quarterly,* 1956, *27,* 97–110.

Spielberger, C. D. Theory and research on anxiety. In C. D. Spielberger (Ed.), *Anxiety and behavior.* New York: Academic Press, 1966.

Spielberger, C. D. Trait-state anxiety and motor behavior. *Journal of Motor Behavior,* 1971, *3,* 265–279.

Spielberger, C. D. *Preliminary test manual for the State-Trait Anxiety Inventory for Children* ("How I Feel Questionnaire"). Palo Alto, Calif.: Consulting Psychologists Press, 1973.

Spielberger, C. D., Gorsuch, R. L., & Lushene, R. E. *The State-Trait Anxiety Inventory (STAI) test manual for form X.* Tallahassee, Fla.: Author, 1969.

Veroff, J. Social comparison and the development of achievement motivation. In C. P. Smith (Ed.), *Achievement-related motives in children.* New York: The Russell Sage Foundation, 1969.

Weiner, B., & Kukla, A. An attributional analysis of achievement motivation. *Journal of Personality and Social Psychology,* 1970, *15,* 1–20.

Wolosin, R. J., Sherman, S. J., & Till, A. Effects of cooperation and competition on responsibility attribution after success and failure. *Journal of Experimental Social Psychology,* 1973, *9,* 220–235.

6

EFFECTS OF REWARDS ON CHANGES IN CHILDREN'S MOTIVATION FOR AN ATHLETIC TASK

Jerry R. Thomas and L. Keith Tennant

A common practice in age-group athletics is to provide many types of rewards (e.g., ribbons, participant certificates, trophies, and allstar teams) as incentives to motivate the participants. The subtle effects of these external rewards on the intrinsic motivation of participants have aroused concern among many social psychologists. Not only is this external reward system prevalent in children's athletics, but tangible rewards are an integral part of many classroom settings. It is not uncommon for a teacher to reward her pupils with gold stars, bonus points, or free time for completing a task or a job well done.

A person who is intrinsically motivated to perform an activity or task will probably have better persistence, completion rate, and performance level for the task than a person who is extrinsically motivated. This suggests that the most desirable form of motivation is internally, as opposed to externally, controlled. People are said to be intrinsically motivated if they engage in an activity simply for the "fun of it" or for no apparent external reason. Extrinsic motivation implies that performance or participation is controlled by external forces (e.g., ribbons, grades, or certificates); and if these forces were not present, the person would cease to engage in the activity or engage at a reduced rate and quality. Most operational definitions of intrinsic motivation basically involve the premise that no external rewards are present. A viable definition was proposed by Roberts (1976), who stated that intrinsically motivated behavior was really behavior caused by a person's need to feel competent and self-determining in relation to his environment. Consequently when external rewards are present, the participant may feel a loss of control in his environment.

A similar approach to motivation was developed by deCharms (1968) as part of his work on determinants of behavior. He proposed that the locus of causality experienced by a person was the determining factor in motivational assessment. If the locus of causality experienced is internal, then the motivational pattern is said to be intrinsic; however, if the locus of causality is external, then the motivational pattern is said to be extrinsic. Nevertheless, this semantic game is not the real problem.

The real dilemma appears to be that children's intrinsic motivation for an activity or task may be seriously undermined through some of the present reward systems. In our reward-oriented society, where we persistently give reward after reward, we may be inadvertently enhancing an undesirable motivational force as a result of these external reinforcements. Though it is apparent that an external reward may induce a participant to achieve at a higher performance level or engage in an activity temporarily, the long-range effect of this practice may not be so desirable. In fact, it is uncertain that a participant would continue in an activity where salient external reinforcement had been given if this reinforcement were removed at a subsequent time. Thus, through our current rewarding systems, we may not only be undermining the intrinsic motivational patterns of the participants, but we may also be increasing the need for external reinforcement to a point where becoming involved in sports is simply the participant's means for attaining the desired reward. This tendency to shift from intrinsic to extrinsic motivation for a task as a result of external rewards was explained using a self-perception theoretical framework originally formulated by Bem (1967).

Bem (1967) and Kelly (1967) originally suggested that self-perception may share a common bond with other-perception. That is, the process of making causal attributions about others' behavior is the same process we use in attributing causes to our own behavior. We make judgments concerning others' behavior by observing the external forces and contingencies impinging upon them. If these forces are salient and sufficient, then behavior is generally attributed to these external factors. Self-perception theory infers that people will use similar techniques to make causal attributions about their own behaviors.

This explanation of self-perception theory was derived from attribution theory (Heider, 1958). Heider theorized that causal inferences are made by persons to understand the behavior of others. These inferences are a result of empirical observations made using the situational factors involved. For example, the inferences one person makes about another's motivation take into account the conditions surrounding the behavior. If behavior is exhibited in a situation where no external reward is apparent, then the perceived locus of control is within the person. The resulting inferences about motivation would then be seen as internal, causing the behavior to be explained as intrinsically motivated. Conversely, behavior perceived in the presence of an external reward will be attributed to that external force, causing motivational inferences to be described with extrinsic terms.

This use of attribution theory by social psychologists in explaining behavior has recently gained attention because it is one of the few theories that is consistent with common sense. This uniqueness has resulted in the terms *naive psychology* or *common sense approach* being used when referring to attribution theory.

Because this attention was focused on attribution theory and more research into behavior was completed, it is easy to see how the transition was made by Bem (1967) from other perceptions to self-perceptions. This self-perception or self-attribution theory simply became a special case of other perception. A pertinent aspect of self-perception theory that was investigated relative to motivational influences was termed the *overjustification* hypothesis. Basically, this hypothesis states that a person's internal motivational level may be undermined by administering an expected and salient external reward for a specified behavior. For example, if a person is intrinsically motivated on a task and is given an oversufficient reward for doing the task, then he may perceive his actions as being motivated by the external reward. Consequently, where the activity was originally intrinsically motivating, the person now perceives the activity as simply a means to achieving an end, that is, the reward. This overjustification hypothesis served as the basis of investigation for several authors.

Deci (1971) was one of the first to directly pursue experimental work using a cognitive approach to examine the negative effects of rewards on intrinsic motivation. In a group of several experiments, Deci found that college students who had been paid to complete a puzzle task had a subsequent decrease in interest on that task at a later time. This portion of the experiment tends to support the overjustification hypothesis; however, experiments that incorporated verbal reinforcement and positive feedback as a reward were less supportive of the hypothesis. In fact, the students in these experimental groups seemed to have an increase in intrinsic motivation for the task. Deci theorized that this was the result of an inferential process whereby students viewed the monetary reward as a "buy off" for their behavior. The groups that received positive feedback and reinforcement viewed these rewards as social approval; consequently, the undermining effect did not occur. This study and a later one by Deci (1972a) served as the framework within which he formulated his cognitive evaluation theory. To explain the effects of feedback and monetary rewards in both paradigms, he relied heavily on the work described earlier by Hieder (1958) and deCharms (1968) using the perceived locus of causality. Additional propositions (Deci, 1975) were later added to his cognitive evaluation theory. These propositions were that changes in feelings of competence and self-determination can be another process through which motivation is affected. Additionally, the theory maintained that every reward has two aspects. It has either a controlling or an informational aspect, and the salience of these aspects will aid in determining the perceived locus of causality.

In a similar study, Deci (1972b) added a noncontingent monetary reward group to the paradigm. Results of this study were consistent with his earlier findings. In addition, the noncontingent reward group had no change in their intrinsic motivational levels for the task. In these studies, Deci (1971, 1972 a,b) demonstrated that there was a negative relationship between the amount of extrinsic reward a person received for an activity and the amount of intrinsic motivation he had for engaging in that activity. Deci, Benware, and Landy (1974) examined the attribution of motivation as a function of output and rewards and supported their hypothesis. Persons attributed greater extrinsic motivation and less intrinsic motivation to others who received higher rewards than to those with lower rewards. Within the self-perception, self-attribution framework (Bem, 1967), people would be expected to make similar attributions about their own behavior.

A more extensive investigation into the overjustification hypothesis within a self-perception paradigm was completed in a subsequent series of studies (Greene & Lepper, 1974; Lepper & Greene, 1975; Lepper, Greene, & Nisbett, 1973). These studies supported the overjustification hypothesis by showing that children in an expected reward group had significantly less subsequent intrinsic interest in the target activity. The experimental paradigms used in each study were similar. Children were selected who had a high intrinsic interest for a particular activity. These activities included picture drawing or puzzle completion in a classroom setting. One group of children was given an expected reward, a second group received an unexpected reward for participating in the activity, and a third group served as a control. One or two weeks later the children were unobtrusively observed for their interest on the same activity in a free choice situation. The results indicated that the unexpected reward and control groups maintained significantly higher interest in the target activity than did the expected reward group. Greene and Lepper's (1974) replication of their previous study (Lepper et al., 1973) adds more credence to the overjustification hypothesis and suggests the importance of examining the potential adverse long-term consequences of an extrinsic reward system.

In a later study, Lepper and Greene (1975) explored the effects of adult surveillance as a form of extrinsic reward. From a self-perception perspective, it was hypothesized that adult surveillance would have the same effect on motivation and interest as would the expectation of a reward. The results of their study indicated support for this hypothesis, and it was further speculated that it made little difference whether the surveillance was constant or only occasional.

Most theorists are in harmony concerning the roles that self-perception and the overjustification hypothesis play in explaining behavioral changes in various reward paradigms. One exception to this, however, is the position taken by Reiss and Sushinsky (1975). Primarily, they attacked the work of Lepper and Greene and the theoretical constructs of other similar studies (Calder & Staw, 1975; deCharms, 1968; Deci, 1971, 1972a). Reiss and Sushinsky maintained that the findings of an overjustification effect in children can be explained more parsimoniously by what is termed the *competing response* hypothesis. They viewed the reward as being only one of many possible responses that can interfere with play behavior. For example, exposure to a salient rewarding stimulus can elicit many responses that interfere with play, including perceptual distractions, cognitive distractions, excitement in anticipation of reward, or frustration from delay of withholding a reward. Reiss and Sushinsky indicted previous investigators who ignored distraction as a possible explanation for the overjustification effect. To support their position, they designed two experimental studies in behavior modification that examined both the overjustification and competing response hypotheses. These experiments, which used listening to songs, followed a paradigm similar to other research in this area. Results, as interpreted by the authors, supported the competing response hypothesis. Their findings also disconfirmed the overjustification hypothesis, since they demonstrated that extrinsic rewards over several task trials caused an increase rather than a decrease on subsequent interest for the behavioral task. Along with these conclusions, they also criticized some of the methodological procedures of Lepper and Greene as well as debated the operational definition for intrinsic motivation.

In a reply to Reiss and Sushinsky (1975), Lepper and Greene (1976) responded point by point to the charges. The focus of their reply was on the distinction between intrinsic and extrinsic motivation, explanation of their previous data, and data relevant to these issues. They concluded that both were addressing different issues; consequently, Reiss and Sushinsky's analysis had missed the mark. This effective reply (Lepper & Greene, 1976) seems sufficient to counter the competing response position even with a subsequent reply by Reiss and Sushinsky (1976).

The use of several types of rewards in the Lepper and Greene studies prompted Ross (1975) to examine the effects that reward saliency has on intrinsic motivation. Ross postulated that an external reward must be salient to a person if it is to cause a decrease in his intrinsic motivation for an activity. Reward saliency was manipulated by altering the position of the reward container. The more conspicuous the container, the more salient it was felt the reward would be. Preschool children who were saliently rewarded showed a subsequent decrease in interest for the target activity. This was in contrast to the no-reward and nonsalient reward groups. Using a similar paradigm, Halliwell (1976a) further attempted to examine the effects of reward saliency on motivation as well as to cross-validate the Ross (1975) findings. Methodological variations in the Halliwell study included differences in age groups, external rewards, and target activity. The results of this investigation failed to replicate Ross's study; however, there were trends in the data that indicated some support for the salency hypothesis. The author pointed out that with the exclusion of three outliers the results would have been significant. Subsequent follow-up by the author indicated these scores were a result of subject artifact, and not treatment.

Other motivation research based within the self-perception theoretical framework yielded consistent findings. Calder and Staw (1975) found an interaction effect between intrinsic and extrinsic motivation for a task satisfaction variable. When a task involved high intrinsic interest, introduction of an extrinsic reward led to the self-perception that one was performing the activity primarily for the reward. When a task involved less intrinsic interest, however, the self-perception effect did not apply. This caused persons with a low intrinsic interest for a boring task to increase their enjoyment rating when given an external reward; whereas those with high intrinsic interest on an enjoyable task decreased their rating of the enjoyment when given an external reward.

Hammer and Foster (1975) conducted similar research and predicted an interaction between intrinsic and extrinsic motivation. They maintained that people in a contingent pay condition would be more intrinsically motivated when performing a boring task than would those in a noncontingent or controlled condition. Also, persons performing an interesting task and receiving a contingent reward would be less intrinsically motivated than similar persons in a control or noncontingent group. Additionally, it was postulated that quantity of performance would decrease in the high interest-contingent reward group; whereas quantity would increase in the low-interest group as a result of contingent reward. Results of their study failed to support the hypotheses. Performance levels increased on both the low-interest and high-interest tasks in the contingent reward group. Also, quantity levels were not adversely affected, and the quality of performance was improved as a result of the extrinsic rewards. This led to the conclusions that intrinsic and extrinsic reinforcements are additive in nature and do not undermine performance.

Kruglanski, Friedman, and Zeevi (1971) also obtained results consistent with self-perception theory. They examined the effects of extrinsic incentive on the qualitatitive aspects of task performance. Task quality was determined by two creativity and two recall measures, plus the Zeigarnik (1927) measures (these were 16 recall measures). Their data supported the hypothesis that extrinsic incentives would reduce the quality of task performance. Further evidence (Kruglanski, Alon, & Lewis, 1972) showed that not only is quality reduced but so is the task enjoyment level. These investigators reported evidence that children tended to incorrectly attribute causality to the prizes received for having participated in competitive games and consequently reported less enjoyment of the games as such.

Evidence for the overjustification hypothesis seems to remain consistent across studies. Paramount to that hypothesis is the distinction between intrinsic and extrinsic motivation as discussed earlier (Reiss & Sushinsky, 1975). This distinction between internal causes versus external causes has led to some conceptual difficulties. Kruglanski, Riter, Amitai, Margolin, Shabtai, and Zaksh (1975) pointed out the conceptual difficulties associated with internality or externality rather well. They maintain the following:

> (a) Any activity seems to have an internal cause, the actor's motive for engaging in it; and (b) many activities seem to have an external cause as well as an internal one, namely, the anticipated change in the environment (reception of the reward, solution of the problem) satisfying the actor's motive for engaging in the activity. For instance, money constitutes an external object, however, the desire for it may be acutely internal. Similarly, interest in a task may be internal, yet the task eliciting such interest is certainly external to the person. (p. 744)

Kruglanski et al. (1975) made a distinction between the content of an activity and the consequence. In a study designed to test this content-consequence hypothesis, using money for intrinsic motivation, the investigators found that when persons were extrinsically rewarded with money and money was an inherent part (content) of the task, the intrinsic motivation level was enhanced rather than undermined. Rewards given when money was a consequence of the task had a reducing effect on intrinsic motivation. This implies that any activity may be intrinsically motivating if the situation that the person is participating in is a result of the activity's content.

Yet another position for viewing the deleterious effects of salient external rewards on intrinsic motivation was advanced by Ross, Karniol, and Rothstein (1976). They attributed the loss in subsequent interest for a task that has been rewarded to the frustration generated by having to wait for the reward. This frustration makes the task somewhat aversive for future participation. This *delay of gratification* hypothesis was sufficiently compelling to merit an investigation. The results of their study proved contrary to the delay-of-gratification interpretation and more consistent with an attributional analysis of intrinsic motivation. The delayed-contingent reward group had a significantly greater interest in the target activity at a later free play period than did the task-contingent reward group.

Another important aspect was pointed out by Ross et al. (1976) while attempting to relate the plausability of the delay-of-gratification explanation. They questioned the ability of a child as young as 3 or 4 years of age to "engage in the rather sophisticated causal reasoning posited by attribution theory." Piagetian (Piaget, 1952) and neo-Piagetian (Pascual-Leone, 1970) theoretical interpretations indicate that children in these developmental years are simply unable to reason within this sophisticated framework. This is due to the child's inability, at such an early age, to handle multiple plausible causes for an event.

Several developmental studies (Karniol & Ross, 1976; Schultz, Butkowsky, Pearce, & Shanfield, 1975; Smith, 1975) were conducted to examine the cognitive processes used in children's causal analysis of reward situations. Smith (1975) found that children did not display any systematic form of attributional analysis; however, due to a methodological problem, the results were questioned by Karniol and Ross (1976). Using a similar paradigm and correcting the methodological problems in Smith's study, Karniol and Ross found that young children tended to systematically employ either an additive schema or multiplicative schema in conducting causal analysis of reward situations.

Therefore, it was hypothesized in several studies (Halliwell, 1976 a,b; Schultz et al., 1975) that children will use the discounting principle more with increased age; whereas the use of the additive rule will decrease with age. In essence, this means that young children using the additive rule will see their intrinsically motivated behavior as fun, while viewing the external reward simply as a bonus with no underminding effect. However, older children tend to use the discounting principle in causal analyses, which results in discounting of their own intrinsic interest in the activity and viewing their behavior as motivated by the external causes.

A good account of the additive and discounting principles relating to children's use of multiple schema was completed by Halliwell (1976b). His data supported the additive versus discounting principle across age. Using an other-perception framework, children were asked to view rewarded actors and respond to questions concerning the actors' participation. Young children saw the actor as having fun and getting a reward too; whereas, by the ages of 7 to 10 years, the children viewed the actor as participating for the reward. These results were explained within the developmental framework of neo-Piagetian theory. It was also suggested that as the focus of attention moves from other-perception to self-perception, the ability of younger children to discount increases. This could possibly be a result of children's attributing their own behavior to salient rewards sooner then they attribute other people's behavior to such rewards.

In summarizing the current literature, it has become evident that there is some disparity between studies; however, the majority of the research tends to support the overjustification hypothesis.

There are two important factors that must be integrated when considerating the effects of external rewards on the intrinsic motivation of children. These variables are the processing capacity of the child and whether the causal reasoning involves self- or other-perception.

The processing capacity is an age- or stage-related variable: there is ample evidence that older children can process greater amounts of information than younger children (Chi, 1976; Newell, 1977; Thomas & Bender, 1977). Thus, with younger children, discounting may be considered as a transformation of internal to external causes relative to the specified behavior. The ability to focus on the internal causes of behavior and attribute these internal factors to external causes is probably more information than the 5- or 6-year-old can process, especially when the processing must be done in reference to another person's behavior. The majority of the literature suggested that discounting will begin to occur at about 7 years of age (early concrete stage).

Additionally, children seem to be able to use causal reasoning about their own behaviors earlier in development than about the behaviors of others. Halliwell (1976b) suggested that this is because their own behaviors are more relevant to them, and greater amounts of the available attention can be used because of this meaningfulness. This would explain the discrepancies in the findings between self-perception studies of young children (5 years) that report undermining of intrinsic motivation and other-perception studies that report discounting of intrinsic motivation beginning about 7 years of age.

These theories and models can be easily understood within the framework of children's sports and physical performance; however, one additional variable must be considered: Is the reward contingent on the quality of performance of the athletic task? This includes rewards that are only available given certain levels of performance as well as when the quality of the reward is directly related to the quality of the performance. Previously reported studies generally do not consider the quality of the person's performance on the target task; the reward is simply given for performance. The literature is well documented with studies indicating that rewards contingent on the quality of performance increase the immediate performance level. The question of importance is, do the contingent rewards that are frequently associated with children's sport undermine the child's intrinsic interest in that sport? However, it is possible that the child may reason differently relative to contingent rewards; that is, since he controls the quality and effort associated with his performance, he also controls to a great extent whether he obtains the reward. Given this situation, an external reward may increase, rather than undermine, intrinsic motivation. The ability of the child to carry out the necessary causal cognitions is also a variable of concern in determining the effects of contingent rewards.

Based on the previous discussion, the present study was an attempt to investigate the following questions:

1. Does a noncontingent reward undermine subsequent performance on an

athletic task, as has been reported in previous research on various nonathletic tasks?

2. Does the effect of a noncontingent reward differ from the effect of a contingent reward on the subsequent behavior?

3. Is the effect of either contingent or noncontingent rewards related to increased age (at which point increased processing capacity would be assumed)?

METHOD

Participants

To investigate the aforementioned questions, 424 boys were screened for their initial interest on a target activity. They were selected from six elementary schools in the area of Gainesville, Florida. This screening process involved showing the children an 8-mm film of a boy their own age performing four athletic tasks. The film sequence for the tasks was dribbling a basketball, tossing bean bags, walking a balance beam, and throwing balls at targets (which was the task of interest in the study). Each task was given equal time on the film that took 2 min to view. The screening film was shown to children in their regular classroom groups. On completion of the film, they were asked to select the task or activity they considered "the most fun." The children indicated their activity preference by checking the appropriate square on a screening form (Figure 1). Including all of those screened, 34% selected the target task; 21%, the balance beam; 15%, the bean bag toss; and 30%, the dribbling. The total number screened at each age level was 127, 147, and 150 for 5-, 7-, and 9-year-olds. The percentage selecting the target activity across each level accounted for 38%, 33%, and 32% of the students screened within those ages. Recognizing that both a recency and primacy effect may exist in memory for children, the target task was placed last in the film sequence, to increase the number of children selecting this task. Only students who selected the task of throwing balls at targets were chosen for the experimental groups. This activity was the target activity; consequently, those preferring this task were indicating a higher degree of intrinsic motivation for this task as opposed to the other choices. The 48 screened children at each age level were randomly assigned within age levels to four experimental groups (total $N = 144$). The mean ages (in months) for each of the three levels were 65.1, 86.1, and 110.2.

Athletic Tasks

The target task, throwing balls at targets, was designed so that performance measures for each boy could be obtained. Values were assigned to each target size, with the smaller target having a higher value. The score for

FIGURE 1   Activity preference screening form.

each child was a cumulative total for each hit the child made on the various targets. The children chose between colorful pictured targets of three different sizes and point values. The value of each target was 1, 2, or 3, with the points increasing as the target size decreased. Target diameters were 1½, 2, and 2½ ft. Children were clearly instructed that smaller targets were worth more points. To help equate throwing differences between age groups, the target distances were varied. Distances of 10, 15, and 20 ft. were used for the 5-, 7-, and 9-year-olds, respectively. A low retaining net was used to keep the children from advancing closer to the target than permitted for their age group. These distances were established through previous pilot work that indicated each parameter was sufficient to allow persons to succeed and yet provide for a reasonable score distribution. A sufficient supply of tennis balls was provided so that ball retrieval was not necessary. The second activity, ball dribbling, involves dribbling a ball through a maze of five standards positioned on a 10-ft. square with one standard on each corner and one in the center. Arrows on the floor served as a directional guide to the subject.

A third task used was a modified balance beam. The beam measured 10 ft. in length and consisted of two 5-ft. sections. The first section had a width of 3½ in. and the second section was 1¾ in. wide, thus providing a walking surface with a decreasing width.

The final activity, a bean bag toss, consisted of tossing bean bags onto a colorful target from a distance of 12 ft. The target provided was a refurbished wastepaper can with a 16-in.-diameter opening.

Reward Treatments

Each child, except those children in the control group, received a reward. This was a monetary reward ranging from a minimum of 8 cents to a maximum of 32 cents, both ranges being established by the contingent reward group. Each point scored was worth ½ cent. By yoking the children in the other two reward groups to a previous performance of a boy in the contingent group, the contingent group served as a reference for rewards to the noncontingent and unexpected reward groups. This insured that individual rewards were matched so that the amount of reward given was equivalent by person across the three experimental groups. Rewards were given on completion of the 5-min testing period.

Before performance, children in the contingent group were told that their reward was directly related to their performance; and the more points they scored on the task, the greater the amount of money they would receive. Children in the noncontingent group were told to perform as well as they could and that for performing the task for 5 min they would receive a reward. It was stressed that this reward was not related to their performance on the target task. Members of the unexpected reward group were told to simply perform as best as they could, and no mention was made concerning a reward. However, the reward was given to them following the 5-min test period. Children in the control groups were told they could play with the task they had previously chosen for 5 min.

Order of Testing

All control children at each age level were tested first, to minimize children's telling each other about the rewards. Following the testing of controls, a contingent reward child had to be tested, to yoke the amount of reward earned to the other two reward groups. A noncontingent and unexpected reward child was tested in alternating order following the testing of each contingent reward child. The order of testing resulted from a decision to control precisely the amount of the reward across groups rather than randomizing the testing order of treatment groups. Since only 3–12 children were obtained within an age level at each school, it appeared that communication about the experiment among children was a minimal problem; and the decision was made that it was more important to equate rewards by individual children across treatment groups.

Procedures

After the initial screening to determine intrinsic motivation for the target task, the children were randomly assigned within each of the three age levels to the following four levels of reward treatment: No reward or control (CL), contingent reward group (CT), noncontingent reward group (NCT), and an unexpected reward group (UE). Each child was then given the appropriate instructions for his respective reward group and allowed to participate on the target activity for 5 min. During this 5-min period, the experimenter recorded the child's number of trials or throws and the score obtained on the target task. Immediately after completing the task, the child received the appropriate reward for his respective group.

Approximately 2 weeks later, each boy returned to the testing area (Figure 2) and participated in a free-choice situation among the original four tasks. He was told to participate in any activity present while the experimenter completed a few minutes of important paper work. The experimenter then "released" the child in a position central to all four tasks and proceeded to position himself at a point where he could observe the performance but be shielded by a screen from the child's vision. Before beginning to posttest, the boys were each informed that the experimenter had no more money; consequently, no rewards could be given to them this time. During this posttest session, the children again participated for 5 min, during which time trials and score on the target task, initial task selection, and persistence at each of the four tasks were recorded from the shielded position.

The first task attempted by the boy after being released by the

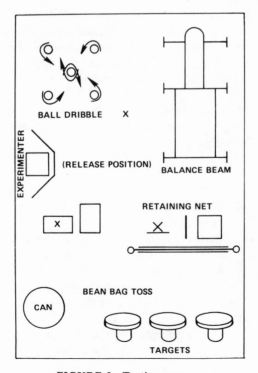

FIGURE 2 Testing area.

experimenter was recorded as his initial contact. This initial contact was noted for future analysis as well as for indicating the activity having the most initial intrinsic interest for the child at that particular time.

Once released, the child's 5 min in the free choice situation was begun. The time spent on each task as well as the intermittent time was recorded to the nearest second. The boy's cumulative time during the 5-min session served as his persistence measure for the task. Time on the task was determined by verbally noting on a tape recorder when contact or termination was complete for each task. The tape was then replayed and timed at a later date. This technique was similar to the one used by Halliwell (1976a). Other data collected during the child's persistence at the target activity included his number of trials and the score obtained.

Analysis

Data collected on the target activity during the initial and subsequent testing sessions was analyzed using a 3 X 4 analysis-of-variance design. This Age X Reward design was used to determine whether significant differences existed between the means, using as the dependent variable performance score, raw score, and number of trials for each of the experimental groups. The performance score was obtained by dividing the child's raw score by the number of trials taken.

Because of the large variances and negatively skewed data obtained on the persistence measure (time on target), the Kruskal-Wallis (Siegel, 1956) one-way analysis of variance by ranks was used to analyze these data from the 12 groups. Scores were ranked from low to high across all children. The large-sample method was used, and the recommended corrections were made for tied observations.

Data obtained during the free choice situation on initial task selection were analyzed using chi-square to determine if treatment groups differed significantly on their initial choice of tasks.

RESULTS

The results obtained from analysis of variance using total score, total trials, and performance scores as the dependent measures during the initial testing period are reported in Table 1. These results indicated there were significant main effects ($p < .05$), but no significant interactions. Each dependent variable was significant across all age effects, and only the performance measure failed to yield any significant effect across treatments. A follow up of the significant age effects, using the Duncan Multiple Range Test, indicated that differences exist between each of the cell means for the dependent variable with one exception (Table 2). This is the mean difference on initial performance between the 5- and 7-year-olds.

TABLE 1 ANOVA table for initial testing effects

Source	Initial score			Initial trials			Initial performance		
	df	ms	F	df	ms	F	df	ms	F
Age	2	3,351	86.60*	2	8,714	135*	2	.7273	23.40*
Treatment	3	168	4.30*	3	287	4.46*	3	.0235	.75
Interaction	6	30	.78	6	26	.40	6	.006	.19
Error	132	38.7		132	64.3		132	.031	

*p < .05.

TABLE 2 Follow up results for age effect using Duncan's multiple range test

Age (in years)	Means[a]			Initial score		Initial trials		Initial performance	
	IS	IT	IP	7	9	7	9	7	9
5	28.50	29.20	1	*	*	*	*	*	*
7	37.70	39.50	1.05		*		*		*
9	45.20	55.90	1.23						

[a]IS, initial score; IT, initial trials; IP, initial performance.

*p < .05.

137

The Duncan Multiple Range follow up for the significant treatment effects on the initial testing data failed to discriminate among the treatment means. The trends in these data, however, were for the contingent reward group to have a higher initial score and the control condition the lowest supporting the frequently reported effects of contingent reward on immediate performance. These mean scores ranged from 34.4 to 38.8 points. A similar situation occurred with initial trials. Even though a significant F ratio was obtained, a subsequent follow up failed to identify the exact source of the difference. Once again, as would be expected, trends in these data pointed toward the contingent group's taking the larger number of trials, whereas the control group took the least. These means for trials ranged from 38.6 to 45.1 points.

An analysis of data obtained during the subsequent free choice period is reported in Table 3. Examination of these data revealed that only one significant F ratio occurred, that being within the age effect on the final performance variable. The multiple-range test follow up failed to determine where the difference occured; however, the trend was for performance to increase steadily across each age level.

The cumulative time data obtained from the children's participation on the target task was ranked from lowest to highest across all experimental and age levels and was subjected to the Kruskal-Wallis (Siegel, 1956) nonparametric test for rank differences. Significant differences were observed ($H = 25$, $df = 12$, $p < .05$) among the 12 groups. The mean rank scores are depicted in Figure 3. The contingent reward group had more time on the target activity than any other group at all age levels. Another obvious point, which will be discussed later but can easily be observed in Figure 3, is the steady decline in time spent on the target task by the noncontingent reward group across age levels. It should also be noted that there is a close proximity in Figure 3 for both the unexpected and no-reward, or control, groups. These scores barely fluctuated across age levels. Data resulting from initial contact with the target activity were analyzed and the subsequent chi-square of .587 ($df = 6$) was not significant ($p > .05$).

DISCUSSION

The reported data support the theoretical positions of other-perception taken by numerous authors (Halliwell, 1976b; Karniol & Ross, 1976; Schultz et al., 1975) in that in the noncontingent reward situation the younger children view the rewards as a bonus (additive). This increases their time on the target task above the control and unexpected reward groups. But with increasing age, greater amounts of discounting occur in the noncontingent group, so that by 7 years they are not different from the control and unexpected reward groups. By 9 years of age, the children view the noncontingent reward as a

TABLE 3 ANOVA table for free choice testing effects

Source	Final score			Final trials			Final performance		
	df	ms	F	df	ms	F	df	ms	F
Age	2	11.5	.24	2	188.4	2.11	2	2.33	4.55*
Treatment	3	67	1.41	3	64.3	.72	3	.19	.38
Interaction	6	13.6	.28	6	19.2	.21	6	.14	.27
Error	132	47.4		132	89		132	.51	

*$p < .05$.

139

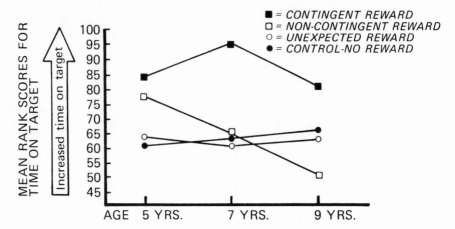

FIGURE 3   Mean rank scores for time on the target task across ages.

bribe to participate in the task; and this seriously undermines their persistence in a free choice situation.

This experiment is not a study of other-perception as are those reported by Halliwell (1976b), Karniol and Ross (1976), and Schultz et al., (1975), but in fact is a study of children's self-perception. As such, the data on the 5-year-old children are in direct conflict with those reported by Lepper and Greene in their various studies. That is, the noncontingent reward does not undermine, but in fact increases time on the target task in the free choice situation. While the undermining process is evident with the older children, why are the effects in the exact opposite direction from data in the three Lepper and Greene studies?

Several explanations are available, but first it is necessary to indicate some methodological differences in the present study and the series of studies by Lepper and Greene. If the contingent reward group is disregarded for the time being, the research paradigms are similar but with two differences. In the Lepper and Greene studies, the level of intrinsic motivation was determined by observing the potential participants unobtrusively in the classroom setting. In the present study, the children selected the activity by viewing a film of a child doing several "fun" activities. This selection procedure is somewhat artificial and resembles procedures in many of the other-perception studies. This may lead to selecting participants with a lower level of "true" intrinsic motivation than did Lepper and Greene's technique. Thus, the noncontingent reward group might have had a lower initial level of intrinsic motivation.

A similar methodological difference exists in the subsequent free-choice situation. Lepper and Greene again observed their participants in the classroom through a one-way mirror, whereas the children in the present study came back to the experimental situation. Even though the participants thought the experimenter could not see them, a point made by Lepper and

Greene (1976) seems pertinent. That is, since the children were not in a naturalistic setting but were in the setting (although rearranged) in which they received the reward, they somehow may have still expected to receive a reward. However, this point is somewhat weakened by observing the effects of the unexpected reward group across ages. An undermining effect does occur with the noncontingent group across age, but not with the unexpected group. Why did not these children also expect the reward in the free-choice situation? In addition, why did their performance parallel the control's performance across age if the experimental situation were the variable of concern?

Thus, based on these data, noncontingent rewards seem to have a motivating effect on initial performance and subsequent interest for 5-year-old children. However, by age 9, a reward simply for participating tends to undermine the child's subsequent interest in the task. Since age group athletics are getting into full swing at about 8 or 9 years of age, rewards such as ribbons or trophies for participation may result in undesirable long-term effects on intrinsic motivation to participate in the sport or activity.

The effects of contingent rewards are relatively clear. Obviously the children at all age levels understood that the reward was contingent on the quality of their performance, since the initial score, trials, and performance all favored the contingent reward group. This reward did not undermine, but in fact increased subsequent persistence at the target task across all age levels. This supports observations by both Deci (1975) and Lepper and Greene (1976, below):

> Rewards may convey information to an individual concerning his ability or competence at a task. . . . To the extent that such information leads a person to believe that he has been successful and is personally responsible for his success, we expect that intrinsic motivation to engage in the task is enhanced. (p. 33)

With reference to age-group athletics, this suggests that rewards based on the quality of performance are not detrimental to subsequent interest and persistence in the sport or activity, but in fact increase the intrinsic motivation to perform. One point of caution seems important here. This enhancement of intrinsic motivation may relate to the success of the child in obtaining the reward. In the present study, every child in the contingent reward group perceived it within his ability to earn the reward by his performance (in fact, every child did earn some level of reward). If certain children in sports programs perceive that the desired rewards exceed their level of performance (e.g., all-star teams, regular playing opportunities), these contingent rewards may in fact undermine their intrinsic motivation to play the game.

Unexpected rewards appear to have no effect on subsequent interest;

children in this group had time on target activity that paralled that of the control group. This is consistent with the earlier overjustification literature.

Data collected on the dependent measures of trials, score, and performance in the free-choice situation fail to support a logical interpretation with respect to the treatment conditions. It was anticipated that significant differences would have been obtained between the contingent reward groups and the other experimental conditions on the performance variable. For the results to have been in agreement with Hammer and Foster (1975), the contingent reward should have had a significantly higher performance score. On the other hand, if the discounting principle is really operating, then those children in the noncontingent reward group should have had significantly lower performance scores as a result of undermining. The trend of the data is toward the expected direction for each condition but not significantly so.

If undermining has occurred on the task, there should be a decreased level of initial interest exhibited on that task at a later time. The results derived using the chi-square analysis for initial contacts with the target fail to support the expectations for undermining. Experimental groups did not vary as a result of treatment on the initial task selection in the free choice situation. To explain this, the experimenters did observe that many children engaged the target activity shortly after experimenting with the various athletic tasks present during the free-choice situation. Consequently, the initial task selection variable may not have been indicative of the children's intrinsic interest, as predicted, but was simply a result of their need to quickly explore each task before engaging in prolonged activity on any one particular task.

In summary, the data from this study support results frequently reported in other-perception studies, that is, young children view a reward for performance of a task as a bonus and this reward serves to increase their subsequent interest in the task. But as children get older, they begin to perceive the reward as a bribe; and this has an undermining effect on subsequent task interest, resulting in a decrease in the motivation to persist at the task. A contingent reward (a reward based on the quality of the performance) increased the subsequent task interest (as measured by task persistence) across the age levels in this study (5-9 years). The results for task performance, however, were not consistent with the persistence findings in that there were no differences among the groups at any age level.

In applying these results to age group sports, children above 8 or 9 years should probably not be given rewards just for participating in the sport. But rewards based on the quality of performance appear to increase intrinsic motivation, at least when the child's own perception is that of having the necessary skill to attain the reward.

REFERENCES

Bem, D. J. Self-perception: An alternative interpretation of cognitive dissonance phenomena. *Psychological Review,* 1967, *74,* 183–200.

Calder, B. J., & Staw, B. M. Self-perception of intrinsic and extrinsic motivation. *Journal of Personality and Social Psychology*, 1975, *31*, 599–605.

Chi, M. T. Short term memory limitations in children: Capacity or processing deficits? *Memory and Cognition*, 1976, *4*, 559–572.

deCharms, R. *Personal causation: The internal affective determinants of behavior*. New York: Academic Press, 1968.

Deci, E. L. Effects of externally mediated rewards and intrinsic motivation. *Journal of Personality and Social Psychology*, 1971, *18*, 105–115.

Deci, E. L. Intrinsic motivation, extrinsic reinforcement, and inequity. *Journal of Personality and Social Psychology*, 1972, *22*, 113–120. (a)

Deci, E. L. The effects of contingent and noncontingent rewards and controls on intrinsic motivation. *Organizational Behavior and Human Performance*, 1972, *8*, 217–229. (b)

Deci, E. L. *Intrinsic motivation*. New York: Plenum Press, 1975.

Deci, E. L., Benwars, C., & Landy, D. The attribution of motivation as a function of output and rewards. *Journal of Personality*, 1974, *42*, 652–667.

Greene, D., & Lepper, M. R. Effects of extrinsic rewards on children's subsequent intrinsic interest. *Child Development*, 1974, *45*, 1141–1145.

Halliwell, W. *Reward salience and children's intrinsic motivation*. Unpublished manuscript, Florida State University, 1976. (a)

Halliwell, W. *The role of cognitive development, perceptual modality and subject gender in children's motivational analyses*. Unpublished doctoral dissertation, Florida State University, 1976. (b)

Hammer, W. C., & Foster, L. W. Are intrinsic and extrinsic rewards additive: A test of Deci's cognitive evaluation theory of task motivation. *Organizational Behavior and Human Performance*, 1975, *14*, 398–415.

Heider, F. *The psychology of interpersonal relations*. New York: Wiley, 1958.

Karniol, R., & Ross, M. The development of causal inferences in social perception. *Journal of Personality and Social Psychology*, 1976, *34*, 455–464.

Kelly, H. H. Attribution theory in social psychology. In D. Levine (Ed.), *Nebraska symposium on motivation* (Vol. 15). Lincoln, Neb.: University of Nebraska Press, 1967.

Kruglanski, A. W., Alon, S., & Lewis, T. Retrospective misattribution and task enjoyment. *Journal of Experimental Social Psychology*, 1972, *8*, 493–501.

Kruglanski, A. W., Friedman, I., & Zeevi, G. The effect of extrinsic incentive on some qualitative aspects of task performance. *Journal of Personality*, 1971, *39*, 606–617.

Kruglanski, A. W., Riter, A., Amitai, A., Margolin, B., Shabtai, L., & Zaksh, D. Can money enhance intrinsic motivation?: A test of the content consequence hypothesis. *Journal of Personality and Social Psychology*, 1975, *31*, 744–750.

Lepper, M. R., & Greene, D. Turning play into work: Effects of adult surveillance and extrinsic rewards on children's intrinsic motivation. *Journal of Personality and Social Psychology*, 1975, *31*, 479–486.

Lepper, M. R., & Greene, D. On understanding "overjustification": A reply to

Reiss and Sushinsky. *Journal of Personality and Social Psychology*, 1976, *33*, 25–35.

Lepper, M. R., Greene, D., & Nisbett, R. E. Undermining children's intrinsic interest with extrinsic rewards: A test of the "overjustification hypothesis." *Journal of Personality and Social Psychology*, 1973, *28*, 129–137.

Newell, K. M. *Motor control: Developmental issues.* Paper presented at the NAPECW-NCPEAM Conference, Orlando, Fla., January 1977.

Pascual-Leone, J. A mathematical model for the transition rule in Piaget's developmental stages. *Acta Psychologica*, 1970, *32*, 301–345.

Piaget, J. *The origins of intelligence in children.* New York: International University Press, 1952.

Reiss, S., & Sushinsky, L. Overjustification, competing responses, and the acquisition of intrinsic interest. *Journal of Personality and Social Psychology*, 1975, *31*, 1116–1125.

Reiss, S., & Sushinsky, L. W. The competing response hypothesis of decreased play effects: A reply to Lepper and Greene. *Journal of Personality and Social Psychology*, 1976, *33*, 233–244.

Roberts, G. C. *Personality and emotional development in children's sports: A reaction.* Paper presented at the AAHPER Symposium, The Child in Sport: Readiness and Effects, Milwaukee, Wisc., March 1976.

Ross, M. Salience of reward and intrinsic motivation. *Journal of Personality and Social Psychology*, 1975, *32*, 245–254.

Ross, M., Karniol, R., & Rothstein, M. Reward contingency and intrinsic motivation in children: A test of the delay of gratification hypothesis. *Journal of Personality and Social Psychology*, 1976, *33*, 442–447.

Schultz, T. R., Butkowsky, J., Pearce, J. W., & Shanfield, H. Development of schemes for the attribution of multiple psychological causes. *Developmental Psychology*, 1975, *11*, 502–510.

Siegel, S. *Nonparametric statistics for the behavioral sciences.* New York: McGraw-Hill, 1956.

Smith, M. C. Children's use of the multiple sufficient cause schema in social perception. *Journal of Personality and Social Psychology*, 1975, *32*, 737–744.

Thomas, J. R., & Bender, P. R. A developmental explanation for children's motor behavior: A neo-Piagetian interpretation. *Journal of Motor Behavior*, 1977, *9*, 81–93.

Zeigarnik, B. Über das Behalten von erledigten und unerledigten Handlungen. *Psychologische Forschungen*, 1927, *9*, 1–85.

7

CHILDREN'S ASSIGNMENT OF RESPONSIBILITY FOR WINNING AND LOSING

Glyn C. Roberts

Recent work concerned with how people perceive or make attributions about the causes of everyday events has been investigated within a body of research known as *attribution theory*. Attribution theory is concerned with how people interpret information about the perceived underlying causes of events. It is assumed that people implicitly or explicitly are constantly making attributions to causes about every salient event that occurs to them. The individual is regarded as a naïve psychologist who is trying to answer questions about the environment, such as why this or that event occurred. Humans are conceived as active, information-processing organisms who use attributional schema or naïve *theories* to make sense of the complex world in which they live. The theory focuses on both the process of making cognitions relative to one's environment and the implications of making such inferences. The essential assumption is that thought precedes action.

Although attribution theory is concerned with causal judgments made in a number of situations about many types of events, the focus of this chapter is on those attributions made after achievement events—more specifically, on the causal attributions people make after their own success or failure at an achievement-oriented activity. Much achievement-oriented research concentrated on academic success and failure, but the basic principles and concepts appear to be applicable in a wide variety of settings (Carroll & Payne, 1975; Elig & Frieze, 1975). Motor performance and sports settings are important achievement events for people because of the competitive or social evaluation components implicit in such settings (c.f., Scanlan, 1977) and the saliency of the outcome. It is important, therefore, to determine whether participation and achievement behavior in sport and motor performance settings are also dependent upon certain belief patterns (Frieze, J. H., McHugh, & Duquin, 1976; Iso-Ahola, 1975; Roberts, 1975, 1976, 1977; Thomas & Halliwell, 1976).

Within attribution theory, Weiner and associates (1971, 1974) proposed a miniature model that focuses on the beliefs individuals have about succeeding or failing at an achievement-oriented activity. Weiner and associates extended Heider's (1958) original attribution theory to provide a model of achievement behavior that assumes beliefs about the causes of success and failure moderate between the perceptions of an achievement task and the final achievement outcome. The differential allocation of responsibility to a particular causal event then guides subsequent behavior. The attributions one makes following a success or failure are seen as having both emotional and behavioral consequences. The attributions one makes affect one's choice of activity, the pride or shame one feels, actual performance levels, and the expectancies of future performance levels.

Weiner and associates (1971, 1974) assumed that people attribute the causes of success and failure to one or more of four causal elements: ability, effort, luck, and task difficulty (Figure 1). Each causal element may be jointly classified as being either internal (ability, effort) or external (luck, task difficulty) and stable (ability, task difficulty) or unstable (luck, effort). Attributions along the locus of control dimension (internal-external) are assumed to influence affective reactions to outcome with internal attributions maximizing personal affect (pride or shame) and external attributions minimizing personal affect (Lanzetta & Hannah, 1969; Weiner & Kukla, 1970). The stability dimension (stable or unstable), on the other hand, mediates expectancies for future performance with stable attributions maximizing outcome expectancies consistent with past outcomes (success or failure) and unstable attributions minimizing outcome expectancies consistent with past outcomes (Feather & Simon, 1971; Fontaine, 1975; Weiner, Heckhausen, Meyer, & Cook, 1972; McMahan, 1973; Simon & Feather, 1973).

The hypothesized attributional process in sports and motor performance situations is illustrated in Figure 2. The attributional process begins with a

Locus of Control

		Internal	External
Stability	Stable	Ability	Task Difficulty
	Unstable	Effort	Luck

FIGURE 1   The dimensions of causal attributions.

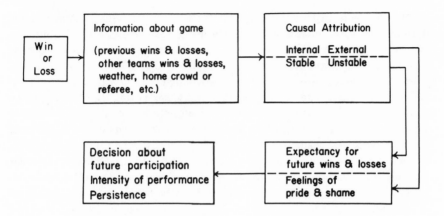

(Modified from Frieze, 1976).

FIGURE 2   The attribution process.

particular win or loss. After the outcome is established, the athlete attempts to determine the cause of the outcome. For example, the athlete may use the previous wins and losses of himself or the team, the opponent's previous wins or losses, the expectancy associated with the outcome, the weather, the home crowd, and the referee to determine the causes of the current win. This information determines the particular causal attributions that the athlete or athletes use and the dimensions along which the causal elements are invoked. These particular causal elements in turn affect the emotional reaction of the athlete to the outcome and the future performance expectancies of the athlete. For example, an athlete who has consistently won in the past and who wins a particular contest against a competent opponent would probably attribute high ability to himself. This is an internal attribute that maximizes pride in the outcome, but ability is also a stable attribute, which indicates that the athlete would expect similar outcomes in future contests. Further, these expectancies and the emotional reaction to the outcome are assumed to affect the athlete's decision about future participation, the intensity of future participation, and persistence at the activity.

Given the taxonomy and causal elements, there are two research directions one can take: Backward to the information that affects the cognitive processes—the antecedents of causal attributions; and forward to the effect these causal cognitions have on subsequent achievement behavior—the consequences of holding certain cognitions. The research reported here deals with the antecedents of causal cognitions. This research investigated some of the factors that were hypothesized to effect causal cognitions in sport and motor performance settings.

It is assumed that ability inferences are made from past history information; and, in particular, the pattern of past performance is important. If an athlete or team has won repeatedly in the past, one infers high ability to that athlete or team. Effort inferences are also made from success outcomes. If an athlete or team succeeds, then usually effort is inferred. Also, a win following previous losses is usually attributed to increased effort. Task difficulty inferences are usually made from social norms. If other teams or athletes lose to a particular team or athlete, then that athlete or team is considered hard to beat. In other words, the task is considered to be difficult. Luck inferences are made if a team or athlete perceives the outcome to be out of their own personal control. For example, the team or athlete may blame the referee, the bounce of the ball, or whatever, and consider that the particular outcome was determined more by luck factors than anything else.

Attribution theory, therefore, considers that people use the available information in an essentially logical fashion to determine the causes of outcomes. Persons analyze success and failure feedback in terms of the information they provide concerning the influence of a given causal factor. Thus, attribution theory assumes an information-processing model based on the covariation of cause and effect (Kelly, 1971; Nicholls, 1975).

The model proposed by Weiner and associates (1971, 1974) assumes that people attribute causes in a manner consistent with reality. However, an alternative position to the information-processing approach assumes that though people may need to process information in a logical way to arrive at decisions about the causes of an event, they also need to maintain self-esteem. The second position assumes that people adopt self-serving attributional strategies—variously called self-enhancement, ego-defensive, ego-enhancing, or ego-biased strategies—because people are strongly motivated to view themselves positively (Beckman, 1973; Hastorf, Schneider, & Polefka, 1970; Miller & Ross, 1975; Nicholls, 1975). Consequently, such persons attribute success and failure to those factors that promote the greater positive view of self. For example, success is attributed to internal factors and failure to external factors because such attributional biases are conducive to maintaining self-esteem. This line of research implies that people are not consistently logical in determining the causes of outcomes in achievement situations. It is important, therefore, to determine the extent to which people employ covariation with outcomes, use covariation with other variables, or simply employ ego-biases as the basis of causal attributions in sport and motor performance settings—so that subsequent research on motivation and achievement change programs is based on the appropriate assumptions.

Empirical investigations of causal attributions following task success or failure yielded data consistent with the self-serving position (Fitch, 1970; Frieze, I., & Weiner, 1971; Fontaine, 1975, Exp. 2; Iso-Ahola, 1976; Simon & Feather, 1973; Streufert & Streufert, 1969; Wortman, Costanzo, & Witt, 1973). Despite such support, the theoretical and empirical underpinnings of such self-serving motivational biases were called into question (Bem, 1972;

Kelley, 1971; Miller & Ross, 1975). To be considered self-serving in their attributions, people must indulge in self-enhancing attributions under success and in self-protective attributions under failure. The extant literature supports ego biases under success but not under failure (Miller & Ross, 1975).

Previous research allegedly supporting the ego-biased position may be questioned on several grounds. First, the typical experiment investigating causal attributions uses a novel task. Miller and Ross (1975) and Ajzen and Fishbein (1975) suggested that internal ascriptions following success and external ascriptions following failure may be emminently rational rather than self-serving in a novel task situation. Success is informative to a person in that it induces perceptions of self-control over the outcome, which exacerbates internal attributions. Failure, on the other hand, is less informative and, hence, yields neither reliable personal nor environmental attributions. In other words, following outcome on a novel task, people may be merely processing the available information in an entirely logical and rational manner in ascribing success to their own attributes and failure to environmental attributes. In real life, however, particularly in motor performance and sport settings, people rarely perform on novel tasks. If the task is one with which people have had previous experience and, thus, have expectations relative to performance in that setting, how do they attribute success and failure? If a person has previous experience with the activity, then this previous experience seems an important source of reference that must affect subsequent attributions.

To be consistent with reality, a person should causally attribute outcome so that the attribute reflects previous experience. The immediate success or failure outcome that is consistent with previous outcomes (success or failure) should lead to ability and task difficulty attributions that are relatively stable over time. The immediate outcome, which is inconsistent with previous outcomes, should lead to effort or luck attributions, which are relatively unstable over time. Previous research showed that expected or consistent outcomes (success or failure) let to more stable, internal attributions (high or low ability), whereas unexpected or inconsistent outcomes led to more unstable, external attributions (good or bad luck) (Kelley, 1967; McArthur, 1972; Nicholls, 1975; Weiner et al., 1972). Therefore, to adequately test whether persons are self-serving in their causal attributions or are processing the information in a logical and rational manner, investigations should use tasks with which the person has had previous experience and knowledge of previous outcomes. The degree to which people use the current outcomes as opposed to previous experience in the determination of outcome may be taken as evidence of self-serving strategies.

A second question of importance to causal attributions following outcome is the degree of ego involvement of a person in an activity. Most previous studies used tasks that had importance and relevance to participants only for the duration of the experiment. The trivialness of the tasks and low induced ego-involvement may account for the inconclusive findings of previous research investigating self-serving versus information-processing strategies (Miller & Ross, 1975). Therefore, to test the self-serving as opposed to the information-processing strategies in causal attributions, the task should be one that preferably is of some importance to the participants.

When the task is one in which a person has prior experience and the task is of some importance so that effort will be applied, then we may appropriately investigate whether people invoke self-serving or information-processing causal attributions. One activity used in the present study to investigate this question was Little League competition. In Little League, the participant has prior experience, and the outcome of each game is salient and of real importance to the participants.

Most investigations of causal attributions used individual achievement tasks. In real life, however, a great deal of human activity takes place in groups or teams. This means that two sources of attributions for outcome avail themselves—one is to the team or group, the other is to the self. What are the causal attributions of people when engaged in team activities, and do attributions to the team differ in some meaningful way from attributions to the self? This question is of relevance to attribution theory and to attribution research in sports and motor performance settings. It is plausible that persons may be entirely rational and logical in attributing reasons for winning and losing to the team while still maintaining self-serving attributions to the self. The purpose of the first study, therefore, was to observe the effect of prior experience and present outcome on team and self causal attributions when children were engaged in Little League baseball.

The self-serving position differs from the information-processing position in terms of predicting causal attributions (Nicholls, 1975). For ability attributions, the information-processing position assumes that feedback is more attributable to ability if the outcome is consistent with previous wins or losses. In Little League competition, winning following previous win experiences should be attributed to high ability more than a win following previous losses. A loss following previous losses should be attributed to poor ability more than a loss following previous win experiences. The self-serving position, on the other hand, predicts that players attribute ability in accord with winning and losing the present game regardless of previous experience.

It is difficult to predict effort attributions in a sport activity such as Little League. The players are instructed by the coach to apply effort, the players are ego involved so that effort will be applied, and effort is directly perceived rather than inferred. Therefore, the information-processing approach and the self-serving position do not differ in their predictions of effort attributions. It is predicted that players attribute effort in accord with the outcome regardless of the previous win-loss history of the team.

Luck is an unstable dimension and, as such, may be more readily invoked to explain outcomes inconsistent with previous experience rather than outcomes consistent with previous experience. Thus, the information-processing position maintains that losing after win experiences and winning after loss experiences should be attributed to luck more than winning following win experiences and losing following loss experiences. The self-serving position, on the other hand, predicts that winning or losing alone determines causal attributions. Losing is attributed to luck more than winning regardless of previous win-loss experiences.

In predicting task difficulty ascriptions, the capabilities of the opposing team determine the difficulty of the task at hand. Therefore, it is expected that task-difficulty attributions are outcome related in that losing teams invoke task difficulty attributions to a greater extent than winning teams.

STUDY 1

Method

Participants

A total of 202 Little League baseball players (all boys) participating in the Champaign-Urbana Little League comprised the sample for this study. They came from 18 teams and data were gathered at nine different ball games. The teams participated in five leagues and all teams participating in those leagues were used, with the exception of one team whose coach refused to participate. This meant the loss of two teams. The other four leagues in the total nine-league association were used by a colleague for a separate study. The five leagues used in the present study were chosen at random from the nine leagues. All members of each team participated for at least a few innings of the game. Therefore, all members of each team who were suited up were used.

A pregame questionnaire was given to all players to determine their expectancies for the game and their degree of confidence in their stated expectancies. Despite the possible source of confounding with previous scores, all players were also asked to estimate the number of runs they would score and the number of runs their opponents would score against them.

The postgame attribution questionnaire consisted of questions pertaining to the perceived reasons for the outcome of the game. Two questionnaires were actually used. One questionnaire was developed for the teams that won their game; the statement for each question requested that players say why they won that particular game. A second questionnaire was developed for those teams that lost; the statement for each question asked subjects to tell why they lost that particular game. Questions were asked on team and self-ability, effort, luck, and task difficulty attributions on 5-point Likert scales.

Procedure

Before testing, each Little League president was contacted, and permission was sought to contact each coach and manager for each team within that particular league. When permission was granted, before each game, each coach and manager was asked if they would participate in the study. When permission was obtained (one coach refused) the experimenter requested the coaches to inform their own teams that following the game, the teams must return to its dugout so that each player could complete a short questionnaire.

Just before the game, the experimenter gave a short questionnaire to each player. The pregame questionnaire probed the expectations of winning of players and their confidence in their expected outcome.

On conclusion of the game and the traditional handshake, the players returned to the dugout, and the experimenter gave the appropriate questionnaire to the players. Each player sat in the dugout and individually completed the questionnnaire. The questionnaire took about 5–8 min to complete. Every attempt was made to gently prevent any adult from assisting or instructing a player (one father insisted on helping his son fill in the questionnaire; that player was not included in the analyses). The players completed the questionnaires and returned them to the experimenter.

The history of win-loss experience of the teams was determined by the win-loss records of the teams before the game in which the data were collected. The win-loss record of the teams for the previous four games was taken as the criterion, as opposed to considering the games of the season to date. The arbitrary selection of the last four games was determined to some extent by the previous win-loss records of the teams. Using more than four games eliminated too many teams from the analyses. To be considered as a team that had a history of past success experiences, teams had to have won the last four games. Conversely, to be considered a team with a history of past failure experiences, a team must have lost the last four games. This produced a population of eight teams. Ten teams had to be omitted from the analyses, using past success-failure experiences, because they did not meet the criteria. Teams were therefore categorized as being either previously successful or previously unsuccessful.

Outcome was obviously determined by whether the team won or lost that particular game. These criteria produced the following teams, which supplied the data that were used in subsequent 2 × 2 (History of win-loss experiences × Outcome) analyses: Two previously successful teams that won the current game (22 players); two previously unsuccessful teams that won the current game (27 players); three previously unsuccessful teams that lost the current game (31 players); and one previously successful team that lost the current game (12 players).

Results

To determine the veracity of the procedure by which teams were categorized as either having winning or losing histories, analyses were conducted on the questions asked on the pregame questionnaire. When asked to predict the outcome of the game ("definitely win" to "definitely lose"), all players responded that they would win; the teams with a history of winning were somewhat more positive in their predictions, but the difference was only marginally significant, F (1, 90) = 2.299, $p < .13$. When asked to rate their confidence in the predicted outcome, however, teams with a history of winning were reliably more confident of winning than were teams with a history of losing, F (1, 90) = 6.090, $p < .01$. Despite the obvious confounding with runs scored both for and against in previous games, teams with a history of winning predicted reliably greater scores in the upcoming game than did teams with a history of losing, F (1, 90) = 6.319, $p < .01$. When asked how many runs the opposing team were going to score, winning teams predicted smaller scores, but the difference was only marginally significant, F (1, 90) = 2.606, $p < .10$.

The causal attribution data are given in Table 1 and the analyses were conducted separately on the team and individual causal attributions.

Team attributions

The data were first analyzed by the multivariate analysis of variance (MANOVA) procedure in a 2 X 2 (History of win-loss X Outcome) factorial design including luck, task difficulty, ability, and effort ascriptions as the dependent variates. This method was justified by the use of multiple criterion measures for causal attributions. MANOVA yielded a significant main effect for outcome, F (4, 85) = 5.779, $p < .001$, and a significant interaction between outcome and history of win-loss experiences, F (4, 85) = 4.647, $p < .01$. Discriminant function analyses were conducted on the data. Discriminant function analyses identify the dimension or dimensions along which the teams differed most clearly in terms of the criterion measures used (Tatsuoka, 1971). The discriminant function coefficients revealed that for outcome, ability (.9031) and luck (.4712) were the most discriminating variates between winning and losing teams. The step-down F analysis supported the discriminant function analyses, in that ability, F (1, 88) = 27.28, $p < .001$, and luck, F (1, 88) = 5.835, $p < .01$, emerged as the only significant variates. For history of win-loss experiences, the discriminant functions revealed that task difficulty (−.7370) was the most discriminating variable for win-loss experiences. This was also supported by the step-down F analyses, F (1, 88) = 9.64, $p < .01$. The interaction discriminant function analysis revealed that ability (−.5000) and task difficulty (−.4911) were the most discriminating variates. The step-down F analysis, however, revealed that ability was the only significant variate, F (1, 88) = 10.480, $p < .01$.

To render these results more meaningful, univariate analyses of variance (ANOVA) were run on each of the variates comprising the Weiner et al. (1971) model. The team causal attributions are illustrated in Figure 3.

Task difficulty The only reliable main effect for task difficulty was for past experience, F (1, 82) = 10.573, $p < .001$. Teams that consistently lost

TABLE 1 Team and individual causal attributions to ability, effort, luck, and task difficulty

| | Team attributions | | | | | | | | Individual attributions | | | | | |
| | History of winning | | | | History of losing | | | | History of winning | | | History of losing | | |
Outcome	Ability	Effort	Luck	Task ability	Ability	Effort	Luck	Task difficulty	Ability	Effort	Luck	Ability	Effort	Luck
Won	1.54	2.05	1.73	2.43	1.55	1.30	2.07	2.74	3.43	2.32	1.62	3.67	1.52	1.85
Lost	1.90	1.82	3.33	2.13	2.77	2.10	2.77	3.40	2.18	1.42	2.82	2.43	1.71	2.61

Note. Attributions were measured on a 5-point Likert scale. Individual attributions for task difficulty were not asked due to the team nature of baseball.

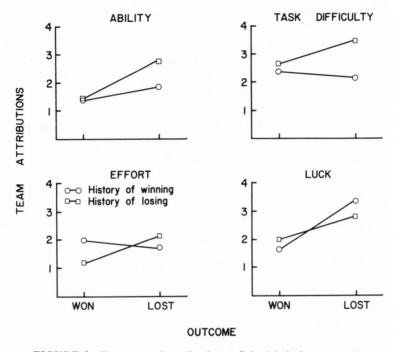

FIGURE 3   Team causal attributions of the Little League study.

invoked task difficulty as a reason for the team's losing reliably more than did teams that consistently won. The interaction, however, was significant, F (1, 82) = 3.890, $p < .05$, which warranted investigation of the simple main effects. Post hoc individual-comparison F tests were conducted on the data and revealed that teams with a history of winning, that just lost the current game, responded that they considered the task reliably less difficult than did teams with a history of losing, that also just lost the game, F (1, 36) = 10.561, $p < .01$. Teams with a history of losing who also lost the present game considered the task to be reliably more difficult than teams with a history of losing who had just won their present game, F (1, 55) = 5.31, $p < .05$. Teams with a history of winning did not differentially attribute task difficulty as a reason for the outcome, regardless of whether they won or lost.

Ability   The main effects of outcome, F (1, 85) = 26.53, $p < .001$, and past history, F (1, 85) = 8.32, $p < .01$, were statistically significant. A statistically significant interaction, however, also emerged, F (1, 85) = 7.941, $p < .01$, which warranted analysis of the simple main effects. The individual-comparison F tests revealed that teams with a history of losing who also lost the current game considered themselves reliably less able than did teams with a history of losing who won, F (1, 37) = 48.62, $p < .001$, and reliably less able than did teams with a history of winning who also lost, F (1, 38) = 13.264, $p < .01$. Teams with a past history of winning did not consider themselves to be lower in ability after losing than did teams with a history of winning who won, F (1, 30) = 1.979, $p > .05$.

Effort Effort attributions analyses revealed that neither past experience, F (1, 85) = 1.699, $p > .05$, nor outcome, F (1, 85) = 1.088, $p > .05$, were reliably different. The significant interaction, F (1, 85) = 5.406, $p < .05$, however, indicated analyses of the simple main effects. These analyses revealed that teams with a history of losing who won the current game invoked team effort as a reason for winning to a reliably greater extent than did teams with a history of winning who also won, F (1, 49) = 6.971, $p < .05$, and teams that also had a history of losing who also lost, F (1, 54) = 9.42, $p < .01$. Interestingly, teams with a history of winning did not invoke team effort as a reason for losing to a greater extent than did teams with a history of winning who won ($F < 1$).

Luck When asked how much luck had been a factor in winning or losing, outcome was the only reliable main effect, F (1, 88) = 11.565, $p < .001$. Losing teams ascribed luck as a causal attribute for losing to a reliably greater extent than winning teams. The history of past success-failure outcomes did not interact with present outcome, F (1, 88) = 1.785, $p < .05$.

Individual Attributions

The individual causal attributions of outcome data were also analyzed by means of the MANOVA procedure. In the analyses of causal attributions to self, however, the factor of task difficulty was not included. The team nature of Little League baseball allowed team causal attributions to task difficulty to be collected, but mitigated against asking self task difficulty attributions in a meaningful way. The MANOVA yielded a significant main effect for outcome, F (3, 85) = 13.615, $p < .001$. The main effect for history of win-loss experiences, F (8, 86) = 1.174, $p > .05$, and the interaction of history of win-loss experiences and outcome, F (3, 86) = 1.178, $p > .05$, were not statistically significant. Discriminant function analyses revealed that for outcome, ability (−.8940) was the most discriminating variate between winning and losing teams. The step-down F analyses supported the discriminant function analysis in that ability, F (1, 88) = 23.705, $p < .001$, was statistically significant. Because of the lack of reliable differences for the main effect of history of win-loss experiences and the interaction between outcome and history, neither the discriminant functions nor the step-down F tests for these variables are reported.

To render the preceding results more meaningful, the data of causal attributions to self were also subjected to ANOVA procedures. The causal attributions to effort, luck, and ability are illustrated in Figure 4.

Effort No significant main effects for outcome, F (1, 88) = 2.180, $p > .05$, or previous win-loss experience, F (1, 88) = 1.109, $p > .05$, materialized when causal attributions to self-effort was analyzed by ANOVA. A statistically

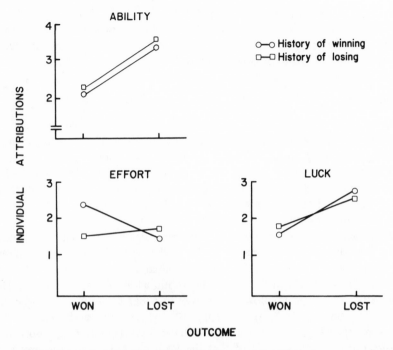

FIGURE 4 Individual causal attributions of the Little League study.

significant interaction emerged, F (1, 88) = 5.159, $p < .01$, which, when analyzed by individual-comparison F tests, revealed that teams with a history of winning stated that they exerted more effort when they *lost* then when they won, F (1, 32) = 5.373, $p < .05$. Teams with a history of winning also stated that they exerted less effort when they won than did teams with a history of losing who won the current game, F (1, 47) = 6.625, $p < .05$. The other simple main effects were not reliably different ($F < 1$). Apparently, teams with a history of losing exerted effort regardless of outcome, but teams with a history of winning exerted reliably less effort when they won than when they lost. Teams that lost apparently did not invoke self-effort as a causal element in losing.

Ability Interestingly, when players were requested to attribute their own ability (high or low) as a causal agent in the team's outcome (win or loss), only outcome was statistically significant, F (1, 84) = 23.142, $p < .001$. Players in teams that won considered that their abilities were a contributing element to the victory of the team to a reliably greater extent than players on teams that lost considered that their *low* abilities were a contributing element to the defeat of the team. No interaction between past win-loss experiences and outcome was evident ($F < 1$).

Luck Similarly, only the main effect of outcome was statistically significant for luck attributions, F $(1, 86) = 9.978, p < .01$. Players on teams that lost considered that their own luck (bad luck) contributed to the team's loss to a reliably greater extent than players on teams which won considered that their own luck (good luck) contributed to the team's victory.

Discussion

Generally, the results of the multivariate and univariate procedures revealed that Little League participants adopt self-serving strategies when causally attributing outcome to themselves, but adopt an information-processing approach when attributing outcome to the team. When attributing outcome to themselves, the players ignored the previous win-loss history of the team, but did take the previous win-loss history of the team into account when causally attributing team outcome.

Two factors may account for the differences between self and team causal attributions. First, the team nature of baseball is such that one cannot know the exact role one had in determining the outcome of the game. One's own contribution is submerged within the contributions made by teammates. The team nature of the game allows the player to adopt self-serving strategies for their own contributions without apparent contradiction with reality. The results of the analyses on team- and self-effort attributions support this interpretation. Players considered that the team did not try hard when losing a game, but all players attributed high effort to themselves. Second, the team nature of baseball may have reduced the degree of ego involvement of players when attributing responsibility of team outcome. The attribution of responsibility for outcome to the team allows the player to diffuse his own responsibility for the outcome. The attribution of outcome to the team becomes more of an external causal attribute than does self-attribution. Therefore, the players were able to adopt a more rational and information-processing approach to team causal attributions; allocation of responsibility to the team is less ego involving because of the diffusion of responsibility.

The univariate and multivariate analyses supported the information-processing position for team attributions. This was particularly true of the ability factor, which the discriminant function analysis identified as being the most discriminating variate for team causal attributions. It was predicted that to support the information-processing position, players should attribute ability in accord with the consistency of the outcome with previous losses. A loss following previous losses would be attributed to low ability to a greater extent than would a loss following previous wins. This was supported in the present study. Teams that lost and had a history of losing recognized and were prepared to admit that they were poor in ability. Teams that lost, but had a history of winning, considered themselves to have just as much ability as did teams with a history of winning that also won. These players probably assumed that the unusual loss was a temporary state of affairs for them and therefore did not consider themselves diminished in ability. Rather, other factors accounted for their losing.

It was expected that team attributions to effort would be attributed in accord with outcome. The previous outcome experiences of the teams, however, had an effect on team effort attributions. Teams with a history of winning that won the current game attributed the outcome to effort less than did teams with a history of losing that won. To account for their inconsistent win, players on losing teams attributed greater effort to themselves than did players on teams that consistently won. This is in accord with an information-processing position.

Luck attributions supported the self-serving position. Winning or losing, and not the previous win-loss experiences of the teams, determined the luck attributions. Winning teams used attributions to good luck less than did losing teams, who used attributions to bad luck to account for the outcome. However, the pattern of the outcomes is in accord with the predictions of Simon and Feather (1973). Inconsistent outcomes (winning or losing) were attributed to luck more than were consistent outcomes; but the interaction of this analysis was not statistically significant ($p > .05$).

The task difficulty data partially supports the information-processing position relative to team causal attributions. When engaged in an ego-involving task in which the players have experience, it was expected that the opposing teams would be judged as being difficult as a function of the outcome of the game. The outcome main effect was not significant ($p > .05$), but the history of previous win-loss experiences was significant. Teams that consistently won considered the task relatively easier than teams that consistently lost. This, in retrospect, must be considered to be support for the information-processing approach.

Although it is plausible for a player to process the information in a rational and logical manner for team attributions, individual attributions are obviously more ego involving and, therefore, may be more susceptible to self-serving attributions. This study provided data to support that reasoning.

The individual luck causal attributions were outcome related only. Players on teams that won considered that their own good luck was less effective in winning than players on teams that lost considered that their own bad luck was a factor in losing. Therefore, this result supports previous research in that players invoked an external element when attributing their own contribution to the loss.

The effort attributions are interesting in that players on teams that lost were quite prepared to admit that the team did not try as hard as it should, but that they as players exerted a great deal of effort. In other words, players may have used team-effort attributions as an external attribute in that the responsibility for losing is diffused through the other players. The players themselves, on the other hand, considered that they had tried very hard, implying that the loss was really the responsibitiey of other teammates. This reasoning is supported by the fact that the players on teams that lost individually attributed greater effort to themselves than did the players on teams that won. The players considered that their own effort was not in dispute when losing. This supports the self-serving position in causally attributing wins and losses.

The ability attributions also support the self-serving posture. Players on teams that won attributed their own ability as being a factor in winning to a greater extent than players on teams that lost attributed their low ability to the loss.

The results of the present study generally support the notion that Little League baseball players attribute team causal attributions in accord with a logical, information-processing approach, while making individual causal attributions with a self-serving bias. The measure for these differential attributions may be due to the diffusion of responsibility for ego involvement of the players, referred to previously; but the differential attributions may be due to methodological reasons peculiar to this study. First, the experimenter had no control over the number of innings a player participated in during any one particular game. Therefore, many of the players were making their own attributions to the outcome on the basis of a few innings. This obviously places the player in something of a dilemma, because he does not have more information on which to judge his own contribution to the team outcome.

This situation may facilitate self-serving biases. First, some evidence suggests that in minimal-information situations, people are more likely to perceive a relationship between behavior and positive outcomes than between behavior and negative outcomes (Jenkins & Ward, 1965; Miller & Ross, 1975; Smedslund, 1963). Second, the arbitrary means by which previous win-loss behaviors of the team had been determined may have weakened the effect of that variable on the individual attributions in some way. Only the previous four games of the teams were used to determine the win-loss histories, and post hoc investigation revealed that all teams used had experienced at least one loss and one win in the league.

Therefore, to investigate the veracity of the results of the Little League study and to alleviate some of the difficulties, a second study was conducted. A novel team activity was used, which controlled for the previous success-failure experiences of the participants and the amount of participation in the activity.

STUDY 2

Method

Participants

A total of 41 boys, aged between 9 and 12 years, who were participating in the University of Illinois Summer Youth Fitness Program, were all randomly assigned to one of four treatments: (1) boys who succeeded but who had previously failed at the task; (2) boys who had continually succeeded at the task; (3) boys who failed, after having previously succeeded at the task; and (4) boys who had continually failed at the task. Thus, a 2 × 2 (History of success-failure × Outcome) factorial design was created.

Procedure

The experimenter, a 35-year-old man, greeted the participants, who were brought to the testing site in pairs of the same age by a confederate. On arrival at the testing site, the boys were told that they were going to be a team who were to be tested for their quickness and coordination at a motor task. The experimenter emphasized the team nature of the task and informed the boys that their quickness and reactions were going to be compared with those of other children of their own age. The children were used to being tested, and some competition for scores had been fostered within the fitness program. They were also told that their scores would be compared to their other tests to see if their scores matched up and to see if their sports performance could be determined.

When the experimenter completed the cover story, the team was shown the motor task. The task consisted of two Dekan pressure plates mounted on the floor, 5 ft. apart, as illustrated in Figure 5. On a table placed alongside the pressure plates was an apparatus clearly labeled "Human Performance Analyzer." Emerging from each pressure plate were two cables which mounted

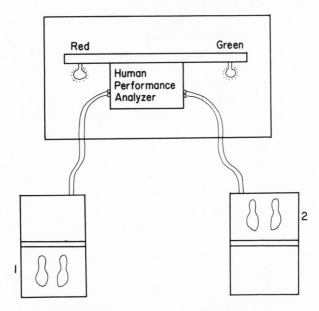

FIGURE 5 The two-person relay game.

the table and entered into the back of the apparatus. Above the apparatus was a black panel with one green bulb and one red bulb clearly visible.

The experimenter explained that the task was a team relay-type activity and demonstrated task performance. He stood on the portion of the first pressure plate with his back to the apparatus. To assist the boys in assuming the correct stance, foot shapes were painted on the pressure plates, as shown in Figure 5. The experimenter explained that, in his own time, as time was not recorded until the boy's feet left the pressure plate, the boy should attempt to run across to the unmarked portion of the second plate and put at least one foot on that portion of the pressure plate. The experimenter demonstrated the activity. The experimenter then stood on the second pressure plate where marked, again with his back to the apparatus. The experimenter emphasized the team nature of the task and told the participants that when it was their turn to stand on the second pressure plate, they were not to move until after the first subject had struck the pressure plate and put at least one foot on that portion of the pressure plate. They were told that the time started when the first boy left the first pressure plate and the time stopped when the second boy touched the first pressure plate. All were told that if they cheated and left the second pressure plate before the other subject had touched, then that trial would not count.

Each child then modeled the experimenter until the experimenter was satisfied that each one knew and understood the task adequately. The boys were informed that they would take turns at initiating the trial and also turns at reacting to the initiator.

The boys were then informed that the apparatus on the table was a minicomputer and that the minicomputer would be used to let them know how they compared to other boys of their own age who had done this task. They were informed that the minicomputer would compare their time to that of all other boys that had been tested. The minicomputer would give them feedback through the two lights that were mounted on the panel above the apparatus. If one team were as fast or faster than the other teams, then the green light would come on indicating a fast time. If the team were slower than the other, then the red light would come on, indicating slower performance. The experimenter illustrated the task by asking the children to walk through one trial. The red (poor) light came one, and the experimenter explained that the red light came on because they had walked slowly through the task. In actual fact the experimenter was in control of the feedback lights and the lights came on in the order designated by the experimenter according to the treatment to which the team was randomly assigned.

If the boys had no questions, the first series of trials was given. This series was given to establish a history of success or failure at the task. Half the teams were given all-success feedback for 15 trials, and half were given failure feedback for 15 trials. After each trial the computer lit up one or the other of the two feedback lights and the children were told to attend to the feedback.

Once the feedback light was given, the boys then changed places, to initiate the next trial. Following each trial, the experimenter verbally reinforced the feedback with such statements as "That's slow—concentrate a little more," "A little slow that time," "Good—pretty good that time," and "Ok, way to go."

Following the 15 trials, the children went to a table in the experimental room and were asked to complete a questionnaire. The questionnaire probed their responses to the amount of fun they had, whether they liked the game, and also asked team and individual causal attributions.

After completing the questionnaire, the children returned to the task and were given 10 more trials at the task. Half the boys who had succeeded in the first half of the experiment were given continued success feedback, whereas the other half were given failure feedback. Similarly, half the boys who had failed in the first half of the experiment were given continued failure feedback, and the other half were given success feedback. This procedure generated the treatment conditions identified previously. Again, the experimenter gave verbal reinforcement following the trials.

After all teams had completed their 10 trials in the second phase of the experiment, the children were asked to complete a short questionnaire. The questions asked both team and individual causal attributions for the second series of trials; these were the data used for this experiment.

Debriefing

All children who had continually succeeded or who had failed then succeeded in the later part of the experiment were escorted back to their respective stations in the fitness program and thanked for their participation. However, since predetermined false feedback had been given, the boys who failed in the second phase of the experiment were given a further treatment to debrief them.

The experimenter first asked all children verbally what reasons they thought accounted for their failure, especially the ones who had previously succeeded. The experimented wanted to determine whether the boys were suspicious of the manipulation. One team in the previous success and eventual failure group was eliminated from the experiment because of suspicions of the treatment.

For the children on teams that continually failed, the experimenter then stated that they had performed quite slowly as compared with boys of their own age group. The experimenter always mentioned an age group 2 years older than the actual age of the boys in that particular team. The boys always protested hotly that their ages were lower than that stated, and the experimenter feigned surprise and questioned each boy about his age. He then asked them if they would like to try again with a correct age comparison on the minicomputer. All the previously failing teams were then given positive feedback for at least 10 trials and often more if they wished to continue.

For the children who had previously succeeded and then failed, the experimenter used two procedures to debrief the subjects. First, for some boys, the experimenter wondered aloud whether the machine was operating correctly. He investigated the machine and always discovered the "problem" and then asked the boys if they wished to redo the task. These children then received success feedback for at least 10 trials. The second procedure was for the experimenter to "confess" that he had programmed the minicomputer to compare the team to a higher age group because they were doing "so well" in the initial phase. The experimenter then "corrected" the minicomputer; on the subsequent trials, the boys all succeeded.

All children were instructed not to discuss the experiment with anyone in the program. These debriefing procedures were apparently successful because when the experiment was completed, many boys from all conditions came in to try again at the task. Some children had actually changed partners to see if they could be faster with a new partner. Also, several teams wanted to see if they could establish new "records." Where possible, many of these boys were allowed to redo the task, and the experimenter maintained the deception about the minicomputer.

Results

Team attributions

The data were first analyzed by a multivariate analysis of variance (MANOVA) procedure in a 2 × 2 (History of success-failure × Outcome) factorial design including luck, task difficulty, ability, and effort attributions as the dependent variates. The MANOVA yielded significant mean effects for outcome, F (4, 34) = 21.996, $p < .001$, and history of success-failure outcomes, F (4, 34) = 2.809, $p < .05$. The interaction between outcome and history of success-failure experiences was marginally significant, F (4, 34) = 2.206, $p = .08$. Discriminant function analyses were conducted on the data. The discriminant function coefficients revealed that for outcome, luck (.6630) and task difficulty (.5784) were the most discriminant variates between winning and losing teams. The step-down F analyses supported the discriminant function analyses, in that luck, F (1, 37) = 7.592, $p < .01$, and task difficulty, F (1, 37) = 18.770, $p < .001$, were the most significant variates. For history of success-failure experience, the discriminant function analyses revealed that luck (1.0277) emerged as the most significant variate, which was also supported by the step-down F analyses, F (1, 37) = 6.049, $p < .01$.

To render the above results more meaningful, univariate ANOVAs were run on each of the variables. The team causal attributions are illustrated in Figure 6.

Task difficulty The only reliable main effect for task difficulty was for outcome, F (1, 37) = 19.682, $p < .001$. This merely meant that teams which failed considered the task more difficult than teams which succeeded.

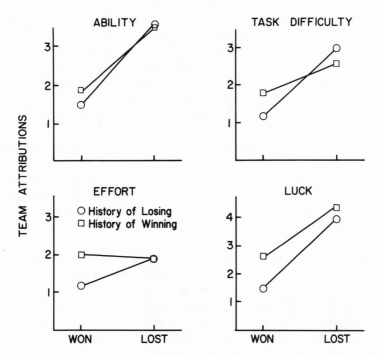

FIGURE 6 Team causal attributions of the relay game.

Ability For attributions to team ability, only the main effect of outcome, F (1, 37) = 55.072, p < .001, was significant. This merely meant that, in terms of ability, teams that succeeded considered themselves to be greater in ability than did teams that failed.

Effort The effort attribution analyses revealed that neither past experience, F (1, 37) = 1.138, p = .29, outcome, F (1, 37) = .598, p = .44, nor the interaction of past experience and outcome, F (1, 37) = 1.138, p = .29, were statistically significant. The children considered that they applied effort regardless of whether they succeeded or failed and regardless of whether they had previously succeeded or failed.

Luck When asked how much luck had been a factor in succeeding or failing at the motor task, both outcome, F (1, 37) = 9.05, p < .01, and past history, F (1, 37) = 70.3, p < .001, were statistically significant. Teams that succeeded considered luck to be less a factor in the outcome than did teams that failed. Similarly, teams with a history of failing considered luck to be more of a factor in attributing outcome than did teams with a history of succeeding.

Self attributions

Attributions to the self were also analyzed by means of the MANOVA procedure. In these analyses, however, the element of task difficulty was left out for the same reasons as stated in the first study. The MANOVA yielded significant main effects for outcome, F (3, 35) = 21.108, $p < .001$, and for history of success-failure experiences, F (3, 35) = 3.804, $p < .05$. The interaction of outcome with previous history was not significant, F (3, 35) = 2.092, $p > .05$. The discriminant function analyses revealed that for both outcome and previous history analyses, luck (1.0080 and .9490, respectively) was the most discriminating variate, which was supported by the step-down F analyses.

The data were also analyzed by ANOVA procedures. The causal attributions to ability, effort, and luck are illustrated in Figure 7.

Ability Only the main effect of outcome, F (1, 37) = 31.801, $p < .001$, materialized in the analyses of ability attributions. Children on teams that succeeded considered that they contributed to the team outcome to a greater extent than did those on teams that failed.

Effort No significant main effects for outcome ($F < 1$), or history of success-failure ($F < 1$), or a significant interaction ($p < .05$) occurred for effort attributions. All boys considered that they exerted great effort regardless of the previous success-failure history or outcome.

Luck Interestingly, both the main effects of outcome, F (1, 37) = 9.424, $p < .01$, and previous success-failure history, F (1, 37) = 64.898, $p < .001$, were statistically significant. However, a statistically significant

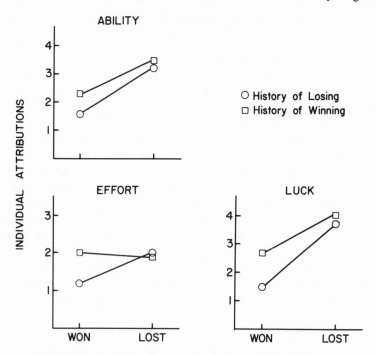

FIGURE 7 Individual causal attributions of the relay game.

interaction, F (1, 37) = 4.680, $p < .05$, occurred that warranted investigation of the simple main effects. Newman-Keuls procedures revealed that when teams succeeded in the later trials, teams with a history of previous failure attributed the outcome to luck more than did teams with a history of previous success. Boys on teams that failed considered that luck contributed to the failure more than individuals on teams that succeeded considered that luck accounted for their success.

Discussion

The second study was conducted to control for the possible confounding that may have occurred between the team and self causal attributions in the Little League study. First, all participants were involved in the game for the entire length of the experiment and, therefore, would have similar participation bases from which to make self and team causal attributions. Second, a two-person team relay game was used to increase the saliency of each child's contribution to the team outcome. Third, the history of previous success-failure of each team was controlled. Fourth, to counteract the task-novelty effects that may occur (Miller & Ross, 1975), the study attempted to ego involve each child in the game through the cover story. Subjective, casual observation of the children during the game and after the experiment was over when many children requested to attempt the game again suggested that the cover story was reasonable successful. The effort data also support this contention in that all children attributed high effort to themselves regardless of the manipulations of the experiment.

It was hypothesized that children would use the available information in the game in a logical and consistent manner when causally attributing outcome to both team and self. Contrary to hypothesis, the results of the second study, taken as a whole, offer only weak support for the logical, information-processing strategy when attributing causes of the outcome. Although both outcome and previous history of success-failure experiences did contribute to self-causal attributions for luck, generally, the results of the present study support the self-serving position for both team and self-causal attributions.

It is relatively easy to account for the similarity of the team and self-causal attributions in the second study. The game was a two-person team relay game where the contribution of each person to the team outcome was apparently important. It is less easy to account for the self-serving bias of children in the face of conflicting information. They apparently were more concerned with maintaining self-esteem than they were in interpreting reality.

A possible reason for the self-serving bias evident in both studies may be due to a factor mentioned earlier—the ego involvement of the individual in the activity. The self-causal attributions in the Little League study and both team and individual causal attributions in the second study are directly impinged on the skills and abilities of the individual participant. Therefore, it may be hypothesized that the self-serving nature of these causal attributions may be a function of the ego involvement of the children in the activities in which they were attempting to maintain self-esteem. Recent evidence confirms that ego involvement affects causal attributions. Students who participated in university examinations (Simon & Feather, 1973), persons involved in therapy service (Arkin, Gleason, & Johnston, 1976), people in real-life tasks as opposed to simulated situations (Fontaine, 1975), and participants in a study where level of ego involvement was directly tested (Iso-Ahola, 1976), all gave self-serving attributions following performance outcome. All the preceding studies used activities that were important to the people concerned. Sports and motor-performance settings are known to be an important source of social comparison for boys in the age range under discussion (Scanlan, 1977; Veroff, 1969); therefore, it is reasonable to assume that it was the degree of ego involvement of the children in the activities that affected their causal attributions.

This interpretation is supported in a study conducted by Duval and Wicklund (1973). Duval and Wicklund found increased self-serving causal attributions when the attributions were directed at the self as opposed to being directed away from the self. The results of the present investigation support this finding. When the attributions were directed at the self in the Little League study and in the two-man relay game in the second study, self-serving attributions resulted. It may be hypothesized that self-serving biases are facilitated in tasks where the focus of attention is to the self. Most physical activity and motor performance situations focus attention to the self because of the skill orientation of the tasks. As Miller and Ross (1975) noted, most tasks used in previous research were neither skill oriented nor focused on the self.

The preceding discussion closely follows the mini-max principle of causal attributions advocated by Luginbuhl, Crowe, and Kahan (1975). Luginbuhl et al. suggested that people use a principle that takes the form of a desire to maximize present and future positive outcomes and minimize present and future negative outcomes. The importance of the outcome to a person on a given task directly affects the use of the mini-max principle. It successful performance on a given task is unimportant to the person, or the outcome does not focus on attributes that impinge directly on the self, then causal attributions may follow a more rational and logical sequence. For example, in the Little League study, team success may be attributed to high ability, and team failure to low ability, without undue concern because the attributions do not focus on the self.

If successful performance is important to the individual, however, or the outcome focuses directly upon the self, or a valued skill is being used, then the mini-max principle suggests a different set of attributions. A child may maximize present and future outcomes by attributing success to ability—a stable, internal attribute implying that success is to be expected in the future. On the other hand, a child may minimize present and future outcomes by attributing failure to a lack of effort or, particularly, to bad luck—both unstable attributes implying that the outcomes may change in the future. The results of the present study are consistent with the mini-max principle. When attributing outcomes that directly impinged on the self in motor activities assumed to be valued and important to the child, the children in the present investigation attributed success to ability and failure to bad luck.

Much of the previous research supporting the logical, information-processing approach to causal attributions typically used simulations with within-participant designs that also encourage a person to be *logical* over time (Fontaine, 1975). Such studies have indicated that people can be logical, but as soon as the person becomes ego involved for some reason, the logical, information-processing model proposed by Weiner and associates (1971; 1974) becomes less valuable as a predictor of attributions. This is not to imply that people are not logical in attributing the causes of events; it merely suggests that they are less so in some situations. The challenge remains for future investigators to assess the relative explanatory powers of the motivation (self-serving) and nonmotivational (information-processing) interpretations of causal attributions.

It becomes an empirical question to determine the extent to which people employ various strategies in explaining to themselves the causes of events in sports and motor performance settings. But it is important that these empirical questions be resolved in concert with gathering evidence pertaining to the behavioral consequences of holding certain cognitions before we begin to advocate attributional-retraining or achievement-change programs. Such programs are important for maintaining and heightening the motivation of children to participate in physical activity and sport pursuits, if we assume that this is desirable; but it is imperative that we found such programs on sound and appropriate causal attributional assumptions.

REFERENCES

Ajzen, I., & Fishbein, M. A Bayesian analysis of attribution process. *Psychological Bulletin,* 1975, *82,* 261–277.

Arkin, R. M., Gleason, J. M., & Johnston, S. Effect of perceived choice, expected outcome and observed outcome of an action on the causal attributions of actors. *Journal of Experimental Social Psychology,* 1976, *12,* 151–158.

Beckman, L. J. Teachers' and observers' perceptions of causality for a child's performance. *Journal of Educational Psychology,* 1973, *65,* 198–204.

Bem, D. J. Self-perception theory. In L. Berkowitz (Ed.), *Advances in experimental social psychology.* New York: Academic Press, 1972.

Carroll, J., & Payne, J. W. *Judgment of criminality: An analysis of the parole decision.* Paper presented at the meeting of the American Psychological Association, Chicago, 1975.

Duval, S., & Wicklund, R. A. Effects of objective self awareness on attribution of causality. *Journal of Experimental Social Psychology,* 1973, *9,* 17-31.

Elig, T., & Frieze, I. H. A multi-dimensional scheme for coding and interpreting perceived causality for success and failure events: The coding scheme of perceived causality (CSPC). *JSAS Catalog of Selected Documents in Psychology,* 1975, *5,* 313. (Ms. No. 1069)

Feather, N. T., & Simon, J. G. Causal attributions for success or failure in relation to expectations of success based upon selective or manipulative control. *Journal of Personality,* 1971, *39,* 527-541.

Fitch, G. Effects of self-esteem, perceived performance, and choice on causal attributions. *Journal of Personality and Social Psychology,* 1970, *16,* 311-315.

Fontaine, C. Causal attribution in simulated versus real situations: When are people logical, when are they not? *Journal of Personality and Social Psychology,* 1975, *32,* 1021-1029.

Frieze, J. H., McHugh, M., & Duquin, M. *Causal attributions for women and men and sports participation.* Paper presented at the meeting of the American Psychological Association, Washington, D.C., 1976.

Frieze, I., & Weiner, B. Cue utilization and attributional judgments of success and failure. *Journal of Personality,* 1971, *39,* 591-605.

Hastorf, A., Schneider, D., & Polefka, J. *Person perception.* Reading, Mass.: Addison-Wesley, 1970.

Heider, F. *The psychology of interpersonal relations.* New York: Wiley, 1958.

Iso-Ahola, S. E. A test of attribution theory of success and failure with Little League baseball players. In C. Bard, M. Fleury, & J. Salmela (Eds.), *Mouvement 7.* Quebec: Association des Professionels de Activite Physique de Quebec, 1975.

Iso-Ahola, S. E. *Self enhancement and consistency as determinants of causal and trait attributions of outcome.* Unpublished doctoral dissertation, University of Illinois, 1976.

Jenkins, H. M., & Ward, W. C. Judgment of contingency between responses and outcomes. *Psychological Monographs,* 1965, *79* (1, Whole No. 594).

Kelley, H. H. Attribution theory in social psychology. In D. Levine (Ed.), *Nebraska symposium on motivation.* Lincoln: University of Nebraska Press, 1967.

Kelley, H. H. *Attribution in social interaction.* Morristown, N.J.: General Learning Press, 1971.

Lanzetta, S. T., & Hannah, T. E. Reinforcing behavior of "naive" trainers. *Journal of Personality and Social Psychology,* 1969, *11,* 245-252.

Luginbuhl, E. R., Crowe, H. H., & Kahan, J. P. Causal attributions for success and failure. *Journal of Personality and Social Psychology,* 1975, *31,* 86-93.

McArthur, L. A. The how and what of why: Some determinants and consequences of causal attributions. *Journal of Personality and Social Psychology,* 1972, *22,* 171-193.

McMahan, I. D. Relationships between causal attributions and expectancy of success. *Journal of Personality and Social Psychology,* 1973, *23,* 108-114.

Miller, D. T., & Ross, M. Self-serving biases in the attribution of causality: Fact or fiction? *Psychological Bulletin*, 1975, *82*, 213-225.

Nicholls, J. G. Causal attributions and other achievement-related cognitions: Effects of task outcome, attainment value, and sex. *Journal of Personality and Social Psychology*, 1975, *31*, 179-189.

Roberts, G. C. Win-loss causal attributions of Little League players. In C. Bard, M. Fleury, & J. Salmela (Eds.), *Mouvement 7*. Quebec: Association des Professionels de Activite Physique de Quebec, 1975.

Roberts, G. C. *Personality and emotional development in sports: A reaction*. Paper presented at the AAHPER symposium, The Child in Sport: Readiness and Effects, Milwaukee, Wisconsin, March 1976.

Roberts, G. C. *Children in competition: Assignment of responsibility for winning and losing*. Paper presented at the NCPEAM-NAPCEW Conference, Orlando, Fla., January 1977.

Scanlan, T. K. *Children in competition: Examination of anxiety and social comparison responses in the laboratory and the field*. Paper presented at the NCPEAM-NAPCEW Conference, Orlando, Fla., January 1977.

Simon, J. G., & Feather, N. T. Causal attributions for success and failure at university examinations. *Journal of Educational Psychology*, 1973, *64*, 46-56.

Smedslund, J. The concept of correlation in adults. *Scandanavian Journal of Psychology*, 1963, *4*, 165-173.

Streufert, S., & Streufert, S. C. Effects of conceptual structure, failure and success on attribution of causality and interpersonal attitudes. *Journal of Personality and Social Psychology*, 1969, *11*, 138-147.

Tatsuoka, M. M. *Multivariate analysis*. New York: Wiley, 1971.

Thomas, J. R., & Halliwell, W. *Personality and emotional development in children's sports*. Paper presented at the AAHPER symposium, The Child in Sport: Readiness and Effects, Milwaukee, Wilconsin, March 1976.

Veroff, J. Social comparison and the development of achievement motivation. In C. P. Smith (Ed.), *Achievement-related motives in children*. New York: The Russell Sage Foundation, 1969.

Weiner, B. *Achievement motivation and attribution theory*. Morristown, N.J.: General Learning Press, 1974.

Weiner, B., Frieze, I., Kukla, A., Reed, L., Rest, S., & Rosenbaum, R. M. *Perceiving the causes of success and failure*. Morristown, N.J.: General Learning Press, 1971.

Weiner, B., & Kukla, A. An attributional analysis of achievement motivation. *Journal of Personality and Social Psychology*, 1970, *15*, 1-20.

Weiner, B., Heckhausen, H., Meyer, W. V., & Cook, R. E. Causal ascriptions and achievement behavior: A conceptual analysis of effort and reanalysis of locus of control. *Journal of Personality and Social Psychology*, 1972, *21*, 239-248.

Wortman, C. B., Costanzo, P. R., & Witt, T. B. Effect of anticipated performance on the attributions of causality to self and others. *Journal of Personality and Social Psychology*, 1973, *27*, 372-381.

8

COACHING BEHAVIORS IN LITTLE LEAGUE BASEBALL

Ronald E. Smith, Frank L. Smoll, and Bill Curtis

Organized athletic experiences are generally regarded as important in a child's development, and participation is believed to have direct relevance to the development of such important factors as attitudes toward achievement, perseverance, risk taking, and the ability to tolerate frustration and to delay gratification. The situation is one in which cooperation, unselfishness, and important motivational factors such as achievement motivation and fear of failure may be at least partially developed. Also, the physical health benefits of athletics are obvious.

However, the desirability of organized athletic competition for children has been a controversial issue for a number of years. Most research in the area has focused on considerations such as the influence on physical growth of children, physiological maturity of participants, injuries, and psychological characteristics of participants (see Seefeldt, Gilliam, Blievernicht, & Bruce, this volume, for a review of the studies). Although much has been written about the hazards of competitive athletics for young children, research findings indicate that these have been exaggerated (Rarick, 1969). Rather, the results of organized athletic experiences seem to be variable and to depend on a host of factors, including the way in which the program is structured and supervised.

In a policy statement released jointly by American medical and physical

This research was supported by grant MH24248 from the National Institute of Mental Health. The contributions of Earl Hunt, David Coppel, and Samuel J. Clarke are gratefully acknowledged, as is the cooperation of Little League Baseball, Inc., Washington District 8 (H. E. Pohlman, District Administrator).

education associations (AAHPER, 1968), it was asserted that "the issue in question is not whether athletics are good for school age children, but rather the kinds of athletic programs which are provided for children of elementary school age and the conditions under which the programs are conducted" (p. 2). Although emphasis is placed on the importance of "high quality supervision," research pertaining to coaching behaviors and their influence on children is virtually nonexistent. The empirical question thus becomes one of determining the way in which various types of organized athletic experiences affect attitudes and behavior of participants.

Because of the limited number of positions on interscholastic teams, most children receive their only coaching from typically untrained amateur coaches in youth sports programs. Singer (1972) noted that "the adult coach typically knows his sport and the skills involved quite well. But does he understand his athletes? Can he relate to children?" (p. 24) In terms of the overall impact on the child, the coach's role in teaching skills and techniques relevant to the sport in question may not be as crucial as the type of relationship that is formed with players. The coach-player relationship is a social interaction, and like all such interactions, the responses of one person influence the responses of the other. In addition to giving technical instruction, coaches may be important adult models for transmitting attitudes and behaviors to their players. They also employ a variety of response-contingent behaviors that are rewarding or punitive in nature, and therefore should shape the behavior of young players. Both laboratory and naturalistic studies of child-rearing practices have indicated the nature of child responses that might be anticipated on the basis of certain parental behaviors. On the other hand, virtually nothing is known about how specific behaviors on the part of coaches influence the attitudes and behavior of children. The project described herein is being conducted in an attempt to specify the manner in which coaches' responses affect the attitudes and behaviors of their players. On the basis of such data, an experimental training program designed at assist coaches in relating more effectively to children has been developed.

METHOD

The basic conceptual model that guided the development of our methodology is shown in Figure 1. It is assumed that players' evaluative reactions to the coach's behaviors are mediated by their perception and recall of

FIGURE 1   Cognitive-behavioral model.

those behaviors. A complex of cognitive and affective processes are involved at this mediational level. These processes are influenced not only by the coach's behaviors, but also by other factors, such as the child's previous athletic experiences, personality and attitudinal variables, and by the evaluative reactions themselves. As the latter relationship implies, the unidirectional nature of the mediational model is an oversimplification. Players' evaluative reactions are likely to influence their subsequent perceptions and recall; but also, to the extent that they are perceived by the coach, these reactions may be expected to influence his or her subsequent behaviors toward the children. Other factors that influence how coaches behave include their coaching goals, their expectancies concerning the ways in which particular behaviors relate to goal attainment, their perceptions of player motives, and the sport and competitive level at which they are coaching.

A number of measurement approaches were taken to quantify coach and player variables, including behavioral assessment, interview, and self-report. The major coach and player variables are as follows.

Coach measures	*Player measures*
1. Coaching Behavior Assessment System (CBAS) observed behaviors	1. Perception of coach's behaviors
2. Coach recall of behaviors	2. Attitudes toward coach and participation
3. Coaching goals	3. Attraction toward teammates
4. Perceived behavioral instrumentalities	4. General self-esteem
5. Perception of players' motives	5. Athletic self-esteem

Coach Variables

Coaching Behavior Assessment System

The CBAS was developed to permit the direct observation and coding of coaches' behavior during practices and games. Both the measurement approach and the behavioral categories of the CBAS are an outgrowth of social learning theory (Goldfried & Sprafkin, 1974; Mischel, 1973). The categories, though empirically derived, tap behavioral dimensions that have been shown to affect both children and adults in a variety of nonathletic settings (Bales & Slater, 1955).

The CBAS was developed over a period of several years. Initially, soccer coaches were observed during practice sessions and games to determine the range of behaviors that occurred. The observers carried portable tape recorders and essentially did a "play-by-play" of the coaches' behaviors using a time sampling procedure. The behavior descriptions were transcribed and content analyzed in light of concepts from social learning theory to develop an initial set of scoring categories from which the present system eventually evolved. Subsequent use of the system in observing and coding the behaviors of basketball, baseball, and football coaches indicated that the scoring system is sufficiently comprehensive to incorporate the vast majority of coaching behaviors, that individual differences in behavioral patterns can be discerned, and that the coding system can be used easily in field settings.

Behavior categories In the CBAS, we deal with two major classes of behaviors. *Reactive* behaviors are responses to immediately preceding player or team behaviors, whereas *spontaneous* behaviors are initiated by the coach and are not a response to an immediately preceding event. These classes are roughly analogous to the distinction between *elicited* behaviors (responses to identifiable stimuli) and *emitted* behaviors (behaviors that do not have clear-cut antecedents). As shown in Figure 2, reactive behaviors are responses to either desirable performances, mistakes, or misbehaviors on the part of players, while the sponteneous class is subdivided into game-related and game-irrelevant behaviors initiated by the coach. The system thus involves basic interactions between the situation and the coach's behavior.

CLASS I. REACTIVE BEHAVIORS

A. DESIRABLE PERFORMANCE
    1. POSITIVE REINFORCEMENT   (R)
    2. NONREINFORCEMENT   (NR)

B. RESPONSES TO MISTAKES/ERRORS
    3. MISTAKE-CONTINGENT ENCOURAGEMENT   (EM)
    4. MISTAKE-CONTINGENT TECHNICAL INSTRUCTION   (TIM)
    5. PUNISHMENT   (P)
    6. PUNITIVE TIM   (TIM + P)
    7. IGNORING MISTAKES   (IM)

C. RESPONSE TO MISBEHAVIORS
    8. KEEPING CONTROL   (KC)

CLASS II. SPONTANEOUS BEHAVIORS

A. GAME-RELATED BEHAVIORS
    9. GENERAL TECHNICAL INSTRUCTION   (TIG)
    10. GENERAL ENCOURAGEMENT   (EG)
    11. ORGANIZATION   (O)

B. GAME-IRRELEVANT BEHAVIOR
    12. GENERAL COMMUNICATION   (GS)

FIGURE 2   Response categories of the Coaching Behavior Assessment System (CBAS) (adapted from Smith, Smoll, & Hunt, 1977b).

The CBAS contains 12 behavioral categories:

I. Reactive Behaviors
    A. Responses to desirable performances
        1. Positive Reinforcement or Reward (R). A positive reaction by the coach to a desirable performance by one or more players. R may be verbal or nonverbal in nature. Examples include congratulating a player or patting a player on the back after a good play.
        2. Nonreinforcement (NR). A failure to reinforce a positive behavior; the coach essentially fails to respond. An example would be a player getting a base hit and the coach showing no reaction.
    B. Reactions to mistakes
        3. Mistake-contingent Encouragement (EM). Encouragement of a player by a coach following a mistake.
        4. Mistake-contingent Technical Instruction (TIM). Telling or showing a player who has made a mistake how to make the play correctly. TIM behavior *requires* that the coach instruct the player in some specific way. An example is showing a player how to field a ball after an error has been made.
        5. Punishment (P). A negative response by the coach following an undesirable behavior. Like R, P may be either verbal or nonverbal. Examples include making a sarcastic remark to a player who has just struck out or the coach waving in disgust after a player has made an error.
        6. Punitive TIM (TIM + P). Sometimes TIM and P occur in the same communication, as when a coach says, "How many times do I have to tell you to catch the ball with two hands!" Whenever a coach gives TIM in a punitive or hostile manner, P is also scored (TIM + P).
        7. Ignoring Mistakes (IM). A lack of response, either positive or negative, to a mistake on the part of a player or the team. Essentially, IM occurs when a coach does not respond with EM, TIM, P, or TIM + P to a mistake.
    C. Response to misbehaviors
        8. Keeping Control (KC). Responses that are designed to maintain order. Such behaviors by a coach are ordinarily elicited by unruly conduct or inattentiveness by the players.
II. Spontaneous Behaviors
    A. Game-related spontaneous behaviors
        9. General Technical Instruction (TIG). A communication that provides instruction relevant to techniques and strategies of the

sport in question. As in the case of TIM, the purpose of these communications is to foster the learning of skills and strategies for dealing with game situations. The message must clearly be one of instruction. Unlike TIM, TIG is not elicited by an immediately preceding mistake by a player or the team. Rather, it is coach initiated. Baseball examples include telling or showing a player how to bat or field, telling a fielder which base to throw to, telling a pitcher to take more time between pitches, and shifting the infield or outfield in a strategic manner.

10. General Encouragement (EG). Encouragement that does not immediately follow a mistake. EG differs from the R and EM categories in that it is not a response to specific actions by the players. It relates to future hopes, rather than to the behaviors of the past. It differs from Technical Instruction in that the coach makes requests with which the players may not necessarily be able to comply (e.g., "Come on, team, let's get some runs.").

11. Organization (O). Behavior directed at administrative organization, such as reminding the players of the batting order, announcing substitutions, reassigning positions, and telling players to coach on the bases. It involves organizational behavior that is not intended to influence play immediately. Thus, putting in a new shortstop is scored O, while positioning the shortstop closer to second base is scored Technical Instruction.

B. Game-irrelevant spontaneous behavior

12. General Communication (GC). Interactions with players that are unrelated to game situations or team activities, such as joking with players, conversation about family matters, daily activities, etc.

In using the CBAS, observers stationed themselves at a point from which they could observe the coach in an unobtrusive manner. Observers did not introduce themselves to the coach, nor did they indicate in any way that they would be observing him. Observations were recorded by writing the behavioral codes (e.g., R, P, TIM) as the behaviors occurred.

Training procedures In using any behavioral assessment system, it is essential that observers be well trained and competent. Unless independent observers can agree on how a particular behavior is to be categorized, the system cannot be scientifically useful. Thus, a major goal of any training program should be to establish high interrater reliability. A training program developed by the authors to achieve this goal includes: (a) extended study of a training manual (Smith, Smoll, & Hunt, 1977a), containing an explanation of the CBAS and instructions for its use; (b) group instruction in use of the scoring system, including viewing and discussion of an audio visual training module (Smith, Smoll, Hunt, & Clarke, 1976); (c) written tests in which trainees are required to define the CBAS categories and score behavioral examples; (d) the scoring of videotaped sequences of coaching behaviors; and (e) extensive practice in the use of the CBAS in actual field settings.[1] A high degree of demonstrated expertise in the use of the CBAS was required before an observer was permitted to collect data.

Reliability studies Several studies have been performed to assess the reliability of the CBAS coding system as well as to evaluate the effectiveness of the observer training program. In the first study, 31 trainees viewed a viedotaped sequence of 48 randomly ordered discrete coaching behaviors performed by an actor. In each instance, the game situation was verbally described by a narrator, and the coach's behavior was then shown. Each of the 12 CBAS categories was represented four times. Scoring accuracy was defined in terms of agreement with scoring of the behaviors by the authors. The number of scoring errors ranged from 0 to 5, with a mean of 1.06 errors per observer. This yielded an average-with-expert scoring of 97.8%.

The consistency of scoring over time was assessed by readministering the videotape of the 48 coaching behaviors to 24 of the trainees 1 week after the first viewing. The trainees had been given no feedback about their initial codings. The index of consistency was the percentage of behaviors that were scored identically on the two administrations. These percentages ranged from 87.5% to 100%, with a mean consistency score of 96.4%.

Two studies were performed to assess interrater reliability of CBAS scoring in field settings. In the first, five observers independently and simultaneously coded the behaviors of a female Little League baseball coach during a 6-inning game that lasted 84 min. An average of 250 behaviors were coded. The correlation coefficients between the coding frequencies of observer pairs across the 12 CBAS categories ranged from +.77 to +.99. The average interrater reliability coefficient was +.88.[2]

A second interrater reliability study was undertaken, in which 2 of the authors (R. E. Smith and F. L. Smoll) and 19 trained observers used the CBAS to independently code the behaviors of a male Little League baseball coach during a 5-inning game that lasted 91 min. An average of 208 behaviors were coded during this time interval. The authors scored each behavior in consultation to provide a basis for assessing the accuracy of the observers. Reliability coefficients were computed between all possible pairs of observers, which resulted in a total of 171 coefficients reflecting the degree of

---

[1] Information regarding the *CBAS Audio Visual Training Module,* which includes videotaped instruction in the categories, examples of the various coaching behaviors, and a videotaped proficiency test on the CBAS, is available from the authors.

[2] Experience in using the CBAS suggests that the most useful and reliable behavioral index is the relative frequency of behaviors within each coding category. The reliability data are based on this index.

correspondence of coding frequencies across the behavioral categories. The mean interrater reliability coefficient for the 171 observer pairs was +.88.

Reliability coefficients computed between the 19 observers and the criterion codings of the authors indicated a high level of accuracy in the observers' coding of the data. The coefficients ranged from +.62 to +.98, with a mean reliability coefficient of +.86.

Self-report measures

Several self-report measures were developed to assess coaches' beliefs, attitudes, and perceptions. These were combined into a Coaching Philosophy Questionnaire, which was completed by the coaches at the end of the season.

To assess the relative importance of various coaching objectives, a set of eight goals were paired, each with every other, in a 28-item forced-choice format. The goals, which had previously been assigned similar social desirability ratings by a sample of 50 male and female Little League baseball coaches, were as follows:

1. Developing good qualities in youngsters.
2. Interest in the sport.
3. Developing a winning team.
4. Providing a recreational experience for children.
5. Teaching players to master techniques.
6. Working with youngsters.
7. Being involved in an enjoyable leisure-time activity.
8. Giving leadership and direction to others.

Coaches were asked to indicate which of each pair of goals was more important to them, and this yielded a summed preference score, ranging from 0 to 7, for each of the goals.

Coaches' self-perception of their behaviors was assessed by describing and giving examples of the 12 CBAS behaviors and asking them to indicate on a 7-point scale ranging from "Almost never" to "Almost always" how often they engaged in the behaviors. They were also asked to indicate the extent to which each behavior was instrumental to each of the eight coaching goals on a 7-point scale ranging from (−3), "Very negative" to (+3), "Very positive." The summed products of these rating and the importance scores assigned to each of the goals yielded an Expectancy × Value instrumentality measure for each CBAS behavior.

A measure of perceived player goals was constructed by pairing each of eight potential motives with one another in a 28-item forced-choice format and asking the coaches to indicate which reason of each pair was of greater importance in motivating the average player to achieve good performance. The goals were as follows:

1. Personal pride in performing well.
2. Avoiding failure or embarrassment.
3. Impressing the other kids.
4. Developing baseball skills.
5. Hoping to become a great athlete.
6. Pleasing parents.
7. Having a winning team.
8. Pleasing the coach.

As on the coaching goals measure, a summed preference score was obtained for each of the perceived goals.

Player Variables

The player variables were assessed in a structured interview in the childrens' homes conducted by trained interviewers at the conclusion of the season. Children were assured that their data were confidential and that coaches would never be told how their players responded to the questions.

The measure of the player's perception of the coach's behavior was presented as a recall test in the hope of minimizing distortions in reporting ("We've observed your coach, and now we want to see how well you and your teammates can remember what he did."). The player was given a description and examples of each of the 12 CBAS behaviors and indicated how frequently his coach had engaged in that behavior on a 7-point "ladder" scale ranging from "Never" (bottom rung) to "Almost always."

Following the recall section of the interview, the children used another set of ladders to indicate their reactions to their participation. The children were given a clipboard and recorded their own responses in such a way that the interviewer could not view them. The following questions were asked:

1. How much do you like baseball?
2. How much did you like playing for your coach?
3. How much would you like to have the same coach again next year?
4. How much do you like your coach?
5. How much do your parents like your coach?
6. How much does your coach like you?
7. Do you like baseball more or less than you did at the beginning of the season?
8. How much does your coach know about baseball?
9. How well did the players on your team get along?
10. How much did you like the other players on your team?

The players' level of self-esteem was assumed to be a potentially important moderator of their reactions to the behaviors of their coaches. A measure of general self-esteem was derived from Coopersmith's (1967) Self-Esteem Inventory. A total of 14 items was selected, which correlated highly with total score on the Coopersmith measure and which reflected global self-evaluations. The children rated themselves on each item on a 5-point scale ranging from "Very much like me" to "Not at all like me." Six of the items were keyed in the negative direction, eight in the positive direction. Children also used 11-point scales to evaluate themselves on 10 specific abilities, 5 of which were relevant to baseball. The item on which the players evaluated their "ability in baseball" served as the measure of their self-esteem relative to that sport.

SUBJECTS

The present study involved 51 male coaches in three Little League baseball leagues in the Seattle area. The leagues were each divided into three levels: minors (mainly 8-9-year-old boys), majors (mainly 10-12 years old), and seniors (13-15 years old). There were 23 minor coaches, 17 major coaches, and 11 senior coaches. With their written consent, coaches were observed and their behaviors coded during at least three games (mean = 3.96 games). An average of 1,122 behaviors were coded for each coach during the course of the season. At the conclusion of the season, the coaches completed the Coaching Philosophy Questionnaire privately in their homes. A total of 13 coaches refused to participate in the project.

After the season ended, 542 players (238 minors, 187 majors, and 117 seniors) were interviewed. This total represented 83% of the youngsters who played for the 51 coaches. The interviewers were University of Washington undergraduates who had not been involved in the behavioral coding phase.

RESULTS AND DISCUSSION

Coaching Behavior Patterns

A total of 57,213 behaviors of the 51 coaches was coded. Table 1 presents the distribution of behaviors within the CBAS categories. Nearly two-thirds of the behaviors fell into the categories of Reinforcement, General Technical Instruction, and General Encouragement. Although the relative frequency of punitive behaviors was relatively low in comparison with other categories, about 20% of the observed mistakes were responded to with either Punishment or Punitive Technical Instruction.

To determine the dimensions along which the CBAS categories patterned themselves, a factor analysis was performed with a Varimax rotation. The orthogonal factor structure is presented in Table 2. Four factors emerged,

TABLE 1 Distribution of coach behaviors in the Coaching Behavior Assessment System (CBAS) categories

	CBAS category	Rate per 100 behaviors
R	Reinforcement	17.1
NR	Nonreinforcement	4.2
EM	Mistake-contingent Encouragement	3.1
TIM	Mistake-contingent Technical Instruction	4.2
P	Punishment	1.8
TIM + P	Punitive Technical Instruction	1
IM	Ignoring Mistakes	3.7
KC	Keeping Control	1.7
TIG	General Technical Instruction	27.3
EG	General Encouragement	21.4˙
O	Organization	8.4
GC	General Communication	6.1

Note. From Smith, Smoll, & Curtis (1977).

which accounted for 69% of the response variance. Factor 1 is essentially an activity level index. (Rate is simply the total number of observed behaviors, excluding Nonreinforcement and Ignoring Mistakes, divided by the total number of minutes of observation.) Factor 2 reflects the degree to which the coach is punitive and gives General Encouragement versus the extent to which he organizes and keeps control. Factor 3 reflects an instructional orientation versus one involving General Encouragement and General Communication. Factor 4 is a supportive pattern involving Reinforcement and Mistake-contingent Encouragement.

Perceived Behaviors

The players' ratings of how frequently their coaches engaged in the CBAS behaviors were also subjected to a factor analysis, and the results are presented in Table 3. Three factors emerged, which bore little resemblance to the observed behavior factors. The first factor involved supportive and structuring behaviors (Reinforcement, General Encouragement, General Technical Instruction, and Keeping Control). Punishment, Punitive Technical Instruction, and Nonreinforcement loaded on Factor 2, suggesting that all three are perceived as aversive. Factor 3 reflected the tendency to respond to mistakes with technical instruction versus the tendency to ignore them.

Of greater interest than the overall factor structure of the perceived behaviors were the results of factor analyses performed for each of the three age-ability levels (minors, majors, and seniors). Table 4 shows that the first factor for the youngest children comprised the two punitive categories and

TABLE 2 Orthogonal factor structure and factor loadings of Coaching Behavior Assessment System (CBAS) behaviors

Factor 1		Factor 2		Factor 3		Factor 4	
Behavior	Loading	Behavior	Loading	Behavior	Loading	Behavior	Loading
NR	(.86)	*P	(.61)	*TIM	(.64)	*R	(.86)
IM	(.85)	*TIM + P	(.61)	TIG	(.73)	*EM	(.72)
Rate	(−.85)	EG	(.58)	EG	(−.58)		
		KC	(−.59)	*GC	(−.76)		
		O	(−.77)				

Note. $N = 51$ coaches. Asterisks identify player-perceived behaviors that significantly differentiate between coaches who were beyond ±1 SD on the behavioral factors. (See text.) From Smith, Smoll, & Curtis (1977). Following is a key to symbols of behaviors.

R	Positive Reinforcement	TIM + P	Punitive TIM
NR	Nonreinforcement	IM	Ignoring Mistakes
EM	Mistake-contingent Encouragement	KC	Keeping Control
		TIG	General Technical Instruction
TIM	Mistake-contingent Technical Instruction	EG	General Encouragement
		O	Organization
P	Punishment	GC	General Communication

TABLE 3 Orthogonal factor structure and factor loadings of perceived behaviors

Factor 1		Factor 2		Factor 3	
Behavior	Loading	Behavior	Loading	Behavior	Loading
EG	(.68)	TIM + P	(.79)	TIM	(.57)
TIG	(.61)	P	(.75)	IM	(−.87)
R	(.56)	NR	(.52)		
KC	(.56)				

Note. $N = 542$ players. From Smith, Smoll, & Curtis (1977). Following is a key to symbols for behaviors.

R	Positive Reinforcement	TIM + P	Punitive TIM
NR	Nonreinforcement	IM	Ignoring Mistakes
EM	Mistake-contingent Encouragement	KC	Keeping Control
		TIG	General Technical Instruction
TIM	Mistake-contingent Technical Instruction	EG	General Encouragement
		O	Organization
P	Punishment	GC	General Communication

TABLE 4 Factor structure and loadings of perceived behaviors by age and ability level

Factor 1		Factor 2		Factor 3	
Behavior	Loading	Behavior	Loading	Behavior	Loading
Minors ($N = 238$)					
P	(.74)	EG	(.67)	TIM	(.68)
TIM + P	(.76)	TIG	(.59)	GC	(.55)
NR	(.58)	O	(.57)	IM	(−.55)
(17%)					
Majors ($N = 187$)					
R	(.74)	TIM	(.67)	P	(.82)
EM	(.61)	GC	(.63)	TIM + P	(.81)
EG	(.74)	IM	(−.52)		
(21%)					
Seniors ($N = 117$)[a]					
TIM	(.78)	P	(.87)	R	(.79)
TIG	(.51)	TIM + P	(.85)	EG	(.49)
O	(.58)	EM	(−.55)	NR	(−.81)
IM	(−.75)				
(19%)					

Note. From Smith, Smoll, & Curtis (1977). Following is a key to symbols for behaviors.

R	Positive Reinforcement	TIM + P	Punitive TIM
NR	Nonreinforcement	IM	Ignoring Mistakes
EM	Mistake-contingent Encouragement	KC	Keeping Control
		TIG	General Technical Instruction
TIM	Mistake-contingent Technical Instruction	EG	General Encouragement
		O	Organization
P	Punishment	GC	General Communication

[a]In addition, for the seniors: Factor 4, KC (.86); Factor 5, GC (.90).

Nonreinforcement, indicating that perceptual differentiation occurred primarily in terms of these aversive behaviors. Reinforcement and Mistake-contingent Encouragement did not appear in any of the three factors that emerged in this age group, despite the fact that these positive behaviors had high loadings on the first factor that appeared when the observed behavioral data of the coaches at this level were factor analyzed. In the intermediate (major) group, the positive behaviors of Reinforcement and the two encouragement categories appeared as the most important of three factors. At the senior level, the first factor contained the two Technical Instruction categories and Organization. At the senior level, perception was more differentiated, and the five factors that emerged accounted for 70% of the variance, as compared with 44% and 48% at the minor and major levels, respectively. The pattern of results obtained from the factor analyses suggests that the youngest children are chiefly attuned to variations in negative behaviors, the intermediate age group to positive and supportive behaviors, and the seniors to a technically instructional-organizational orientation.

Attitudinal Measures

The overwhelming majority of the children interviewed expressed favorable attitudes toward their coaches. The mean responses to the items relating to liking for the coach and desire to play for him next year were 6.25 and 6.03, respectively (the sixth point on the scale was labeled "Like a fair amount"). Fewer than 7% of the players interviewed evaluated their coach below the neutral points ("Neither like nor dislike") on either or both of the scales.

A factor analysis of the attitude items for the total player sample yielded two factors, which accounted for 50.8% and 11.5% of the variance, respectively. The first factor included all items relating to attraction toward the coach, whereas the second factor comprised the items dealing with liking for the sport and attraction toward teammates.

Factor analyses of the attitudinal responses at each age and ability level indicated that, as in the case of perception of coaching behaviors, attitudes became increasingly differentiated with age. Only one factor emerged for the minors, and all of the items had high loadings on it. At the major level, two factors were found. The first involved attraction toward the coach, whereas the second involved liking for baseball, attraction among teammates, and perceived liking by the coach. For the seniors, three factors emerged involving attraction toward the coach, intrateam attraction and perceived liking by the coach, and liking for baseball, respectively. It is interesting to note that not until the 13-15-year-old level did liking for the sport become differentiated from other evaluative aspects of participation.

Relationships among Coach and Player Variables

Coach perceptions

Correlation coefficients reflecting the relationships between CBAS observed behaviors and coaches' rating of how frequently they performed the behaviors were generally low and nonsignificant. The only significant correlation occurred for Punishment ($r = +.45$). It thus appears that self-perceptions by coaches show correspondence with externally observed behaviors only for punitive behaviors.

Correlations between coaches' and players' ratings of the coaches' behaviors were also low and generally nonsignificant. The highest correlation again occurred for Punishment ($r = +.26$), but the relationship was even lower than when the coaches' self-ratings of this behavior were correlated with the CBAS Punishment score. It is clear that the ability of coaches to give self-ratings of their behaviors that correspond with the perceptions of others is limited indeed. Whether self-perception skills can be improved through training, feedback, and self-monitoring procedures is a question deserving of empirical attention, since behavior change in coaches may be highly dependent on accurate self-monitoring and social comparison skills.

Coach instrumentalities

For each of the 12 coaching behaviors, an Expectancy X Value instrumentality measure was derived from the coach's importance scores on each of the eight coaching goals and the coach's rating of the instrumentality of each behavior in attaining the goal. These instrumentality measures were then correlated with the coaches' self-perceptions of how frequently they performed the behaviors, the player perceptions of behavioral frequency, and their observed CBAS behavior scores.

The instrumentality measure tended to correlate highly with the coaches' perceptions of their own behavior. The E X V of Reinforcement correlated $+.72$ with self-perception of reinforcement frequency. The corresponding correlations for Mistake-contingent Encouragement, Punitive Technical Instruction, Keeping Control, and Organization were $+.62$, $+.62$, $+.49$, and $+.48$, respectively. The mean E X V correlations with coach-perceived behaviors was $+.42$. On the other hand, the instrumentality scores showed low and generally nonsignificant relationships with the CBAS observed behaviors and with player perception measures. The average correlation with the CBAS observed behaviors was $-.02$, while the average correlation with the player perception scores was $+.10$. It thus appears that the perceived instrumentality of behavior as measured in this study is related only to the coaches' cognitive representations of their own behavior. Coaches believe that they are behaving in a way that will be instrumental to achieving their goals, but this rationality is not reflected in the eyes of other beholders.

Player perceptions

Correlations between the mean behavioral ratings of each team and the observed CBAS behaviors of the 51 coaches yielded significant coefficients for Punishment ($r = +.54$), Punitive Technical Instruction ($r = +.37$), Mistake-contingent Technical Instruction ($r = +.31$), and General Communication ($r = +.26$). None of the coefficients for the other categories exceeded

+.20. It thus appears that players most accurately perceive supportive behaviors, reactions to mistakes, and game-irrelevant communicative behaviors of the coach.

The relationships between observed and player-perceived behaviors were assessed in two other ways. In the first of these analyses, the ratings of players who played for coaches whose factor scores fell 1 standard deviation above or below the means on each of the four CBAS factors were subjected to a simple discriminant analysis. The six perceived behavior categories on which the extreme groups of coaches differed are identified by asterisks in Table 3. These data, like the correlational data, indicate that the highest levels of agreement occurred for Reinforcement, the reaction-to-mistakes categories, and for General Communication.

A final analysis of observed-perceived behavior relationships used the method of canonical correlation analysis. The two major canonical variates derived from the two sets of measures correlated +.89 with one another. The correlations of the variates with the observed CBAS scores are presented in Table 5. The behavior canonical variate reflects a dimension having Reinforcement, Mistake-contingent Encouragement and Organization on one

TABLE 5 Correlations between observed behaviors and canonical variates derived from observed and player-perceived behaviors

| | | Variate Pair 1 | |
	Behavior	Observed variate	Player-perceived variate
R	Positive Reinforcement	$-.47^{***}$	$-.46^{***}$
NR	Nonreinforcement		
EM	Mistake-contingent Encouragement	$-.49^{***}$	$-.62^{***}$
TIM	Mistake-contingent Technical Instruction		
P	Punishment	$.65^{***}$	$.52^{***}$
TIM + P	Punitive TIM	$.73^{***}$	$.51^{***}$
IM	Ignoring Mistakes		
KC	Keeping Control		$-.31^{*}$
TIG	General Technical Instruction		
EG	General Encouragement	$.35^{**}$	
O	Organization	$-.38^{**}$	
GC	General Communication		$.47^{***}$

Note. $N = 51$. From Smith, Smoll, & Curtis (1977).
$^{*}p < .05.$
$^{**}p < .01.$
$^{***}p < .001.$

TABLE 6 Correlations between player-perceived coaching behaviors
and team attraction toward the coach

	Behavior	r
R	Reinforcement	.16
NR	Nonreinforcement	−.04
EM	Mistake-contingent Encouragement	.43*
TIM	Mistake-contingent Technical Instruction	.29*
P	Punishment	−.34*
TIM + P	Punitive Technical Instruction	−.35*
IM	Ignoring Mistakes	−.07
KC	Keeping Control	.14
TIG	General Technical Instruction	.35*
EG	General Encouragement	.34*
O	Organization	.19
GC	General Communication	.06

Note. From Smith, Smoll, & Curtis (1977).
*$p < .05$.

end and the punitive categories and General Encouragement on the other.
General Encouragement also loaded with the punitive categories in the factor
analysis of the CBAS categories. This may be because some behaviors coded
EG are given in a haranguing or sarcastic fashion that players may find to be
aversive. The perceived behavior canonical variate, like the observed one,
reflects a dimension ranging from Reinforcement and support following
mistakes to punitive behaviors.

Perceived behaviors and player attitudes

Relationships between player perceptions of coaching behaviors and their
evaluative reactions toward the coaches were assessed in two ways. The
evaluative measure was the team's mean factor score on the first attitude
factor (attraction toward the coach). The correlations between the mean
attraction score and the mean behavioral ratings given by each team are
presented in Table 6. Significant positive correlations were found for
Technical Instruction and both Encouragement categories, whereas Punishment
and Punitive Technical Instruction correlated negatively with attraction toward
the coach.

A second analysis involved a comparison of perceived behavior ratings
given by 87 players on 9 teams whose coaches had elicited extremely positive
reactions from their players ($\geqslant +.7$ SD above the mean on the first attitude
factor) and those given by 109 players on 11 teams whose coaches had been
evaluated .5 SD or more below the mean. A discriminant analysis of these
data yielded significnat ($p < .01$) differences on 9 of the 12 behaviors. As
shown in Table 7, the best-liked coaches were rated as giving more frequent

TABLE 7 Player-perceived behaviors that differentiate between coaches
eliciting extremely positive reactions and those eliciting less positive
reactions from their players

Less positive ($N = 109$)	Extremely positive ($N = 87$)
P	R
TIM + P	EM
	TIM
	KC
	TIG
	EG
	O

Note. All *p*'s < .01. The behaviors were viewed as occurring more frequently in the coach
category under which they are listed. From Smith, Smoll, & Curtis (1977). Following is a
key to the symbols for behaviors.

R	Positive Reinforcement	TIM + P	Punitive TIM
NR	Nonreinforcement	IM	Ignoring Mistakes
EM	Mistake-contingent Encourage-	KC	Keeping Control
	ment	TIG	General Technical Instruction
TIM	Mistake-contingent Technical	EG	General Encouragement
	Instruction	O	Organization
P	Punishment	GC	General Communication

Reinforcement, Mistake-contingent Encouragement, General Encouragement,
Mistake-contingent Technical Instruction, and as engaging in more Organization and Keeping Control behaviors. The least popular coaches were rated as
more frequently engaging in Punishment and Punitive Technical Instruction
following mistakes.

Observed behaviors and player attitudes

In general, the correlations between the observed CBAS behaviors and
player attitudes were lower than they were for the perceived behaviors. Since
the factor analysis of the CBAS behaviors indicated that the behaviors
patterned themselves along meaningful dimensions, an analysis was undertaken
comparing coaches who fell ±1 SD above and below the mean on each of the
four factors. To assess the role of general self-esteem as a potential moderator
variable in coach behavior-player attitude relationships, the players were
divided into high, moderate, and low self-esteem groups on the basis of their
scores on the modified Coopersmith scale. A series of 2 (extreme coach
group) X 3 (player self-esteem level) analyses of variance were performed for
each of the four factors with the two attitude factor scores (attraction toward

coach and attraction toward team and sport) serving as the dependent variable measures.

No significant main or interaction effects were found for the first two factors shown in Table 2. On Factors 3 and 4, however, significant main effects for coaching behaviors were found for both attitude factors. The mean attraction scores obtained by coaches having extreme scores on Factor 3 as a function of players' self-esteem levels are presented in Figure 3. These data indicate that coaches oriented toward technical instruction were evaluated more positively than were coaches who engaged in more General Encouragement and General Communication, $F (1,165) = 12.37, p < .001$, particularly by players who were low in self-esteem. As Figure 4 indicates, players who played for the technically instructive coaches also evaluated their teammates and the sport more positively, $F (1,165) = 6.45, p < .02$. On this measure, a significant main effect was also found for self-esteem, $F (2,165) = 3.05, p < .05$, with low-self-esteem children evaluating teammates and the sport less positively.

Factor 4 reflects the tendency for the coach to engage in the supportive behaviors of Reinforcement and Mistake-contingent Encouragement. As Figure 5 shows, coaches scoring high on this dimension were evaluated more positively by

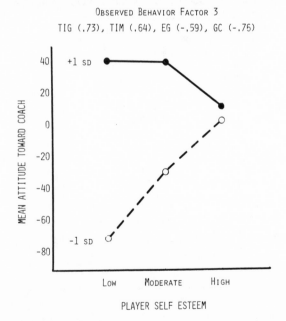

FIGURE 3   Mean attraction toward the coach as a function of coaches' Factor 3 scores and players' levels of self-esteem (from Smith, Smoll, & Curtis, 1977).

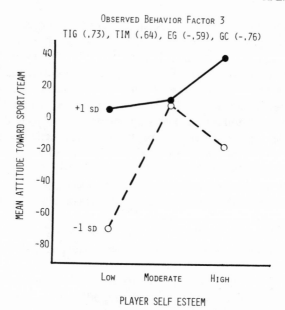

FIGURE 4 Mean attraction toward baseball and teammates as a function of coaches' Factor 3 scores and players' levels of self-esteem (from Smith, Smoll, & Curtis, 1977).

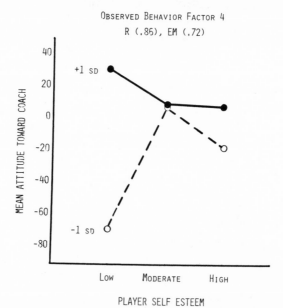

FIGURE 5 Mean attraction toward the coach as a function of coaches' Factor 4 scores and players' levels of self-esteem (from Smith, Smoll, & Curtis, 1977).

their players, $F(1,132) = 4.95$, $p < .05$. This significant main effect was produced primarily by the marked difference at the low-self-esteem level. Figure 6 indicates that players, particularly those high and low in self-esteem, evaluated their teammates and the sport more positively if they played for coaches who gave high levels of reinforcement and support, $F(1,132) = 12.88$, $p < .001$.

The results of the analyses involving coaches with extreme factor scores indicate that coaches who fall at the technically instructive and supportive ends of the statistically independent Factors 3 and 4 were evaluated more favorably by their players. In addition, low-self-esteem players appeared to be affected more by differences on these coaching behavior dimensions than were players higher in general self-esteem. The failure of the punitiveness factor (Factor 2) to yield significant results may be partly the result of a range attenuation on the punitive behaviors resulting from the refusal of 13 coaches to allow us to code their behavior. Informal observation indicated that a number of these coaches were far more punitive than were any of the coaches on whom behavioral data were collected.[3]

Coaching behaviors and post-season self-esteem

In the previous analyses, general self-esteem served as an independent variable. Also of interest, however, were relationships between coaching

[3]Subsequent studies have consistently shown the punitive factor to be negatively related to attitudes toward the coach.

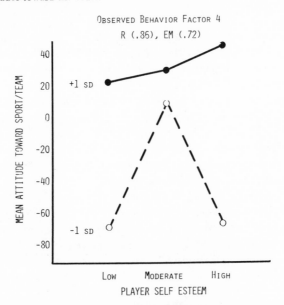

FIGURE 6 Mean attraction toward baseball and teammates as a function of coaches' Factor 4 scores and players' levels of self-esteem (from Smith, Smoll, & Curtis, 1977).

behaviors and player self-esteem scores obtained after the season ended. A discriminant analysis was performed on the general self-esteem scores and the baseball ability self-ratings of players who played for coaches ±1 SD above the means of the four behavior factors. No significant differences on either general or baseball self-esteem were found for the first two factors. On the third (instructional orientation) factor, a significantly lower mean self-rating of baseball ability was found for players who played for the technically instructive coaches, $F(1,165) = 4.15$, $p < .05$, but no difference was found in general self-esteem. Apparently, an emphasis on technical instruction makes players more aware of their skill limitations than does a nontechnical orientation.

The fourth factor (reinforcement-support) was unrelated to postseason baseball self-esteem, but a highly significant difference was found in general self-esteem scores. Youngsters who played for coaches who gave high levels of Reinforcement and Mistake-contingent Encouragement had higher scores on the modified Coopersmith scale at the end of the season, $F(1,132) = 9.52, p < 0.1$. Although the absence of preseason measures precluded the assessment of self-esteem changes over the season, the fact that player assignment to teams was a basically random process suggests the possibility that certain coaching behaviors may affect levels of general and athletic self-esteem. This is clearly an issue deserving of future empirical attention.

Importance of Winning

"Winning isn't everything. It's the only thing." Or is it? In the case of attitudes toward the coach, is it indeed true that everyone loves a winner? We have already seen that certain coaching behaviors are related to how positively coaches are evaluated by their players. To examine the importance of team record, the won-lost percentages of the 9 best-liked and the 11 least-liked coaches were compared. The best-liked coaches had a mean winning percentage of .422 (SD = .277), compared with a mean of .545 (SD = .329) for the least-liked coaches. The difference did not approach significance. Clearly, the extent to which the teams won cannot account for the differences in attraction toward the two groups of coaches.

A second analysis compared the interview responses of players who played for very successful teams (winning percentage > .667) and those who played for losing teams having a winning percentage of less than .333. A discriminant analysis disclosed that winners and losers did not differ in any of their attitudes toward the coach.[4] There were a number of significant differences, however, on other measures. Players from winning teams stated that they liked baseball more, liked their teammates more, felt that their coaches liked them more, and felt that their parents liked the coach more. On the perceived behavior measures, players from winning teams rated their

---

[4] Data from this and subsequent studies show winning to become more important with age. By ages 13–15 winning is significantly related to desire to play for the coach.

coaches as giving significantly more Reinforcement, Mistake-contingent Encouragement, and Mistake-contingent Technical Instruction, but a discriminant analysis of the CBAS data of the winning and losing coaches yielded no significant differences on these or any other behaviors.

Role of Coaches' Beliefs Concerning Player Goals

Coaching styles and the subsequent reactions of children may be influenced by the values and beliefs held by coaches. Among the beliefs that may affect interactions with players are those concerning the goals that motivate players to strive for good performance. The forced-choice instrument described previously was used to measure each coach's beliefs about the relative importance of eight potential player motives. The mean number of times each goal was judged more important than another is shown in the first column of Table 8. Though these scores represent the average ratings across the 50 coaches who provided complete data, individual coaches varied considerably in their motive scores. A minimum variance cluster analysis was therefore performed to determine if there were groups of coaches who shared similar views regarding the importance of the various motives, i.e., who had similar motive profiles. A three-cluster solution proved optimal with regard to interpretability. It yielded two major coach clusters, comprising 28 and 17 coaches, respectively, and a residual cluster in which motive scores were highly variable. The mean motive scores for the two major homogeneous clusters are presented in Table 8. The two clusters differed significantly on all motives except "Pleasing the coach."

In order of importance, the coach in the first cluster believed that the most salient motives for their players were (a) Personal pride in performing

TABLE 8 Means of coaches' importance ratings of player motives by all coaches and by the two coach groups identified by cluster analysis

Motive	Means		
	All coaches ($N = 50$)	Cluster 1 ($N = 28$)	Cluster 2 ($N = 17$)
Personal pride in performing well	5.66	6.46	4.82
Having a winning team	4.56	4.14	5.65
Developing baseball skills	4.26	5.57	3.06
Impressing the other kids	2.92	1.96	3.94
Pleasing parents	2.76	2.04	3.41
Pleasing the coach	2.62	2.71	2.82
Hoping to become a great athlete	2.58	3.14	1.12
Avoiding failure or embarrassment	2.56	1.89	3.06

Note. With the exception of "Pleasing the coach," the means for all motives were significantly different between Clusters 1 and 2. From Curtis, Smith, & Smoll (1977).

well, (b) Developing baseball skills, (c) Having a winning team, and (d) Hoping to become a great athlete. Coaches in the second cluster believed that their players' most important motives were (a) Having a winning team, (b) Personal pride in performing well, (c) Impressing the other kids, and (d) Pleasing the parents. Although coaches in both clusters felt that personal pride in performing well and having a winning team were important motives for their players, coaches in the first cluster also emphasized the importance of developing baseball skills and hoping to become a great athlete. Coaches in the second cluster emphasized instead the importance of impressing peers and pleasing parents. Thus, the major differences among these two types of coaches would appear to revolve around the extent to which they viewed their players as being motivated to achieve intrinsic (athletic) goals versus extrinsic (social approval) goals.

There were no strong differences between the two clusters of coaches in their observed CBAS behaviors, their players' ratings of their behavior, or in the players' attitudes toward the coach and team, with the exception that coaches in the intrinsic cluster were rated by their players as knowing more about baseball than were coaches in the extrinsic cluster, F (1,43) = 12.99, $p < 0.1$. There were some intriguing differences, however, in the relationships of observer- and player-rated behaviors with other measures.

Table 9 presents the correlations between observed behaviors and both the won-lost record and the players' scores on the first attitude factor for both clusters of coaches. In these data, the only consistent relationships were observed for coaches in the extrinsic cluster. There is a series of moderately strong correlations between mistake-contingent behaviors and the won-lost record. It seems reasonable to assume that players on losing teams are generally making more mistakes than players on winning teams; and since there were no differences in the average won-lost records of coaches in the two clusters (54% versus 52%), it would appear that coaches in the extrinsic cluster are more reactive to the mistakes of their players.

For coaches in the extrinsic cluster, strong relationships were evident between observed behaviors and the players' attitude factor scores. Though there was a positive relationship between Reinforcement and the players' liking for the coach, the strongest relationships were the negative correlations for General Communication and Keeping Control. These latter two behaviors are nongame-related and usually occur in or around the dugout. It would appear that there is something in the style or content of the interaction between coaches in the extrinsic cluster and their players that is not well received. Thus, the more often these coaches had to Keep Control or engaged in General Communication, the less favorably their players responded to them. This pattern of results may reflect the effect of expressing in word or manner a less-than-favorable impression of why children want to perform well. That is, the extrinsic coaches may express, either explicitly or implicitly, their belief

TABLE 9 Correlations of observed coaching behaviors with won-lost record and players' attitudes toward the coach within coaching clusters

		Correlations			
		Won-lost record		Players' attitude factor	
	Observed behavior	Intrinsic cluster	Extrinsic cluster	Intrinsic cluster	Extrinsic cluster
R	Positive Reinforcement				.41*
NR	Nonreinforcement				
EM	Mistake-contingent Encouragement		−.58**		
TIM	Mistake-contingent Technical Instruction		−.39		
P	Punishment	−.37*	−.55**		
TIM + P	Punitive TIM		−.51*		
IM	Ignoring Mistakes				
KC	Keeping Control				−.50*
TIG	General Technical Instruction		.40		
EG	General Encouragement				
O	Organization				
GC	General Communication				−.73***

Note. Cluster 1 ($N = 28$), Cluster 2 ($N = 17$). From Curtis, Smith, & Smoll (1977).
*$p < .05$.
**$p < .01$.
***$p < .001$.

that children play baseball to impress or please other people rather than because they are interested in the game and want to become better at it.

Correlations between the players' perceptions of the coaches' behaviors and both the won-lost record and the players' attitude factor scores are presented in Table 10. The patterns of relationships apparent in these data differed from those obtained for the observed behavior in that the significant correlations occurred among coaches in the intrinsic cluster. Thus, the better the won-lost record, the more reinforcing, encouraging, and technically instructive the players perceived these coaches to be. Further, the players' liking for the coach was positively related to how reinforcing and encouraging the coach was perceived to be. While there was little relationship between the won-loss record and the players' attitude factor across all coaches, a correlation of +.40 ($df = 26$, $p < .02$) was obtained between these measures for coaches in the intrinsic cluster.

TABLE 10 Correlations of player-perceived behaviors with won-lost record and players' attitudes toward the coach within coaching clusters

		Correlations			
		Won-lost record		Players' attitude factor	
Player-perceived behavior		Intrinsic cluster	Extrinsic cluster	Intrinsic cluster	Extrinsic cluster
R	Positive Reinforcement	.62***		.38*	
NR	Nonreinforcement	−.48**			
EM	Mistake-contingent Encouragement	.52**		.41*	
TIM	Mistake-contingent Technical Instruction	.31		.30	
P	Punishment	−.37*			
TIM + P	Punitive TIM	−.43**			−.51*
IM	Ignoring Mistakes				
KC	Keeping Control				
TIG	General Technical Instruction			.30	
EG	General Encouragement	.46**		.63***	
O	Organization				
GC	General Communication				

Note. Cluster 1 (*N* = 28), Cluster 2 (*N* = 17). From Curtis, Smith, & Smoll (1977).
*$p < .05$.
**$p < .01$.
***$p < .001$.

Data reported here suggest that within the two identifiable coach clusters, different factors exert influence on the players' attitudes toward the coach and the game. For coaches in the intrinsic cluster, both the players' attitude and their perceptions of the coaches' behavior were related to the won-lost record, and attitudes were also related to perceptions of coaching behavior. For coaches in the extrinsic cluster, however, the players' coach attraction scores were related primarily to the coaches' interactions around the bench. Additional research is clearly necessary to replicate these relationships and to clarify factors underlying them, but there is evidence here of stylistic differences related to differences in sources of influence on players' attitudes.

DEVELOPMENT OF EXPERIMENTAL COACHING CLINICS

The data obtained during the baseball study described here are basically correlational in nature. To justify conclusions involving causal relationships, it is essential that attempts be made to experimentally manipulate coaching behaviors and measure the effects of such manipulation on childrens' reactions. In the best of all possible worlds, this would be accomplished by creating our own leagues and programing experimenter-coaches to behave in particular ways. Given the practical impossibility of such an undertaking, we are establishing experimental coaching clinics and using a variety of behavior-change techniques in an attempt to train coaches to relate to their players in ways that our initial data indicate will create a more positive experience for the youngsters.

The effects of our first experimental clinic are currently being assessed in a study involving 34 Little League baseball coaches and the approximately 400 players who comprise their teams. All the coaches are involved at the major and senior levels in the same leagues that were studied during the project described above. They were randomly assigned to an experimental group consisting of 18 coaches and a control group numbering 16. The coaches in the experimental group were contacted by telephone and invited to participate in an evening clinic in which the results of the previous year's study would be described and coaching guidelines would be presented and discussed. All coaches who were invited agreed to participate.

During the clinic, which lasted approximately 2 hr, the CBAS categories and their relationships with the player variables were described. In particular, the positive relationships between player attitudes toward the coach and the Reinforcement, Encouragement, and Technical Instruction categories were emphasized. Also discussed was the role of winning. Many of the coaches were surprised that won-lost record was unrelated to attitudes toward the coach. This finding also appeared to make a number of them more receptive to the coaching guidelines.

The guidelines were presented both verbally and in a brochure. In addition, modeling was used to demonstrate the forms that both desirable and undesirable behaviors could take. Basically, the guidelines stressed the desirability of increasing Reinforcement (for effort as well as for good performance), Mistake-contingent Encouragement, Mistake-contingent Technical Instruction (given in an encouraging and supportive fashion), General Technical Instruction, and General Encouragement (given in a selective and nonsarcastic manner). The coaches were urged to decrease Nonreinforcement, the punitive categories, and to avoid having to use Keeping Control behaviors by establishing team rules early and reinforcing compliance with them. The guidelines were placed in a goal context of increasing positive coach-player and player-player interactions, developing team cohesion, and developing a positive desire to achieve rather than a fear of failure in children.

Several measures were taken in an attempt to encourage and maintain compliance with the coaching guidelines. During the first 2 weeks of the season, the experimental coaches were observed and provided with CBAS behavioral profiles after each game. In addition to the behavioral feedback, self-monitoring was employed. The coaches were given a brief self-monitoring form on which they indicated approximately how often they engaged in the recommended behaviors. The coaches were asked to complete the forms immediately after each of the first 10 games and to mail them to us in stamped envelopes that were provided.

The effects of the experimental clinics will be assessed by essentially replicating the initial study. CBAS behavior measures will be obtained by observing experimental and control coaches during four complete games. They will also complete the self-report measures of the Coaching Philosophy scale. The interview procedures and measures described previously will be administered to their players at the conclusion of the season to obtain attitudinal measures. Experimental and control coaches can thus be compared on all of these measures. In addition, data from last season are available on 13 of the experimental coaches and 9 of the control coaches (and an initial analysis indicates that the two groups of coaches were virtually identical in attractiveness to their players). It will therefore be possible to assess changes on the experimental measures as a function of clinic participation.

In the future, a variety of approaches to increasing desirable coaching behaviors will be implemented and assessed. We hope to establish, on a broad scale, an instructional program for youth coaches having three basic components. The first component will be technical, with coaches known for their teaching ability offering instruction in how to teach children basic sport skills. The second will be medically oriented, with sports medicine experts instructing coaches on how to prevent and deal with injuries. The third will have the psychological focus of our present efforts, and will be designed to assist coaches in providing the children with a psychologically positive participation experience.

Organized youth sports will continue to flourish and proliferate. They clearly constitute an area deserving of greater attention on the part of community psychologists. Our experience has been that those involved in administering youth sports programs are eager to provide a positive experience for youngsters and are receptive to constructive efforts by professionals to assist them. It is to be hoped that psychologists will seize on the inviting opportunities to positively influence such programs. Our profession as well as the children and adults involved in youth sports will be the ultimate winners.

REFERENCES

AAHPER Committee on Athletic Competition for Children of Elementary School Age. *Desirable athletic competition for children of elementary school age.* Washington, D.C.: AAHPER, 1968.

Bales, R. F., & Slater, P. Role differentiation in small decision-making groups. In P. Parson & R. F. Bales (Eds.), *Family, socialization, and interaction process.* Glencoe, Ill.: Free Press, 1955.

Coopersmith, S. *The antecedents of self-esteem.* San Francisco: Freeman, 1967.

Curtis, B., Smith, R. E., & Smoll, F. L. *Relationships between coaching behaviors and children's attitudes as a function of coaches' perceptions of player motives.* Unpublished manuscript, University of Washington, 1977.

Goldfried, M. R., & Sprafkin, J. N. *Behavioral personality assessment.* Morristown, N.J.: General Learning Press, 1974.

Mischel, W. Toward a cognitive social learning reconceptualization of personality. *Psychological Review,* 1973, *80,* 252–283.

Rarick, G. L. Competitive sports for young boys: Controversial issues. *Medicine and Science in Sports,* 1969, *1,* 181–184.

Singer, R. N. *Coaching, athletics, and psychology.* New York: McGraw-Hill, 1972.

Smith, R. E., Smoll, F. L., & Curtis, B. *Community psychology and youth sports.* Unpublished manuscript, University of Washington, 1977.

Smith, R. E., Smoll, F. L., & Hunt, E. B. Training manual for the coaching behavior assessment system. *JSAS Catalog of Selected Documents in Psychology,* 1977, *7,* 2. (Ms. No. 1406) (a)

Smith, R. E., Smoll, F. L., & Hunt, E. A system for the behavioral assessment of athletic coaches. *Research Quarterly,* 1977, *48,* 401–407. (b)

Smith, R. E., Smoll, F. L., Hunt, E. B., & Clarke, S. J. *CBAS audio visual training module.* Seattle: University of Washington, 1976. (Film)

9

COOPERATIVE GAMES
Systematic Analysis and Cooperative Impact

T. D. Orlick, Jane McNally, and Tom O'Hara

This chapter represents 3 years of research and reflective thinking directed toward the creation of a cooperative games program. The program was conceived as a means of social change directed towards more humane games and lives. The primary aim of co-op games is to increase cooperative behavior both in and out of games. The games have been designed to provide cooperative success experiences, individual feelings of acceptance, and total involvement.

There have been many stages in arriving at the present frame of reference and there are many more steps ahead. This quest began by analyzing the component structure and emphasis of contemporary games and by assessing what kinds of behaviors they are structured to elicit. It was found that to elicit the desired behaviors (i.e., more cooperative behaviors), it was necessary to restructure games. Old games were adapted and new ones created so that their design was more appropriate for eliciting cooperative behaviors. Many questions had to be answered. Did the games actually work? Did they elicit cooperative behaviors from the participants? Did the games provide success experiences? Was there total involvement? Were the games motivationally

J. McNally and T. O'Hara participated primarily in the experimental kindergarten cooperative games study. Without the assistance of the kindergarten teachers (Roberta Haley, Barb Champion, and Bonnie Brooks), the Carleton School Board, other trained observers (Cathy Foley, Kim Stairs, and Glynne Turner), and the kindergarten children, this study would not have been possible. Appreciation is extended to all.

viable for the children? Did they hold the child's attention and interest? Did the children like them?

It was, in fact, possible to formulate a series of behaviorally verified cooperative games that kindergarten children enjoyed playing (Orlick, 1976, 1977). A successful co-op games program had been created and we began to examine a question of great personal and social significance. Can we increase children's cooperative behaviors outside of games through a co-op games program?

The remainder of this chapter is devoted to the exploration of this question. The reader is first exposed to some of the different means of cooperative game analysis; then presented with our first study, which focused on the cooperative impact of cooperative games; and, finally, asked to reflect on future directions.

COMPONENT STRUCTURE OF GAMES

Regardless of its component structure, a game will have some kind of individualistic experience or outcome for the player. Reinforcements or perceived payoffs are experienced by each person even though they may occur in conjunction with others. The important structural distinction relates to how one receives these payoffs—at the expense of others, without reference to others, or by cooperating with others.

The design of a game will largely influence the predominant behavioral response, be it competitive, individualistic, cooperative, or some combination thereof. Consequently, to better understand games and the behavior likely to be elicited by them, each activity can be classified according to its component structure. The following categories have proven to be helpful in classifying the structure of many children's games. Although the categories are neither all-inclusive, nor defined in absolute terms, most activities can be classified according to these paradigms.

1. Competitive Means—Competitive Ends. Everyone is competing against everyone else from the outset to the end. The objective is to beat someone else or everyone else, and the means by which you attempt to do this is by competing against them. Examples are a class race where the first person across the finish line is declared the winner; a group of individuals all fighting to gain sole possession of one ball; to be "King of the Mountain" or "Winner on the Spot."

2. Cooperative Means—Competitive Ends. People engage in cooperation within a group and competition outside the group. Team members are cooperating to beat (or better compete against) another team. An example is any competitive game where teammates help one another in pursuit of a victory and where members of one team share the win and members of the other team share the defeat. In a game like soccer,

cooperative means may be evidenced by teammates passing the ball in preparation for a shot on net. In a regular competitive game, cooperative interdependence and input is not always ensured for all team members. To ensure *Cooperative Interdependent Means*, a rule can be introduced in a game like soccer wherein everyone has to play and wherein everyone has to touch the ball (receive a pass and kick a pass) before a shot on net can be taken. This would ensure cooperative interdependence and input from each team member within the competitive goal structure (Cooperative Interdependent Means—Competitive Ends).

3. Individual Means—Individual Ends. One or more people are pursuing an individual goal without cooperative or competitive interaction and without direct evaluative reference to others. Examples are individual movement activities, creative problem solving where there is no incorrect movement response, and trail skiing along a scenic route.

4. Cooperative Means—Individual Ends. Persons are cooperating and helping each other so that each can achieve an individual end. For example, individual athletes can watch one another, give one another feedback or teach one another new skills so that each person can learn, improve, and perform better. The means are shared, the ends are not. To ensure *Cooperative Interdependent Means* and input from each team member, situations can be set up where athletes pair off and watch one another run through routines giving appropriate constructive feedback. Cooperative interdependence could be ensured during a gym class or activity session by having each group member teach all other group members a unique skill (or rule) for which all are individually responsible for knowing.

5. Cooperative Means—Cooperative Ends. Team members are cooperating with each other from the outset to the end, regardless of what team they happen to be on. "Opposing" team members, if they exist, work together to achieve a common goal. The means as well as the ends are shared. Cooperative interdependence is ensured between teams but not necessarily among all team members within a particular group. An example is collective score volleyball where the objective is to keep the ball on the volley as long as possible. To ensure *Cooperative Interdependent Means* as well as Cooperative Ends, a rule could be introduced in volleyball where each person on a particular side must touch the ball within a collective score game, or games such as Cooperative Musical Chairs, Balloon Balance, Collective Blanket Ball, or Log Roll could be played. In these games, everyone is helping one another for everyone's gain.

Games with both cooperative means and cooperative ends are extremely rare in our culture, but, in fact, are the type of game most desirable for the purposes of this research. By redirecting some thought patterns it was possible to devise two subclassifications of games within this major structural category: Cooperative Games with No Losers and Collective Score Games. Nearly all games created or adapted for the experimental cooperative games program for kindergarten children were Co-op Games with No Losers, a few of which are described as follows.[1]

Sample Cooperative Kindergarten Games with No Losers

Cooperative Musical Chairs Children skip around a row of chairs to music and when the music stops all children must share a chair. Chairs are systematically removed until only one chair remains. The object is to keep every child in the game, even though chairs are being removed. As each chair is removed more children must team up sitting together on parts of chairs, or on top of one another to keep everyone in. Instead of fighting for the sole possession of one chair, kids work together to make themselves part of it.

Turtle A gym mat acts as the turtle shell, and about eight children get under the shell and make the mat move in one direction.

Caterpillar Over the Mountain Children get on their hands and knees and hold the ankles of the child in front of them. One giant caterpillar is formed and it moves around the room and over the mountain (a mat draped over a bench).

Beach Ball Balance Two children are given one beach ball and attempt to hold the ball between them without using their hands. They try to move around the gym or through an obstacle course in this manner. They also see how many different ways they can balance the ball between them and still move around, for example between heads, on side, stomach, back to back and so on.

Numbers and Letters Together The children find one or two partners and are requested to make one specific number, letter or shape using all their little bodies.

BEHAVIOR OBSERVATION

Systematic behavior observation can be extremely helpful in evaluating the frequency with which a particular behavior occurs and in assessing behavioral change. It is not our intent to dwell on the methodology of behavior observation, but rather to expose the reader to some behavioral definitions and to a few observational approaches we have attempted in our cooperation research thus far.[2]

---

[1] All experimental cooperative games used in this study, as well as many others for different age groups, can be found in Orlick (1977, in press).

[2] Researchers interested in more on the measurement of behavior are referred to Hall (1974 a,b).

For the purpose of our systematic observational analysis, cooperation was based solely on the frequency with which a child interacted in a cooperative way with peers. A cooperative social interaction was defined as any behavior directed toward another child that involved some shared, reciprocal, mutual, or helpful quality. More specifically, cooperative social interaction was delineated as follows.

1. Cooperative Task Behavior—One child shares, assists, or executes a task with another child. The emphasis is upon doing things together, working together for a common goal, alternating responses between children, sharing material, or one child's behaving in a manner explicitly to help another child. For example, two or more children work together to solve a problem or to execute a task; two or more children engage in a cooperative activity in which they respond in turn based on the response of the other child.
2. Cooperative Physical Contact Behavior—(a) one child physically supports or is supported by another child. For example, one child carries another child or helps another child up off the ground or over a barrier. (b) Two or more children engage in physical contact of an affectionate nature by, for example, linking arms, holding hands, placing arms around one another, embracing, kissing, or patting another child on the back.
3. Cooperative Verbal Behavior—Verbal interaction is accepted as meeting the criteria for cooperative social interaction only if it has some definite cooperative quality. For example, one child gives another child instruction on how to do something; one child offers to help or share or agrees to a cooperative request made by another child.

This rather encompassing definition of cooperation manifests itself differently in different games and in different settings. For example, during unstructured free time in the kindergarten classroom, a few specific incidences of cooperative social interaction we have observed include tying another child's shoe lace; handing another child an apron or helping him put it on; lifting a block together for a fort or tower; passing scissors, paint brush, glue, and so on; pushing large blocks together to make a big train. One child says, "Let's push the big train over there," two or three others say "OK," and they proceed to help in the push. One child drags a long board across the room, another child picks up the other end to help carry it; one child holds out a jar of paint for another to use; one child holds a bowl or container while another scoops it full of water; and one child pushes another child in a carriage, in a wagon, or on a truck. Other examples include cleaning up—one child squirts soap for another child or holds the water tap on for another child to use—and building together—one child brings or hands a block to another child, two children place or straighten a block together, or one child steadies the structure for another child (not just independent parallel building on the same structure). A final type of cooperative behavior is peer teaching—one child shows another child how to make a toy barn out of construction paper, "You take it like this and cut around like this" (verbalizing and showing); one child says he is having trouble with a puzzle and another child says, "Here, I'll help you," and proceeds to help him with it.

Cooperative behaviors within games may be specific to that game but still fall within the overall definition of cooperative social interaction previously outlined. For example, in Log Roll (Laughing Logs) the act of rolling together as a unit to move a person across the logs is a cooperative act; whereas, for other games, it may be passing a beach ball, linking arms, making a letter together, tapping a balloon to a partner, helping others fit on a chair, leading a friend through an obstacle course, helping build a tower, freeing friends, carrying a teammate, balancing with a partner, moving a big potato sack together, and so on.

Once observers are familiar with cooperative behavior definitions, it is possible to obtain highly reliable behavioral observations from different observers during classroom free time periods, free play periods in the gym, physical education classes, and newly introduced cooperative games. Regardless of the observation method used, within one or two sessions we have consistently attained over 90% agreement between different observers.

In our cooperative game observations, we focused on obvious, overt, gross levels of behavior. We have only recently begun to attempt to categorize the degree or quality of a particular act. In the work presented herein, if something was defined as a cooperative act, it was recorded as such regardless of the circumstances surrounding the event. It is recognized, however, that differences in degree and quality do exist in such things as cooperation, fun, and involvement. For example, passing a soccer ball because two opposing players are converging on you is of a different quality than passing off to a teammate, when both have a clear shot at the net. It is also recognized that some behaviors that have a cooperative intent do not necessarily look like cooperative acts. Consequently, some modifications of our behavioral definitions may be warranted where a more highly refined assessment of cooperation is deemed necessary.

Any behavior can be assessed and recorded if it is clearly defined in observable terms. For example, we have tried to get measures of involvement in various games. Involvement indicates *active* participation in pursuit of the ends of the game. This is represented behaviorally in different ways for different games. For example, in Fish Gobbler, if the participants are either running, diving to the floor, linking together with others, or raising their arms and cheering, they are actively involved in the game. One method we have used to assess active involvement is to do a 10-sec scan, if possible early in the game, toward the midpoint of the game, and toward the end of the game. At the beginning of the session, we generally note the number of players in the gym and then, during the scan, count the number of children not actively involved in the game. If for the duration of the scan, all children are running or rolling or bumping or doing whatever the demands of the game may dictate, there is total involvement. According to our definition of involvement, children sitting or standing motionless, waiting for turns, or attending to something unrelated to the game are not actively involved in the game.

Fun is another concept we have tried to observe in games. It was defined as follows: (a) verbal representation—laughter, shouting, cheering, squeals of glee; (b) facial representation—expressions of joy (e.g., beaming smiles, open mouths, wide open eyes); and (c) gestures representing fun in conjunction with the preceding—stomping feet, clapping hands, jumping up and down, slapping one another on the back or arm. It's fun to observe fun.

In many respects, observing games is easier then observing free play in the classroom or gym. One distinct observational advantage of games is that the structure of the game remains relatively stable, as does the frequency of cooperative behavior emitted. To the contrary, the structure and focus of free play activities (particularly in the kindergarten classroom) is continuously changing. One of the main problems that occurs in observing games is that many games do not last long. Sometimes one must get an assessment of cooperation in a game within a few minutes, whereas free play periods can last much longer.

One method we found successful in observing games is to randomly select one person and count the number of cooperative acts that person engages in over a 30-sec period. A second person is then randomly selected and observed for 30 sec. This continues until the game is concluded. The information can then be analyzed to obtain an estimate of average number of cooperative acts engaged in for a particular game or per minute within a particular game. In instances where cooperation is continuous (e.g., Log Roll), the amount of time cooperating in a 30-sec period can be recorded in place of the number of cooperative acts. Another method we have used in games is to do a series of 30-sec scans across the playing area. Following each scan, the observer notes the number of cooperative acts observed and the number of people engaged in cooperative behavior.

People sometimes have experiences or feelings that are not reflected in their overt behavior. Therefore, it is often advisable to get self-report measures in addition to measures of observable behavior.

ASSESSMENTS OF LIKING

In our cooperative game analysis, once we know a game can elicit cooperative behavior, it is extremely important to determine whether children like the game and whether they feel happy when playing it. Using "smiley faces" (Figure 1) is a quick and comprehensible means of getting some assessment of whether participants of any age like a game. It also gives an assessment of how people feel while playing the particular game. Immediately

In the game I felt

I really liked it   I didn't like it

FIGURE 1   Smiley faces for assessment of liking games.

after the game, the players indicate their feelings by simply marking one of the five faces, which range from very happy to very sad.

The faces are weighted by assigning the value 5 to the happiest face, 4 to the next happiest face, and so on, with 1 being assigned to the saddest face. This procedure provides for calculation of an average level of liking for different games, different ages, and different sexes and can also aid in assessing whether liking increases with repeated exposures. For kindergarten children, we used three faces (happy, in-between, sad) rather than five; and with some retarded groups we used two faces (happy or sad) to ensure comprehension (Figure 2).

A variation of the smiley faces format is the skimetric scale approach

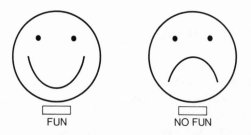

FIGURE 2   Simplified smiley faces format.

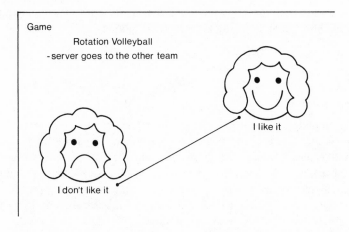

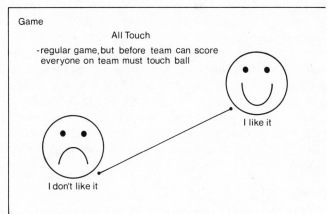

FIGURE 3 Skimetric differential smiley faces.

(Figure 3) wherein players mark how they feel along an 8-cm line between a happy face and a sad face (Orlick, Partington, Scott, & Glassford, 1975). The placing of their mark on the continuum is then measured, giving a score ranging from 0 to 8. We have also used questionnaires and interviews to get more detailed assessments regarding how children feel about playing cooperative games (Orlick, 1977).

KINDERGARTEN STUDY

The primary purpose of the present study was to determine whether, as a result of a cooperative games program, young children would choose to engage in more cooperative behavior in the kindergarten classroom.

Before beginning the study, our observational procedures were refined and a series of cooperative games were field tested to assess their elicitation of cooperation and overall liking by kindergarten children.

Method

Participants

Four intact kindergarten classes from an elementary school in the Carleton School System participated in this study. The school drew primarily from middle-class families living on the outskirts of Ottawa, Ontario. The children attended half-day school sessions (morning and afternoon only). One morning class served as an experimental (cooperative games) group ($N = 24$), and the other morning class served as a control (traditional games) group ($N = 25$). Similarly, one of the two afternoon classes served as an experimental group ($N = 19$) and the other as a control ($N = 19$). The co-op games group had a total combined sample of 43 (24 boys, 19 girls), and the traditional games group had a total of 44 (20 boys, 24 girls). One teacher had her morning class exposed to cooperative games and her afternoon class exposed to traditional games. Both these classes were held in the same room and were observed during free time in the same room with the same basic options of play materials and activity centers to choose from. In the other kindergarten classroom, one teacher taught the morning class and another teacher taught the afternoon class. The experimental and control children were observed in the same room with the same basic options of play materials and activity centers to choose from.

Baseline measures

Two weeks before the introduction of the games program, observers began collecting baseline observation data on cooperative social interaction during free-time periods for experimental and control groups. During the free-time periods, the children participated in self-chosen activities for a period of 30 min in the kindergarten classroom. Preliminary baseline observations were taken on four occasions for each of the four groups of children. These baseline measures were taken early in January 1976, shortly after school resumed following Christmas vacation.

Introduction of games program

To control for the possibility that children perform better or appear happier if they are being treated in a special way, all children (experimental and control) were told they were in a special games program. The games programs were introduced to the experimental and control groups by a qualified games teacher from outside the elementary school for an average of two 30–40 min game periods per group, per week, for 8 weeks. The experimental groups engaged in cooperative activities only; whereas, control groups engaged in a combination of traditional competitive games and individual movements activities found in most primary physical education texts. After 8 weeks, the games programs were conducted by the kindergarten teachers for an average of four 30-min game periods per group, per week, for 10 additional weeks.

Postprogram measures

After the children had been exposed to 18 weeks of either cooperative or traditional games, poststudy observational data on cooperative social interaction were collected. As with baseline data, these measures were taken during 30-min free time periods in the kindergarten classroom. Observations were taken on four occasions for each of the four groups. These procedures began during the last few days in May and continued into early June 1976.

Observation procedures

The specific observation procedures followed in this study are outlined in the following discussion. They form the basis of the findings in the study.

Observers were completely familiar with the behavioral categories and were trained in the reliable use of the rating schedule before baseline measures were taken. Preliminary observations were made on location to enable the raters to adjust to the idiosyncrasies of the children and the situations. During these prebaseline observations, one or two observers and the principal investigator observed the same child for a selected time period, rated his or her behavior, and then discussed results. Training continued until independent interobserver reliability exceeded 90% agreement. This rarely took more than one or two observation sessions. The percentage of agreement was used as an index of reliability (i.e., number of agreements divided by number of agreements plus disagreements). An agreement was a rating of the same behavior (i.e., cooperative interaction or no cooperative interaction) for the same child, in the same observation interval.

After the behavior categories had been learned, practiced, and discussed, uncertainty regarding coding rarely existed. If an observer was really uncertain about whether a particular behavior was cooperative social interaction, it was coded N (no interaction). It was emphasized that approaching cooperative behavior does not meet the criteria of the behavior itself. In addition, if during an observation interval the child was involved with the teacher or had been told to engage in a specified behavior by an adult, a missed trial (MT) was recorded. Later in that same observation session, an attempt was made to make up the missed trial by again focusing on this particular child.

During recording sessions, observers were instructed to get close enough to the child to hear and see what the child was doing or saying. This posed no reactivity problem, because the kindergarten children were accustomed to having different parent volunteers moving about the room. By the time baseline measures began, the children generally ignored the observers.

All observers participating in this study were *blind observers*; they did not know whether the children they were observing were in an experimental or control group, or the details of the specific treatment condition.

Individual observations (10-sec intervals) During observation sessions, approximately 20 children were engaged in free-time activities in a kindergarten classroom. For observational purposes, one child was singled out and watched for a 10-sec interval and either I (for cooperative interaction) or N (for no cooperative interaction) was recorded next to the child's name on a recording sheet. If any cooperative social interaction occurred within the specified 10-sec time period, an I was recorded next to the child's name. If no cooperation occurred, an N was recorded. If the child cooperated during the 10-sec interval, an I was recorded even though he or she may also have engaged in noncooperative behavior during the same time period. After observing the first child, the observer focused on the second child on the list for a 10-sec period, and then continued until all children had been observed once. This cyclical procedure was repeated until the observation period expired (approximately 30 min).

It was necessary for a primary observer to be able to recognize all children in the study before recording baseline measures. To facilitate this process, Polaroid photographs of each child were studied by the primary observer. Preliminary observations were then conducted on location, and finally a miniature photo album was constructed for each class. Initially these photo albums were carried by the primary observer during recording sessions. A primary observer gathered all data and was periodically joined by a secondary observer for reliability checks. In this case the two observers simultaneously gathered data, but were situated so as not to see the other's data sheet. Each observer had a clipboard and a rating sheet. The primary observer had a stop watch and cued the second observer as to who to observe and when to begin and terminate the recording period. During this study, reliability checks were taken on 15 occasions and averaged slightly above 97% agreement. The range of interobserver agreement extended from 92% to 100%.

Group observations (continuous scans) After posttest measures had been taken via the cyclical 10-sec individual observation interval method, a second set of two blind observers, previously trained and checked for reliability, observed each of the experimental and control groups on three occasions. Their observations were conducted during 30–40-min unstructured free-time periods in the kindergarten classroom. The observers used a continuous observation procedure in which one observer continuously scanned each half of the kindergarten classroom in a slow and methodical manner for any incidents of cooperative behavior. If a cooperative act was observed, the specific act, along with the number of children who cooperated in the act, was recorded. For example, if six children helped lift a bench, then "Lifting bench—6 children" was noted.

Results

Individual observations (10-sec intervals)

Baseline measures taken before beginning the games program indicated that the children in experimental and control groups were essentially the same with respect to the percentage of cooperative behavior observed during free activity time in the kindergarten classroom (see Table 1 and Figure 4). The percentage of individual 10-sec observation intervals in which children were observed engaging in cooperative behavior during baseline procedures was 10.5% for the combined co-op games group and 10.2% for the combined control groups. After 18 weeks of treatment, the combined co-op games groups had increased their percentage of observable cooperative behavior from 10.5% to 15.5%. This is a direct increase of 5%, representing a 48% proportional increase over the percentage of observable cooperative behavior at baseline. The combined control groups increased their percentage of observable cooperative behavior from 10.2% at baseline to 11.3% in the posttest. This is a direct increase of 1.1%, which represents an 11% proportional increase over baseline.

Group observations (continuous scans)

Continuous observation scans in the kindergarten classroom revealed that after 18 weeks of treatment, the co-op games groups engaged in an average of

TABLE 1 Pre- and postprogram observational measures during free time in kindergarten classroom (individual 10-sec observation intervals)

	Pretest baseline		Posttest (after 18 weeks)	
Group	No. observations[a]	Cooperation (%)[b]	No. observations	Cooperation (%)
Co-op I	162	11.1	215	14.8
Control I	177	10.3	170	12.3
Co-op II[c]	131	9.9	185	16.2
Control II	242	10.2	200	10.5
Co-ops I & II	293	10.5	400	15.5
Controls I & II	419	10.2	370	11.3

[a]Total number of individual 10-sec observation intervals.
[b]Percentage of individual 10-sec observation intervals where cooperative behavior was observed.
[c]Co-op II and Control II had the same classroom teacher.

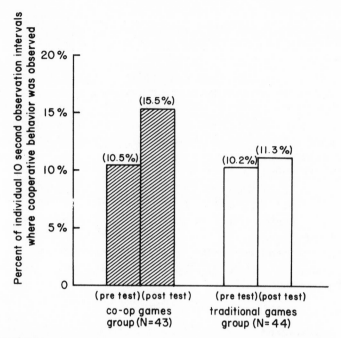

FIGURE 4   Pre- and postobservational measures of cooperative behavior during free time in kindergarten classroom (individual observers—time sampled).

43 observable incidents of individuals cooperating per hour; whereas, control groups engaged in an average of 29 observable incidents per hour (Table 2). Combined co-op games groups averaged 71 incidences of children cooperating over 100 min of observation. Combined control groups averaged 48.5 incidences of children cooperating over 100 min of observation (Figure 5). In short, there were 46% more incidences of children engaging in cooperative behavior observed in the co-op games classes when compared with the traditional games classes. It is clear that on different days, with different blind observers, using different observation techniques, the same trend emerged.

Teachers' informal observations

It is worth noting some of the qualitative comments made by the kindergarten teachers toward the end of the 18-week games program.

Sample Comments—Co-op Games Group

Several times kids say they lost something. Every time now, someone else offers to help that one find the missing article, voluntarily. Does this old heart good!

TABLE 2 Incidence of cooperative behavior during free time in kindergarten classroom after 18-week games program (continuous observation scans)

Group	Time observed (min)	Total incidence of individual cooperation	Average incidence of individual cooperation/sec
Co-op I	110	85	1/78
Control I	100	47	1/128
Co-op II	90	57	1/95
Control II	100	50	1/120
Co-ops I & II	200	142	1/85
Controls I & II	200	97	1/124

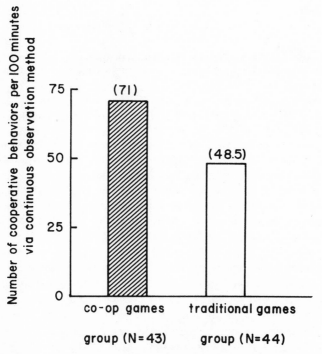

FIGURE 5 Incidence of cooperative behavior during free time in kindergarten classroom after 18-week games program (group observations—continuous scans).

Lloyd spilled a whole jar of purple paint on the floor. Before I got there, there were four kids with sponges, etc., to help him. Amazing!

The most cooperation visible is at clean up time. It constantly amazes me how the majority (all but three or four) team up and help each other. *There is now no discrimination as to whether the mess is theirs or made by someone else.*

These children have learned so well to work in a group that sometimes a job that could be done by one person quickly turns into a 5-minute group effort.

By the end of the co-op games program, peer group sanction for cooperative and helpful behavior seemed to have taken firm hold in co-op games groups. Children who did not help were often encouraged to do so or were told about it in clear terms by their peers and in some cases were not allowed to join in at a play center unless they agreed to help and do their share (see Orlick, 1977).

Although in this particular study we did no systematic pre- and postmeasures in the gym, the teachers' comments indicated that differences between groups were quite evident within this environment, even after 8 weeks of games. This is exemplified by the following comment:

Today was interesting, it was our first day in the gym since Phase I of the games program finished. I had all the equipment out in five separate centers: (1) large climbing apparatus, (2) hoops, (3) bean bags, (4) tunnel, and (5) balls. They were just there for use as each child saw fit, no instructions. Each group of four or five children was at a center for 4 or 5 minutes and then on to another. This afternoon (Co-op II) the children reacted quite differently from the morning (Control II). They experimented with the bean bags carrying them head to head, etc. The hoop group connected themselves and made a long wiggly creature, and over at the ropes on the climbing equipment, children were taking turns helping another child get up and then pushing him and taking turns. There is noticeably more cooperative play in the afternoon class (Co-op II).

The perceived difference in cooperative orientation between groups was simply stated in a meeting with the kindergarten teachers towards the end of the school year. "Now my kids think of everyone being involved" (Co-op I); "Mine don't do that at all" (Control I); "There's a definite difference in my classes. . . . If there are not enough chairs (in Co-op II), the children will share"; "If there are not enough chairs (in Control II), they'll fight." At this point the teacher who had one class exposed to each of the conditions summed up the feeling of the group: "If you're really interested in better citizens, you can't have a control group." So it came to be in this school the following year—all co-op games, no control group.

Discussion

This introductory study indicates that the incidence of cooperative behavior in the kindergarten classroom can be increased through the implementation of a cooperative games program. Perhaps we can explore some possible reasons for this preliminary finding. Cooperative games provide a series of cooperative experience sessions or practice sessions under a variety of circumstances. The children's cooperative efforts generally result in some form of success or reinforcement, whether the task is moving a mountain (a large wooden structure) or becoming part of a giant caterpillar that crawls over the mountain. When children are expected to cooperate to accomplish a task and are subsequently reinforced for this cooperation, through such things as goal attainment, control over environment, feelings of acceptance, expressions of affection, positive social feedback, satisfaction with self, others, and environment, then we might legitimately expect to find increases in cooperative behavior, at least within similar environments. The diversity of cooperative demands and cooperative responses called for in the co-op games program (including cognitive involvement), along with the varied success experiences, may have increased children's overall repertoire of cooperation behavior that could be drawn on in different settings as well. The possibility that some generalization or internalization of the overall value of cooperation occurred merits consideration. Yet, this must be weighed against possible contingency transfers. The fact that there was an increase in cooperative behavior during unstructured free time in the kindergarten classroom may indicate that there was some transfer in contingencies of reinforcement, once children had been thoroughly seasoned within a cooperation contingent environment. For example, once logical consequences within the games environment had helped children learn to reinforce one another for cooperative behavior, then future expectations and resultant consequences from peers could have set in motion, and maintained, contingencies for new codes of acceptable behavior. Thus, peers would have become both models and mediators of a new response paradigm.

It is also possible that during Phase II of the study (latter 10 weeks), the teachers either transferred reinforcement contingencies from the gym to the classroom or that the children expected them to do so. Consequently, if a child was praised by his teacher for sharing or helping move equipment in the gym, it is conceivable that he would expect a similar kind of reaction or reinforcement from his teacher (or from others) for similar kinds of behaviors elsewhere. This expectation itself could serve to initiate a behavior whether or not the expected reinforcement became a reality. Once the behavior has been emitted, any form of positive consequences may serve to maintain it. Such expectations could be operational, even where the same classroom teacher has an experimental and control group in the gym. Finally, it is possible that the transition from cooperative games in the gym to cooperation in the kindergarten classroom is not as dramatic as it may initially appear, because a great deal of play occurs in both settings, particularly during free-time periods.

It is interesting to note that 8 weeks into the program, when some preliminary behavior observations were taken via 10-sec observation intervals, the co-op games groups did not emerge as more cooperative during free time in the classroom. The classroom teachers, however, had begun to report qualitative changes and cited critical incidents of increased cooperative behavior among the co-op games children. A few examples are listed below.

A group of eight!! children cleaning the paint center. They had organized themselves into groups—wet wipers and dry wipers and completed the task. Never have seen this before.

Fran comments of the "good games." She hasn't hit anyone for one week now. This was a daily occurrence. No one has tattled on any of her behaviors for eight school days.

Playing in the sand box. Bobby says to Marc—"Don't grab all the toys, we've got to share." They worked out the problem verbally!! Bobby has never been the verbal type—a good punch has generally been his solution.

When we have story time the children sit in a much smaller group (closer together). There appears to me much less, if any, complaining now about someone bothering another.

The fact that our outside blind observers did not find evidence of these "changes" prompts contemplation of several interesting possibilities:

1. The changes cited by the teachers may have been more of a reflection of their expectations and selective perception of reality than of reality itself.
2. The changes the teachers were observing may not have been strong enough or consistent enough to be picked up by outside observers during individual 10-sec observation intervals.
3. The sensitivity of outside behavior assessors and the behavioral assessments (e.g., the definitions of cooperation and the methods of observation) may not have been refined enough to pick up changes that were in fact occurring.
4. The observation period for outside observers may not have been of a long enough duration to get an adequate sampling of reality.

At that point in time, based on T. D. Orlick's own biased observations and close consultation with the kindergarten teachers who were with the children all day, every day, it was believed that cooperative changes were occurring in the co-op games groups that were not occurring in the control groups. As a result of behavioral scans by Orlick, many borderline cases of cooperative behavior were noted in the co-op games group that were not accepted as meeting the co-op criteria, due to previous instructions to observers (i.e., "if you are uncertain or it is borderline, score it as negative"). These borderline cases were consequently scored the same as clearly noncooperative acts observed in traditional games groups. It appears that the co-op games groups were "pulled over" to this cooperative borderline during Phase II (latter 10 weeks) of the study. It should be noted, however, that during this phase of the study, the teachers, who were now familiar with the games, took over the direction of the games for their own classes; and the games time per week was doubled for the following 10 weeks.

Suggestions for Future Studies

The previous discussion indicates the importance of giving a cooperative games program (or any program aimed at behavior change) enough time to work. It also shows the importance of exploring observational options that provide for a more accurate sampling of reality. The following discussion is addressed to some of these options.

Observational options

When following the individual 10-sec interval observation procedure, the more frequently the observer can go through the list of participants, the closer to reality the picture is likely to be for a particular person and for the group. Nevertheless, observers are likely to underestimate the incidence of a low-frequency behavior, such as cooperation in the classroom. An observer may see several cooperative acts occurring, but records only the one engaged in by the particular child under observation for the isolated 10-sec period. It is also sometimes difficult to assess the intent of an act, because an observer may come in and leave in the middle of an activity. In addition, the observer must be able to quickly identify all participants to use this method efficiently, which should be considered by researchers contemplating its use.

By using continuous observation procedures, observers are less likely to underestimate the incidence of low-frequency behaviors like cooperation in the classroom, particularly if different observers are responsible for different sections of the room. A distinct advantage of this method is that observers record any and all cooperative acts seen. In addition, for continuous observation, the ability to identify each child would be necessary only if data were wanted on individuals as well as groups. Consequently, if one opts to do group observations only, it is much less time consuming to train observers. One problem encountered with this method is that an observer would sometimes like to use more time to understand one scene, and yet to do so may require ignoring other scenes.

With additional observation time per child, with more observers using a continuous observation method, or with a permanent visual recording of children's behavior, we would likely have a better picture of reality. In effect, this would allow us to more dramatically demonstrate differences that do in fact exist and to better explore the contingencies associated with competitive and cooperative behavioral responses. How might we operationalize these possibilities?

We could attempt to set up several videotape recorders in different parts of the room and later play them back, focusing on one child at a time. Unfortunately this is not a practical option in the real world (the community schools) within which we work. Even if the cost were not prohibitive, problems such as setting up unobtrusive cameras in different classrooms and in different schools and securing clearance from administrators to do so would be prohibitive. This may be a valid option for campus schools designed for research.

We could attempt to increase the number of observers in the kindergarten classroom. For example, we might have one observer responsible for each play center. However, although the children are accustomed to having outside adults (in the form of parent volunteers) in their kindergarten rooms, more than two or three outside observers tends to become overwhelming.

We could try to restrict a few children at a time to a particular play area (e.g., sand box, blocks center) for observational purposes. This might be a legitimate option—it ensures that the same number of children always have exactly the same play material for the observation time. However, it may restrict natural free play and the element of choice and may pose some confounding motivational problems. The child may simply not want to be there and may in fact decide not to stay, which alters the play setting considerably.

Another observational option that should be given serious consideration is to select a representative number of children from each group (e.g., 5 boys and 5 girls from each classroom) and to use all available observation time to focus only on these children. Potential participants could be equated by sex and then randomly selected, or could be equated by preliminary observations. Each child selected for observation purposes could be continuously observed on an individual basis for a more substantial period of time, as was the case in the present study. For example, one might devote a minimum of 5–10 min per child on five occasions for baseline and for postprogram observations. This would increase accuracy with respect to the frequency of cooperative behaviors engaged in by each child before and after the program. Because each child would have a pre- and postprogram frequency score, this procedure would also better lend itself to appropriate statistical analysis. It is also likely that the quality of cooperative acts could be more easily detected by this individual-focused procedure.

In an attempt to account for some of the qualitative differences that may better reflect cooperative impact, we are now attempting to distinguish helping behavior as a qualitative subcategory of cooperative behavior. To meet the criterion for acceptance as a helping behavior, the act must have a helping orientation or helping quality. A person must be helping (or trying to help) another achieve a goal, or people must be helping (or trying to help) one another achieve a common goal. The intent of the act as well as the act itself is considered. Behavioral events, such as taking turns, holding hands, and linking arms, certainly meet our criteria for cooperation; but they do not necessarily meet the criterion for helping behavior. Only behaviors clearly aimed at helping another are accepted as meeting this criterion. Behaviors either that do not have a helping component or that clearly show lack of helpful intent do not meet the criterion. For example, if one child hands another child an unwanted toy strictly as a diversion so he can keep the desired toy himself, it does not meet the criterion of helpful behavior. By keeping in the forefront, we have been able to attain over 90% agreement between different observers who were assessing kindergarten children's "helping behavior." It is therefore feasible for observers to assess the overall incidence of cooperative behavior, as defined earlier, and to note next to each incident whether the cooperative act had a helping component.

Other methods and measures

In addition to considering some of the previously mentioned observational options, the following points might be considered for future studies. Pre- and postprogram measures could be taken during free-play and clean-up time in the gym, on the playground, when getting ready (dressing) for recess, during recess, when moving to and from other rooms, as well as during free time and tidy-up time in the classroom. In this case, the play centers, equipment, and playmates available should be the same for all children for pre- and post-measures. Some standardized situations could also be set up during pre- and postprogram observations to provide common occasions "to help or not to help." For example, one could spill a container of paint at the painting center; provide enough chairs, enough balls, or enough cookies for only half the children in the class; and then simply see how the children respond. One could also provide two children with a single toy or allow one child the option to have a toy removed from another child by the experimenter. We could also draw on some standardized experimental table games, such as those devised by Madsen and his colleagues (e.g., marble pull games, cooperation board), to assess children's capacity and willingness to respond in a cooperative manner (Kagan & Madsen, 1971; Nelson & Kagan, 1972). Pre- and postprogram measures could be taken via these procedures and instruments.

It would also be interesting to focus on teacher behavior to assess changes in reinforcement contingencies before, during, and after the program; to assess parents' and siblings' perceptions of children's possible cooperative changes in the home; to do observations in an environment other than the school, such as the home or community playground; to interview children to assess their feelings about the overall value of cooperation or sharing; and to ask them about how they might solve some hypothetical problems.

Some other extremely important but untapped areas of potential impact with respect to cooperative games are their effect on: (a) self-esteem, self-acceptance or liking of self, both in and out of games; (b) liking for each other during the games, general liking for classmates outside the games, and overall liking for other people; and (c) overall liking for games and physical activity as well as the extent to which participation occurs in the future. Pre- and postprogram measures along with follow-up measures could be taken in each area.

CONCLUDING COMMENTS

The concept underlying the cooperative kindergames designed for use in this study can easily be replicated, adapted, or expanded for use in other settings. Consequently, whether one is interested in facilitating cooperative social interaction in games, in classrooms, in work, or in politics, or whether one is interested in researching potential effects of specific programs, the co-op games approach can be of value. Co-op games have the potential to serve as a facilitative tool for normal children, as a preventative tool for potential problems, and as a treatment tool for "problem" children. The games and, perhaps more important, the concept behind the games can be adapted for different ages and populations. We are currently working on a co-op games program for preschoolers (ages 3 and 4) and are experiencing some initial success with our field testing. These youngsters are capable of cooperating surprisingly well. Many of their games can be played in the classroom, in the gym, in the community, or even in the home. It might be worthwhile to have preschoolers or kindergarten children take home a few co-op games to teach to their families. We could also consider directing some of our attention to the other end of the age continuum. Clearly, to increase the overall potential for cooperative learning and living, specific strategies can be employed with different groups and in a variety of behavior settings (Orlick, 1977).

In conclusion, it is hoped that the procedures, preliminary findings, and suggestions outlined in this chapter will provide a beginning for those interested in contributing to the systematic assessment of cooperation and, more specifically, cooperative games. It is through people attempting these kinds of assessments that we will improve our methods of evaluation, better understand the impact of games, and devise more impactful cooperative games.

REFERENCES

Hall, R. V. *Managing behavior 1: Behavior modification: The measurement of behavior.* Lawrence, Kan.: H. & H. Enterprises, 1974. (a)

Hall, R. V. *Managing behavior 3: Behavior modification: Applications in school and home.* Lawrence, Kan.: H. & H. Enterprises, 1974. (b)

Kagan, S., & Madsen, M. C. Cooperation and competition of Mexican, Mexican-American and Anglo-American children of two ages under four instructional sets. *Developmental Psychology,* 1971, *5,* 32–39.

Nelson, L. L., & Kagan, S. Competition and the star-spangled scramble. *Psychology Today,* 1972, *6,* 53–56, 91.

Orlick, T. D. The sports environment: A capacity to enhance—a capacity to destroy. In B. S. Rushall (Ed.), *The status of psychomotor learning and sport psychology research.* Dartmouth, Nova Scotia: Sport Science Associates, 1975.

Orlick, T. D. Games of acceptance and psycho-social adjustment. In T. T. Craig (Ed.), *The humanistic and mental health aspects of sports, exercise and recreation.* Chicago: American Medical Association, 1976.

Orlick, T. *Winning through cooperation—Competitive insanity: Cooperative alternatives.* Washington, D.C.: Hawkins & Associates, 1977.

Orlick, T. *The cooperative sports and games book.* New York: Pantheon, in press.

Orlick, T. D., Partington, J. T., Scott, H. A., & Glassford, R. G. The development of the skimetric differential: A childranistic approach. In C. Bard, M. Fleury, & J. Salmela (Eds.), *Mouvement 7.* Quebec: Association des Professionels de Activite Physique de Quebec, 1975.

IV

SPORT AND THE HANDICAPPED CHILD

ADULT REACTIONS TO
THE SPECIAL OLYMPICS

G. Lawrence Rarick

The Special Olympics Program, since its inception in 1968, has mushroomed rapidly; today it is touching vast numbers of retarded and handicapped children in every state of the union and in several foreign countries. Although the growth of the Special Olympics Program has been remarkably rapid, only limited attention has been given to examining the impact the program has had on the participants or on physical activity and recreational programs in local communities. The statewide questionnaire study in Michigan by Brawer (1969) and the national survey by Cratty (1972) provided considerable data on the reactions of parents and coaches to the Olympics Program in these areas. The evidence from these studies indicated that the participants reacted favorably to the program, implying that there was little reason to believe that participation in the competitive activities of the program led to any undesirable physical or psychological effects. These studies, however, were not designed to yield information on the effects of the Special Olympics on the daily physical activity patterns of the children or on what impact the Olympics might have had on physical activity programs for these children.

The present investigation was designed with four purposes in mind—to determine (1) how the parents of the participants viewed the Special Olympics in respect to its effect on the well being and behavior of their own children; (2) the reaction of teachers who have been associated with the Special Olympics, particularly with respect to the possible impact the program has had on the children in their classes who were participants; (3) the

This investigation was funded by the Joseph P. Kennedy, Jr. Foundation.

reactions of Special Olympics coaches to the program and their impressions of the effects of participation on the children they have coached; and (4) the views of school administrators and civic leaders regarding the impact of the Special Olympics on physical education and recreation programs, facilities, and leadership at the community level.

METHOD

It was decided at the outset to use the interview technique with a limited sample rather than to use questionnaires on a broad front. Though the interview method has recognized logistical limitations, it provides greater flexibility and greater opportunity for probing in depth and for cross-checking replies than can be achieved through questionnaires (Maccoby & Maccoby, 1954). In view of the expense and the logistical problems involved in a nationwide interview study, it was decided to limit the investigation to two heavily populated localities, the metropolitan areas of San Diego, California, and Seattle, Washington.

Sample

The sample of children whose parents, teachers, and coaches were to be interviewed was taken from the Special Olympics files in the San Diego and Seattle areas. In San Diego these files were held by the Association for Retarded Children; in Seattle, by the King County Recreation Department. The files provided data on participants in the Special Olympics at the local, state, regional, and national levels for the period 1968-1970.

No attempt was made to draw a random sample of children whose parents, teachers, and coaches were to be interviewed. Rather, a list of the names of children who had participated in the local and state Special Olympics during 1968-1970 was provided from which the sample was drawn. In drawing the samples in both the San Diego and Seattle areas, an attempt was made to obtain a diversified group, which included children of both sexes and of varying ages who had experienced varying degrees of success in the Special Olympics. The location and number of children in each locality in the San Diego and Seattle samples are shown in Figures 1 and 2, respectively.

A total of 270 interviews were conducted in the San Diego and Seattle areas. A breakdown of the number of interviews in each locality by type of person interviewed is given in Table 1. By far the largest number of interviews was conducted with the parents or guardians of the children, a total of 142. Because more than one child was taught or coached by a single person, the number of teachers and coaches interviewed was substantially less than the number of parents interviewed. Other than the civic leaders who were interviewed, all persons interviewed had immediate contact with the sample of children.

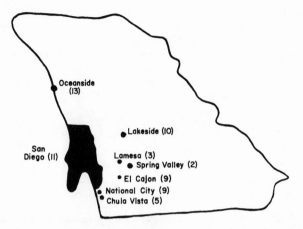

FIGURE 1 Geographical distribution of the sample of children in San Diego County whose parents, teachers, and coaches were interviewed (total sample = 62).

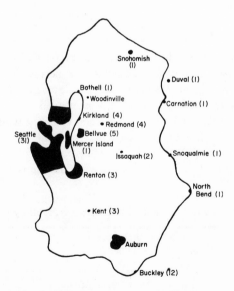

FIGURE 2 Geographical distribution of the sample of children in the Seattle area whose parents, teachers, and coaches were interviewed (total sample = 80). Not included in the illustration, 9 children from Vancouver, Washington.

TABLE 1 Sample sizes in the Seattle and San Diego areas

Interview category	Seattle	San Diego
Parent	80	62
Teacher	37	27
Coach	7	13
School principal	6	0
Civic leader	24	14
Total	154	116

The distribution of the sample of children by sex whose parents, teachers, and coaches were interviewed is given in Table 2. Slightly more boys than girls were included in the sample, the difference corresponding roughly to the relative sex difference in numbers of participants in the Olympics in these areas.

Not all children in the sample were under the immediate care of parents. The distribution of the sample according to parental-guardian relationships is shown in Table 3. By far the most were home-reared children, although a sizeable number were institutionalized.

Interview Instrument

Since four categories of adults were to be interviewed—parents, teachers, coaches, and principals and civic leaders—it was necessary to develop four interview instruments. The first step in the development of the instruments was to decide exactly what information was needed from each category, making reasonably certain that persons in each category would have the information desired or well-founded judgments regarding participants and the Special Olympics Program. The information that was sought related to how adults in each of the four categories viewed the impact of the Special

TABLE 2 Categorization of Seattle and San Diego samples by sex

Metropolitan area	Male	Female	Total no. in sample
Seattle	56	24	80
San Diego	31	31	62

Note. This constitutes the total number of Special Olympics participants whose parents, teachers, and coaches were interviewed.

TABLE 3 Distribution of the sample of Special Olympics participants according to parental-guardian relationships

Parent-guardian relationship	Seattle	San Diego
Sons	38	28
Foster sons	0	2
Daughters	22	22
Foster daughters	0	3
Grandson	1	0
Wards	19	6
Orphans	0	1

Olympics on their own child or on the child under their supervision, and the effect the Special Olympics had on physical activity and recreational programs in their own community. The questions addressed to the parents, teachers, and coaches were designed to provide information on how individual children reacted to the program, changes in their own behavior and physical activity regimen, how they became involved in the program, benefits and drawbacks of the program, and observable effects on concept of self and social interactions with peers. In addition, certain questions were included to obtain data on how the adults viewed the Special Olympics and the influence the program appeared to be having on the communities' attitudes toward the retarded in respect to improving recreational and physical activity programs for these children.

Once the basic information to be sought had been assembled and placed into logical categories, the interview questions were tentatively phrased. Most of the questions were of the structured type, although some were open ended. The University of California Survey Research Center gave valuable assistance in the final development of the instrument. After the instruments were designed, they were administered on a trail basis in the East Bay Area of San Francisco. The formulation, initial testing, and revisions of the instruments required a period of approximately 4 months. The instruments then underwent a final revision before they were used in the San Diego metropolitan area. Minor changes were made in the interview instrument following its use in San Diego.

Interviewing Procedures

The interviews were scheduled in advance by the project assistant and were conducted by a team of five trained interviewers. Interviewing was done in the homes of the parents, at the schools of the teachers, and at locations of convenience for the coaches and civic leaders. Factual information was sought, and in the open-ended responses the person being interviewed was encouraged to give reactions without being interrupted with "leading questions."

RESULTS

The results of the investigation are presented for the most part in table form as the frequency of responses to questions posed during the interviews, with brief comments where explanations and elaboration are appropriate. The data were not appropriate for extensive statistical treatment; the number of interviews by categories of people was relatively small, and the sampling procedures did not meet the criteria needed for the use of probability statistics. It will be apparent, however, as the results are presented, that the frequency and direction of the responses are, in most cases, quite clearly defined.

Parent Interviews

Introduction to the Special Olympics Program

As shown in Table 4, the school was the primary moving force in introducing the children into the Special Olympics Program in both regions (83.75% in the Seattle area and 61% in San Diego). Recreation leaders and, to a lesser extent, community groups were responsible for interesting some of the children.

Training Practices

The data from the parental interviews showed that the majority of participants had been involved in some form of training before the Special Olympics, whereas less than half engaged in post-Olympic training (Table 5).

TABLE 4 Method of introduction to the Special Olympics Program

Method of introduction	Seattle (N)	San Diego (N)
School	67	38
Recreation leader	10	11
Parent	1	3
Parental organization	1	2
Community groups	6	4
Other	0	6
Don't know	1	0

Note. Some respondents indicated that more than one of the sources introduced their children to the Special Olympics.

TABLE 5 Number of participants in training before and after the Special Olympics

Period of training	Seattle	San Diego
Before Olympics		
Yes	63	58
No	0	4
Don't know	17	0
After Olympics		
Yes	25	15
No	34	32
Don't know	21	15

A sizable number of parents in both localities did not know if their children had trained for the Olympics. It is apparent that the Special Olympics is not at this point serving as a stimulus for continuing training for the majority of children. This is not surprising, since this, unfortunatley, is the practice followed by many athletes.

In the Seattle area, data were collected on the type of training the child received. Table 6 shows that most training was voluntary practice provided by persons other than school personnel.

Most parents in both the San Diego and Seattle areas were not familiar with the Special Olympics training program and therefore could not indicate if their children did, in fact, follow the Special Olympics Program of Training (Tables 7 and 8). This is not particularly surprising, because many parents do not follow the details of the educational and recreational programs provided for their children.

TABLE 6 Breakdown of training before and after the Special Olympics, in regard to school-directed and voluntary practice outside the school program (Seattle only)

Supervision of training	Before Special Olympics	After Special Olympics
Total no. who trained	63	25
School-supervised practice only	18	2
Voluntary practice provided through sources other than school	45	23
No knowledge of training program	17	21

TABLE 7   Parental familiarity with Special Olympics Training Program

Familiarity	Seattle	San Diego
Familiar with the training program	6	12
Not familiar with the training program	74	50

TABLE 8   Parental indication of number of children who followed the Special Olympics Training Program

Indication	Seattle	San Diego
Child followed Special Olympics Program	8	12
Child did not follow program	2	14
Not known	70	36

The majority of parent interviews indicated that the training of their children was under the supervision of physical education teachers and recreation leaders (Table 9). Many participants were trained by more than one person. The parents in Seattle were asked about the competence of the coaching their child received. The majority felt that the coaching was adequate (Table 10). Only a small percentage appeared to be dissatisfied.

Parental interpretation of the aims of the Special Olympics

As shown by Table 11, the aims of the Special Olympics seem to have been well understood by the Seattle parents. Improvement of "physical

TABLE 9   Frequency distribution of coaches of participants according to occupations, as indicated by parents of children in Special Olympics Program

Occupation of coach	Seattle	San Diego
Recreational leader	39	14
Physical education teacher	39	77
Teacher	4	25
Parent	6	5
Other	12	15
Not known	3	2

Note. Several children received coaching advice from more than one source.

TABLE 10   Parental opinion of the adequacy of the coaching

Adequacy of coaching	Seattle
Felt the coaching was adequate	64
Felt the coaching was inadequate	8
No opinion	8

fitness" and "concept of self" received the majority of the high ratings (1-2). "Social interaction" was also ranked high. "Community awareness" received many more low ratings (4-5), as did the aim of improving the "parent-child relationship." It is clear that parents sense that the aim of the Special Olympics is to bring about worthwhile changes in the participants.

Parental reaction to the Special Olympics

The interviewed parents in both San Diego County and the Seattle area were, with few exceptions, favorably impressed with the Special Olympics (Table 12). When asked to express their reactions to the Olympics, many stated that it was one of the finest opportunities their child had ever experienced (Table 13). Only 2 of the 142 parents reacted unfavorably, and only 3 were indifferent (no opinion). There were, however, a few adverse comments from a few parents. For example, one parent recounted that at one meet some of the children were observed to be emotionally upset, which in this parent's view was due to faulty preparation. Another commented that for one child success in the program had resulted in the development of an abnormally conceited attitude. Several instances of mildly unfortunate consequences were reported, but the responses of the parents to the program were almost universally enthusiastic.

Physical activity patterns of participants before and after
Olympic participation

One of the major purposes of the Special Olympics Program is to motivate children to become more active in physical activities and to increase their range of recreational pursuits. The parental interviews were designed to obtain information on how the children used their free time before and after participation in the Special Olympics, whether changes did occur in personal recreational pursuits, and whether such changes occurred individually or involved greater parental participation. Frequency of parent responses to questions bearing on these points is summarized in Tables 14, 15, and 16. Insofar as parents are able to make valid judgments on these matters, it is apparent that the majority of the children in both San Diego and Seattle spent their free time chiefly in active outdoor activities before becoming involved in the Special Olympics; and this involvement seemed to have no marked effect in altering their recreational pursuits. In both localities, however, approximately 20%-25% of

TABLE 11 Aims of the Special Olympics as specified by the parent of participant

Aim	No. of 1s	No. of 2s	No. of 3s	No. of 4s	No. of 5s	No response	Don't know	No. of 4–5s[a]
Physical fitness	49	12	13	2	2	2	0	1
Concept of self	35	24	16	3	0	2	0	1
Social interaction	30	27	15	4	1	3	0	1
Community awareness	22	20	6	18	10	4	0	1
Parental Effect[b]	31	13	5	8	18	6	2	4

Note. This table records the responses to a question on the Seattle Questionnaire only. Parents were asked to rate the aims, in accordance with their own priorities, on a scale of importance, with 1 as the high, or grade of most importance; and 5 as the low, or grade of least importance.

[a] Number of 4–5s (this indicates the number of responses split between a rating of 4 and a rating of 5).

[b] This category refers to some improvement in the parent-child relationship, such as increased knowledge of child's capabilities, increased involvement with child, and pride in the child.

238

TABLE 12 Parental reaction to the Special Olympics

Reaction	Seattle	San Diego
Favorable	76	57
Unfavorable	0	1
Indifferent	1	2
Mixed feelings	1	0
No opinion	2	2

TABLE 13 Parental opinion of the value of the Special Olympics for their child

Opinion	Seattle	San Diego
One of the finest experiences the child has had	39	42
A good experience	34	4
Of limited value	5	9
Of no noticeable value	0	4
Harmful	0	2
No opinion	2	1

TABLE 14 Child's use of free time before participation in the Special Olympics

Type of activity	Seattle	San Diego
Passive Indoor	22	13
Passive Outdoor	4	11
Active Indoor	8	11
Active Outdoor	52	33
Not sure	3	0

TABLE 15 Changes in child's recreational pursuits after participation in Special Olympics

Change in participation	Seattle	San Diego
Definite change (toward greater participation)	13	13
No change	64	47
Don't know	2	1
Not sure (Yes and No)	1	0
No response	0	1

TABLE 16   Changes in the number of parent-child activities, after participation in the Special Olympics

Parent-child activities	Seattle	San Diego
Increase in the number of activities participated in jointly by parent and child	14	9
No change from previous parental-child activity involvement	65	52
No response	1	1

the parents indicated that there was a definite change toward greater participation following involvement in the Olympics.

In regard to increased parental-child participation in recreational activities following the Special Olympics, the data show that most parents could see little, if any, change. Approximately 20% from each metropolitan area indicated that the recreational involvement with their children increased subsequent to the child's participation in the program. The nature of this involvement varied from family to family, but in many instances it was related to the Olympic activities.

Teacher Interviews

A total of 64 special education teachers were interviewed, 37 from the Seattle area and 27 from San Diego County. Table 17 shows that most of the teachers became involved in the program because it was something that was of particular interest to them. Only 8 of the 64 saw it as a job to be done, and none indicated that they became involved because of monetary considerations.

The teachers interviewed had a wide range of teaching experience, as much as 38 years and as little as 1 year (Table 18). Similarly, the range of experience in teaching retarded children was great, 1–25 years. The range in

TABLE 17   Teachers' reasons for entering special education area

Reason	Seattle (no. of teachers)	San Diego (no. of teachers)
Interest	25	23
Job to be done	5	3
Advancement	0	2
Pay	0	0
Other	14	0

Note. More than one reason given by some of the teachers.

TABLE 18   Range of teachers' experience and number of children handled by a single teacher

Experience and composition of classes	Seattle	San Diego
Number of years as a teacher	1–38	1–26
Number of years teaching at present school	1–21	1–24
Number of years handling special classes for the mentally retarded:		
Educable mentally retarded	1–25	1–24
Trainable mentally retarded	1–25	1–9
Composition of classes:		
Number of educables taught	3–100	11–20
Number of trainables taught	4–80	6–53

Note. Some teachers taught under departmental systems; hence, they handled many children each day.

numbers of educable and trainable children taught by individual teachers was also large, varying from 3 to 100. The large number of children taught by some teachers can be attributed to departmentalization in the upper grades.

The nature of the teachers' involvement in the Special Olympics is indicated in Table 19. Of the 37 teachers interviewed in the Seattle area, 17 were not involved in the Special Olympics. All 22 of the San Diego teachers were involved. The greatest number served as coaches, with a good many acting as chaperones and as organizers. Those who were involved devoted a considerable amount of time and energy to the program (Table 20). During the active season, the teacher averaged 1½ to 2 hr each practice day, with the number of practice days per week averaging three to five over a period of 2–4 months. In terms of attendance at the Olympics proper, 30 of the Seattle teachers and 16 of the San Diego teachers attended at least once (Table 21).

TABLE 19   Nature of teachers' involvement in the Special Olympics

Nature of involvement	Seattle	San Diego
Coach	10	14
Official	3	2
Organizer	2	5
Chaperone	9	3
Other	7	1

Note. Some involved in more than one capacity.

TABLE 20 Time teachers spent in preparation for the Special Olympics

Time in preparation	Seattle		San Diego	
	Range	Average	Range	Average
Hours per day				
1968	15 min–3 hr	2 hr		
1969	15 min–3 hr	1 hr 15 min		
1970	15 min–3 hr	1 hr 30 min	15 min–5 hr	2 hr
1971	1–3 hr	1 hr 30 min		
Days per week				
1968	1–5	2		
1969	1–5	3		
1970	1–5	3	5–7	5
1971	1–5	3		
Number of months				
1968	1–3	2		
1969	1–5	3		
1970	1–6	4	1–9	4
1971	1–6	4		

Note. This table records estimates of time spent on the Special Olympics for only those teachers who had some active involvement in the program. Refer to Table 18 for the number of individuals and their years of involvement.

Only a few, however, were represented at the state and regional meets, and none at a national meet.

Responses of the Coaches

A total of 20 coaches, 13 in the San Diego area and 7 in the Seattle area, were interviewed. These were the coaches of the 142 children in San Diego

TABLE 21 Teacher attendance at Special Olympics

Attendance at Olympics	Seattle	San Diego
Attended at least once	30	16
Level of attendance		
Local	30	
State	1	
Regional	2	
National	0	
Did not attend	7	11

and Seattle whose parents and teachers were interviewed. Some of the teachers interviewed also served as coaches, but they were interviewed as teachers, not as coaches. When the teacher served as a coach, this was often in an incidental role.

The majority of coaches had prior coaching experience before becoming involved in the Special Olympics (Table 22). The number of years of previous coaching experience ranged from 1½ to 25 years. Six of the seven in the seattle area had previous coaching experience, as compared with 8 of the 13 in San Diego County. The reasons for becoming involved varied; approximately half considered it as a part of their job, and half became involved because of their interest in working with these children (Table 23). The time given by the coaches showed a modal value ranging between 6 and 15 hours per week over a period of 3–10 weeks.

An important part of preparing participants for athletic competition is regularity of practice. As shown in Table 24, 15 of the 20 coaches in the two areas indicated they held regularly scheduled practice sessions during the season, but only 3 followed a regular practice schedule during the off-season. Of those who held regular off-season practice sessions, the frequency of practice per week ranged from once to five times weekly, the average duration of each session being approximately 1 hour.

A special training guide has been prepared and is available for those responsible for training children in the Special Olympics. Of the coaches queried about the manual, 5 of the 7 in Seattle stated they were familiar with it, but only 2 of the group used it as a guide, 3 used it occasionally, and 2 did not follow it at all. In San Diego, 4 of the 13 followed the manual; 8 did not.

TABLE 22 Experience in coaching other than the Special Olympics

Previous coaching experience	Seattle (no. of coaches)	San Diego (no. of coaches)
Prior coaching experience	6	8
No prior coaching experience	1	4
No response	0	1

TABLE 23 Reasons for coaches' involvement in the Special Olympics

Reasons	Seattle (no. of coaches)	San Diego (no. of coaches)
Interested	2	9
Part of job	4	4
No response	1	0

TABLE 24 Practice sessions for the Special Olympics, in-season and off-season, as stated by the coaches

Regularly held practice sessions	Seattle (no. of responses)	San Diego (no. of responses)
In-season		
Yes	4	11
No	3	2
Off-season		
Yes	0	3
No	6	10
No response	1	

Reactions of Principals

Six principals in the Seattle area were interviewed. Five of the six had many years of experience as a teacher and the range of experience as an administrator in schools attended by retarded children ranged from 2 to 17 years. Only one of the six had been closely involved with the Olympics over a period of years, the involvement of the other five being primarily as a spectator. The interviews, however, clearly indicated that the principals were knowledgeable about the Special Olympics Program in their school and sensed the reactions of the participants, teachers, and parents to the program.

The six principals were asked to express freely their reactions to the Special Olympics in terms of its impact on the participants in their schools. Four of the six were enthusiastic; one gave a qualified answer, and one was not supportive of the program. Three of the six felt that the Special Olympics Program had not had much of an impact on physical activity programs in their school or in their community; in fact, one principal was antagonistic. Two of the six viewed the program as a positive influence. Obviously, the sample of principals is too small to show any definite trends, but in view of the split in the opinions expressed here, there is reason to doubt that the program is having the positive impact on school programs that it is designed to have.

Interviews with Civic Leaders

A total of 38 interviews was held with civic leaders and citizens in the San Diego and Seattle areas—14 in San Diego and 24 in Seattle. Those interviewed had a wide range and diversity of occupations; hence, the comments in the aggregate from these two groups served as a reasonably good barometer of the knowledge and the attitudes of a segment of the public (most of whom have some involvement in the program) regarding the Special Olympics. Most of the persons had lived in their respective communities for many years, the range falling between 2 and 56 years in Seattle and between 3 and 51 years in San Diego.

In summarizing results of these interviews, there appeared to be a consensus that the Special Olympics has awakened communities to act in improving physical activity programs for the retarded. The civic leaders recognize that the key to the success of the Special Olympics Program rests with the schools and largely with school personnel; if the program is to be successful, it must be based on a joint school-community effort. The communication with the school personnel is unfortunately not always good, so that many teachers are not aware of the purposes and the program of the Special Olympics.

SUMMARY AND CONCLUSIONS

The following summarizes the major findings of the study:

1. The schools constitute the primary medium of introducing children to the Special Olympics. Over 70% of the children in the two metropolitan areas were introduced through the schools.
2. The parents most frequently mentioned physical fitness as their concept of the aims of the Special Olympics, followed closely by "improved concept of self," opportunity for social interaction, community awareness, and last, as a "morale booster" for them, the parents. The teachers and coaches held similar views, although they saw the "effect on the parents" and "increased community awareness" as less significant than the other three.
3. The parents, teachers, and coaches were in general agreement on the effects of the Olympics experience on the participants. The most frequently mentioned were (a) pride in competition, (b) increased interest in physical activities, (c) improved peer acceptance, (d) improved attitude toward school work, and (e) a negative effect, feeling of frustration.
4. The parents and coaches listed certain undesirable features of the Special Olympics: (a) overemphasis by some on winning, with traumatic effects on the loser, (b) inappropriate grouping for competition, (c) program and meets being too long (inefficient administration), (d) inadequate safety precautions, and (e) parental apathy.
5. The majority (slightly more than half) of the parents, teachers, and coaches were of the opinion that the Special Olympics had brought about improvements in the school physical education program. However, the majority saw little change in community recreation programs for the retarded.
6. The majority of the coaches interviewed (14 of the 20) were experienced

coaches. About half were involved in the Olympics as part of their job, and half as interested volunteers. In general, the parents of the participants and the teachers expressed satisfaction with the coaching.

7. The findings indicate that the Special Olympics training program need to be strengthened. A training manual is available, but the majority of parents and teachers are not acquainted with it. Though many of the coaches were acquainted with the training instructions, only 6 of the 20 indicated that they followed it.

8. The time devoted by the coaches in supervising practice sessions ranged from 6 to 15 hr each week over a period of 3-10 weeks. Fifteen of the 20 coaches held regular practices during the season; only 3 held regular off-season practice.

9. Of the six school principals interviewed in Seattle (none were interviewed in San Diego County) three felt the Olympics had had no noticeable impact on physical education programs, whereas two had observed positive effects in their schools and communities. As a group, the principals were less enthusiastic about the Olympics than were parents, teachers, or coaches.

10. The civic leaders, in general, were of the opinion that the Special Olympics had done much to awaken communities to act in improving physical activity programs for the retarded, emphasizing that the success of the Special Olympics rested on a joint school-community effort.

In conclusion, it is apparent that a majority of the parents, teachers, coaches, and civic leaders interviewed in the two metropolitan areas reacted favorably to the Special Olympics Program. The principals were inclined to be less enthusiastic.

The findings point out rather conclusively that a major weakness in the Special Olympics lies in the inadequate training of the participants. Clearly, more effort needs to be expended in improving the training programs. This means a greater involvement of trained personnel. The schools have both the personnel and the facilities to accomplish this, but as yet these resources have been only partially tapped.

Although the findings of the study are subjective and in some instances colored by personal biases, they show rather clearly how persons intimately involved with the participants feel about this program. One might ask who knows better the impact of programs on children than the parents and others who observe them daily? Obviously, it would be advantageous to have objective data, such as test scores and performance records, for comparative purposes. This is a long, involved, and expensive procedure; and while it would produce data of a different kind, the findings in respect to the problem under investigation would probably not be much different than those reported here.

It should be pointed out that future studies should attempt to determine the number of children who do not participate in the Special Olympics and to learn why they are not involved. Similarly, data should be obtained on those who have not continued to participate in subsequent years and find out why this occurred. This would provide clues for meeting the needs of the less enthusiastic and do much to assure continued involvement.

The major thrust of the Special Olympics should be at the community level. By concentrating the effort here, community interest will be generated, enhancing the likelihood of better physical education programs in the schools and improved recreation services for retarded children and youth. Until major changes are made in school physical education programs with proper attention being given to the retarded, it is doubtful if many of these children will have the skills or the physical fitness for satisfying sports experiences.

REFERENCES

Brawer, M. J. *The Michigan Special Olympics: 1969. A research report.* Unpublished manuscript, Kalamazoo, Mich., 1969.

Cratty, B. J. *The Special Olympics: A national opinion survey.* Unpublished manuscript, Department of Kinesiology, University of California, Los Angeles, 1972.

Maccoby, E., & Maccoby, N. The interview: A tool of social science. In G. Lindzey (Ed.), *Handbook of social psychology* (Vol. 1). Cambridge, Mass.: Addison-Wesley, 1954.

SIGNIFICANT OTHERS AND SPORT SOCIALIZATION OF THE HANDICAPPED CHILD

John H. Lewko

Recent federal legislation (P.L. 94-142) mandated the involvement of handicapped children in physical education and sport activities. Although focused on formal educational routes to this end, the legislation directed attention to the need for understanding the process by which handicapped children are socialized into physical activities and sport in general. However, the social processes that influence children's sport participation have been virtually ignored (McPherson, 1976). The research that does exist has focused on boys in competitive sport programs or on children who drop out of such programs (Orlick & Botterill, 1975). Significant others are critical to the sport socialization process. When participating in sports, the child is exposed to a number of significant others, each of whom exerts an influence on the child and who is in turn affected by the child. The implications of this interaction are the primary focus of this chapter.

The rationale behind the provision of normalized or integrated sports activity for handicapped children is that sports require participants to encounter and deal with variable outcomes, the two extremes being success or failure. When handicapped children are excluded from normalized sports, they lose an opportunity to master an important survival mechanism. A crucial part of any experience of success or failure is the reactions of significant others to these outcomes. This is especially true for children and is critical to their willingness to go on participating and learning.

One could typify the interaction of a significant other and a child in a sports situation as follows:

Child wins/loses
Significant other reacts to win/loss
Significant other reacts to child
Child reacts to significant other

The reaction of the significant other depends on how he perceives and explains the child's performance. This perception will determine the feedback given to the child and what will be expected from the child in the future.

Based on these assumptions, this chapter explores the need for a new approach to the preparation or education of significant others who are primary socializing agents for the handicapped in sport. First, a conceptual framework is presented for the development of a procedure to be called Attribution Awareness Training. The framework is based on two areas of literature, teacher expectancy effects and attribution theory. Recent data are then presented as a first stage in developing this approach. The data focus on two major areas. The first is the way in which significant others explain low performance by disabled children. Attention is directed to the patterns of explanations and their relationship to future expectancy. The second major area is the nature of feedback given to handicapped children after low performance. Of particular interest are the reasons or purposes that significant others assign to various types of feedback. For the sake of clarity, the chapter does not deal with the question of sex differences.

TEACHER EXPECTANCY

The notion that teacher expectation influences student performance has received much attention since the seminal study of Rosenthal and Jacobson (1968). The basis of the "self-fulfilling prophecy" or the "Pygmalion effect" is that variability in student performance is a positive, linear function of the expectancies a teacher has developed for that particular student (Smith & Luginbuhl, 1976). Although scrutiny and criticism was directed to the original findings of Rosenthal and Jacobson, the basic notion of the interaction between teacher expectancy and children's learning is widely recognized (Mendels & Flanders, 1973; Snow, 1969; Thorndike, 1968). Sufficient evidence has accumulated to warrant treatment of the expectancy phenomenon as a major factor when studying interactions between children and significant others (Braun, 1976; West & Anderson, 1976). As Seaver (1973) indicated, "The real concern has been the possibility that pupils might be prevented from attaining levels of achievement they were capable of merely because of the stifling effects of low teacher expectancies" (p. 341). Three studies in particular lend insight into the expectancy phenomenon in teacher-child interactions.

Meichenbaum, Bowers, and Ross (1969) worked with a group of 14 institutionalized female juvenile offenders to isolate the cause of the positive expectancy effect. Six girls were identified to their teachers as "late bloomers," purportedly based on tests that could predict later academic performance better than teacher evaluation. Whereas the teachers agreed with the new label for three of the girls, they were surprised that it applied to the other three. However, discussion among the teachers soon resulted in their recalling incidents that validated the "late bloomer" label for all six. The major finding of the study was a significant difference in the quality, but not the quantity, of teacher-student interaction. Teachers tended to give the high-expectancy girls more positive attention and decreased the amount of positive attention given the low-expectancy girls, although the total amount of attention remained the same for both. The high-expectancy girls showed significantly increased academic performance and decreased frequency of disruptive behavior. The investigators concluded that the expectancy effect was due to a change in the quality of the interaction between teacher and student.

Brophy and Good (1970) observed first-grade teachers interacting with their students after the children had been ranked by the teachers on achievement. These rankings were interpreted as teacher expectation for the students. The investigators reported that low-expectancy boys got fewer correct answers, scored lower on the Stanford Achievement Test, and received less praise and more criticism than did the high-expectancy boys. Some specific teacher behaviors of interest were that teachers tended to be less persistent with low-expectancy children than with high-expectancy children in eliciting correct responses and more often supplied them with answers or called on another child. There was also a difference in the amount of feedback given to the low-expectancy children. The teachers failed to give *any* feedback whatever to the high-expectancy children significantly less often than to the low-expectancy children. Thus, the low-expectancy children were being deprived of important information for evaluating their behavior.

Seaver (1973) investigated the effects of naturally induced teacher expectancies on children's performance. A total of 79 pairs of siblings of average intelligence were identified in elementary and junior high schools. The young siblings were classified according to whether their older siblings had been high or low performers in the first grade. The expectancy group was identified as those younger siblings who were being taught by the same teacher who had taught their older siblings, and the control group consisted of younger siblings who were being taught by teachers other than those who had taught their older siblings. Seaver found that when the older sibling's performance had been high, the expectancy group scored higher than did the control group on all dependent variables, which consisted of six standard achievement measures plus two teacher-created measures. When the older sibling's performance had been low, the expectancy group scored lower than the controls on all variables except word study skills. No sex differences were reported. The author interpreted these findings in terms of a teacher expectancy effect, but he also recognized another potential contributing factor: a reverse expectancy effect, whereby the older sibling might have created an expectancy in the younger sibling regarding possible contact with a teacher.

The three studies indicate that the way in which a teacher, or significant other, interacts with a child is in part related to the expectancy they hold for the child. These expectancies could be viewed as labels that are either consciously or unconsciously attached to children. That the label given a child can influence the perception of the teacher was demonstrated in the "late bloomer" study (Meichenbaum et al., 1969), and more recently in a study by Foster, Schmidt, and Sabatino (1976), in which elementary school teachers were asked to observe videotapes of normal boys engaged in various activities. Before viewing, one group was informed that the boy was "learning disabled." After viewing, all teachers were required to fill out referral forms for the child. The teachers who viewed the learning disabled child provided significantly more negative ratings than did the control group. The investigators concluded that the label generated negative expectancies in the teachers, which affected their objective observations of the child's behavior. It appears that labeling tends to be reductive and can result in multidimensional problems (i.e., learning disabilities) being reduced to unidimensional problems.

Seaver (1973) characterized the potency of the teacher expectancy effect succinctly as follows:

> When teachers expect pupils to succeed, the pupils are likely to do better in school than if their teachers had no expectancies. When teachers expect pupils to perform poorly, the performance of these pupils is likely to suffer. (p. 341)

If expectancies of teachers can influence child performance in school-related activities, there is every reason to assume that a similar effect could hold for the sport context. Regarding the handicapped child and sport, the question must be one of the extent to which significant others and especially professionals either knowingly or unknowingly hold lowered expectancies of success for the children with whom they interact. In fact, one could argue for the probability of an even greater expectancy effect with the handicapped child, based on the general premise of their having been exposed to more failure experiences than the nonhandicapped child, with consequent development of heightened sensitivities and expectations for failure on their part (Richardson, 1971; Zigler & Harter, 1971). This belief has been based on and supported by research in the past (i.e., Cromwell, 1963; Keogh, Cahill, & MacMillan, 1972; MacMillan & Keogh, 1971). However, recent findings that mentally retarded children have the same expectancies for failure as do nonretarded children (MacMillan, 1975) raise the old specter of a self-fulfilling prophecy. In a similar vein, Churchill (1971) proposed that the reactions of psychotic children to failure are no different from those of nonpsychotic children, except that they "emerge at unexpectedly low levels of task complexity, and perhaps immediately after the onset of a 'failure condition'" (p. 214).

The fact remains that in recent years handicapped children, especially the mentally retarded, have been depicted as expecting to fail at tasks more than nonretarded children. If we believe that the handicapped expect to fail and that they have had a history of failure experiences, might we not begin to respond to these children on the basis of this information? Finally, Brophy and Good (1970) pointed out that evaluative feedback is the mediating factor between the teachers' expectancy and change in the pupils' behavior. The more effective the communication process, the more likely teacher expectations will affect pupil performance. This raises a second concern, that of communicating expectancies to the handicapped child by the significant other in the sport situation.

ATTRIBUTION THEORY AND THE SIGNIFICANT OTHER

Jones (1976) stated that "our responses to others are affected by the reasons, or attributes, we assign for their behavior" (p. 300). Therefore, in communicating our expectations to handicapped children, the content of our communication will be based on how we have explained the child's behavior to ourselves. A substantial literature is accumulating in which attempts have been made to understand the dynamics of such explanations. Using the work of Bem (1972) and Jones and Nisbett (1972) as a basis, questions were asked about the manner in which actors and observers attribute the same outcome. In general, it was reported that actors and observers proffer different explanations. Actors attribute outcome to situational factors, whereas observers attribute the same outcomes to personal dispositions. These basic conclusions were questioned recently as to their generality (Monson & Snyder, 1977). Moreover, much of the research focused on an observer who is unfamiliar and uninvolved with the actor and as such, provides limited insight into interactions where the significant other is more than an observer but is very much involved with the actor, as is often true in handicapped sports.

TEACHER ATTRIBUTION OF STUDENT PERFORMANCE

One body of research providing more direct information about the manner in which significant others might attribute behavior of handicapped children is based on several studies of teacher explanations of student performance. These investigations employed an attributional model based on research by Heider (1958) and Kelley (1967). Most of the studies used a simulation technique, in which a person was required to teach an academic task to a nonexistent child they believed to be behind a one-way mirror. They were informed about the child's progress (success or failure) and asked to explain the child's performance. This paradigm closely parallels the situation in which a significant other is involved in teaching a handicapped child a sport skill and then explaining the child's performance. According to Jones (1976), the attributes this significant other assigns to the child's performance will affect his response to the child. Although the results of the studies are not entirely consistent, general patterns have been discerned. In some instances, teachers accept credit for a child's successful performance but tend to avoid blame for a child's failure by attributing the failure to the situation or to the dispositional character of the child (Beckman, 1970; Johnson, Feigenbaum, & Weiby, 1964). Under certain conditions, teachers showed counterdefensive attributions, that is, attributing both the child's failure and success to themselves (Beckman, 1973) or rating the teacher factors as more important in failure than in success conditions (Ross, Bierbrauer, & Polly, 1974).

In a more recent investigation, Beckman (1976) provided further insight into the way that significant others explain variable performance of children. Parents and teachers were requested to respond to both open-ended and structured questions regarding children who had been identified as either low, moderate, or high in true performance. In contrast to Ross et al. (1974), Beckman reported that teachers mentioned their own efforts more in the case of high performance (success) than for low performance (failure) of children, which is consistent with the Johnson et al. (1964) and Beckman (1970) findings. In fact, on the open-ended questions, teachers made no reference to themselves as a causal factor for low performance of the children, which could be interpreted as an ego-relevant attribution. In response to the structured questions, the parents of the low- and moderate-performance children rated teaching as an important factor more than did the teachers themselves. If such is the case, it reinforces the need to examine more carefully the manner in which significant others explain variable performance of children.

The findings of studies in which an involvement significant other was required to attribute variable outcomes for a child can be summarized as follows: When the child fails or exhibits low performance, there is a tendency to make attributions to the situation or the difficulty of the task; when the child succeeds or exhibits high performance, the attributions of the significant others tend to be directed toward the teacher. But how would such attributions influence the expectancy the significant other forms for the child's future performance?

Insight into the link between causal attributions and expectancy of success comes from investigations that use an attributional model for achievement behavior (see Weiner, 1974). Based on the work of Heider (1958), Weiner proposed a model in which four factors (ability, effort, luck, and task difficulty) are used to explain variable achievement behavior. The four factors are viewed along two dimensions, stability and locus of control.

Several investigations have shown that the stability dimension of causal attributions is most directly related to expectancy of success (McMahan, 1973; Weiner, 1976; Weiner, Heckhausen, Meyer, & Cook, 1972). Stability involves ability and task difficulty as fixed or stable attributions, whereas effort and luck are variable or unstable factors. Therefore, if a person attributes low performance or failure to low ability or to the difficulty or the task, there would be little expectation of future success on that or similar tasks since both are considered to be stable and unchanging factors. By the same token, when poor performance is attributed to effort or luck, future expectation is less adversely affected, because both factors are susceptible to change before the next encounter with the task situation. The attribution-expectancy linkage is presented in Figure 1.

Although studies of attribution primarily were concerned with a person explaining personal success or failure, they have direct relevance for the types of attributions that a significant other might make for a handicapped child, and the information that might be communicated, since both actors and observers use these factors to explain achievement behavior. For example, a significant other who is working in a sport situation where a child has performed poorly might attribute the child's performance to a lack of ability or to the difficulty of the task (which also is an indirect attribution of low ability). According to the Weiner paradigm, a low expectancy for the child's future performance would develop, particularly if an ability attribution was made, because task difficulty could be altered to facilitate future success.

Once having perceived the child's performance and made some link between the event and its underlying condition, the significant other will probably respond to the child with some type of feedback. The attributional nature of this feedback of significant others is a critical concern for understanding the handicapped child in sport. This is because evaluative feedback offered to the child will be used by the child in attributing personal

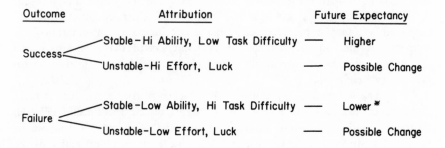

*This pattern could be considered dysfunctional for the handicapped child in sport. A more functional pattern would involve attributing failure to the unstable factors of effort and luck.

FIGURE 1   Attribution-expectancy linkage for success and failure.

performance. Consequently, attributions of low ability, when communicated to the child, become part of the child's own attribution of the outcome. In addition to this influence, Dweck (1976) stated that "certain modes of interaction with social agents promote particular patterns of attributions and that these agents can come to serve as cues for these attributions in achievement situations" (p. 109). Thus, the significant other actually becomes a cue for the child to make certain attributions in achievement situations. The very presence of the significant other could, therefore, be sufficient to remind a child of his lack of ability if this was the feedback the child received in previous interactions (Lewko, in press).

Parke (1976) extended the potential influence of the significant other in stating that "On the basis of past interactions, children formulate attribution 'rules' for success and failure feedback from particular agents; they then use these rules to interpret evaluations they receive from similar agents in new situations" (p. 118). Parke suggested that the influence of one significant other is generalized to similar others, and further, that explanations for success or failure based on the feedback from significant others are generalized to new situations. Such being the case, it is critical that the reactions of significant others to a handicapped child's variable performance be clearly understood, and some procedure be developed to sensitize the significant other to dysfunctional attributions and the harmful feedback that results.

Recent work on attribution retraining (Dweck, 1975; Chapin & Dyck, 1976) demonstrated that deliberate manipulation of information given to a child can significantly increase performance. In both studies, children were provided with explanations for success or failure such as: "That was very good, you tried" (success) and "No you didn't get that, that means you should have tried harder" (failure) (Chapin & Dyck, 1976, p. 512). In both studies, failure outcomes were deliberately attributed to low effort. Because effort is an unstable factor, the effect on the child's future expectations of success is less debilitating than is an attribution to low ability. In everyday life, most people are not familiar with the notion of causal attribution and would therefore not be able to adequately evaluate the content of their communication to determine whether it provides functional or dysfunctional information for a recipient. A method of creating greater awareness of the effects of causal attribution would be invaluable, particularly for people working with handicapped children.

The research cited previously on teacher attributions for student performance can now be interpreted in terms of the relationship between attribution and expectation. It was reported that the low performance or failure of a student was often attributed to the situation or difficulty of the task. If the situation was highly unusual, it was found that there should be little effect on expectancy of success in future situations. When such performance was attributed to task difficulty, however, the teachers' expectation for the child could have been lowered. Attribution of success or high performance by the teachers to themselves produces some interesting implications for feedback to the child. Such an interpretation gives little credit to the child's ability or effort in attaining the success. In fact, if such an attribution were actually communicated to the child (i.e., that the child's success was due largely to the teacher), an important opportunity is lost to guide a child to a stable positive attribution and the positive expectations that could imply. This is related to Weiner's model (1974), which indicates that attributions made along the locus of control dimension (ability and effort-internal; luck and task difficulty-external) results in differential feelings of pride and shame. By providing the child with an external attribution for success, the teacher might be undermining a feeling of pride—which might of its own accord result in the child's choosing not to participate in similar activities in the future. What type of feedback would significant others such as these teachers provide to a handicapped child? Would it reflect the notion that the child was good at the sport, or that the child tried hard? Would it permit the child to feel good about the performance, regardless of the outcome? Or would it be somewhat neutral, in which case a child would not be able to interpret in any fashion, other than perhaps that the significant other was not too interested in the child or the activity? At present there are no answers available for these questions.

The potential influence of a significant other on a child within an attributional framework is presented in Figure 2. It should be noted that the child could also be included in this process, since he or she also engages in some form of explanation of the outcome and has both thoughts and feelings about the present outcome that influence expectations. The focus is primarily

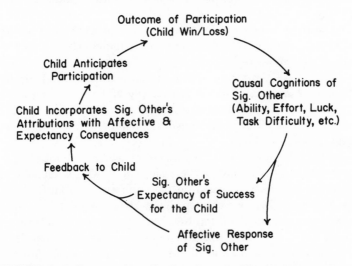

FIGURE 2   Influence of attributions by a significant other on the child in sport.

on the significant other, on the assumption that this person is a powerful influence. As Gergen (1971) noted, children tend to adopt orientations toward themselves that are consistent with the way in which significant others respond to them.

ATTRIBUTION AWARENESS TRAINING

To this point, evidence was presented that suggests the following:

1. Teacher expectancy affects a child's performance, usually in a linear fashion.
2. Expectancies are based, in part, on the types of attributions one makes for some outcome.
3. Significant others make differential attributions for student outcome that have potentially negative effects in terms of future expectancy and affective reactions.
4. Feedback provided to a child by a significant other regarding performance will become incorporated into the child's belief system and used to explain the same outcome.
5. By direct communication of certain causal explanations from a significant other, a child can learn to reattribute outcomes with a concurrent increase in performance.
6. The significant other may come to serve a cue function, which would elicit similar explanations on the part of the child even without feedback.
7. The ways in which the child learns to explain success and failure will be used to deal with similar outcomes across significant others and situations.

That significant others can influence a child's perception of and reaction to some event would be difficult to dispute. If the effects of such influences were clearly understood to be only positive, then no further attention would have to be given to the matter. However, such is not true. If, in fact, the attributions of a significant other can adversely affect a child's performance, then some method of sensitizing the significant other to these potential effects would be of value. The attributional framework provides the basis for developing such a procedure.

In pursuing the notion of a sensitizing or awareness process, the direct implication is that attributions will be manipulated. Whereas current schemas for "attribution retraining" focused on the performer or actor (Dweck, 1975; Valins & Nisbett, 1976), this chapter directs attention toward the significant other who interacts with the actor. Nevertheless, the process suggested here is essentially a form of cognitive behavior modification (Meichenbaum, 1976). The goal is a deliberate modification of the cognitions of people involved with handicapped children in sports contexts. The goal is not to turn these persons into therapists for the children with whom they are interacting. This is, they should be discouraged from engaging in the direct and systematic manipulations of a child's cognition (i.e., attribution retraining). Nevertheless, a greater sensitivity to the possible bias of the feedback they provide might well be invaluable to their real effectiveness.

The attribution-awareness-training approach accepts the child as the final focus, but places greater emphasis on the person interacting with the child. The purpose of this approach is to make the significant others aware of both the role of communication feedback in the formulation of the child's attributions, and the potential effect of their own attributions in biasing the feedback. This is similar to suggestion by Braun (1976) who called for "preventive action" and suggested that teacher training courses and in-service programs be developed to sensitize teachers to the potential biasing effects of expectancy. However, the array of potential factors identified by Braun did not include attributional biases.

Smith and Luginbuhl (1976) provide evidence for the effectiveness of an awareness-training approach on teacher expectancies. A simulation technique was used, where one person (the teacher) was to help two others (the students) solve a problem. The interaction between teacher and students was rated by the "student" and also by two observers who were concealed from the teaching situation. Expectancy of student performance was manipulated by the experimenter, who informed the teacher of recent test results that identified one student as quite bright and the other as relatively deficient in analytic ability, a factor deemed important in solving the problem. Half the teachers also received additional information about the tendency to treat high- and low-ability students differently. This information constituted the experimental manipulation. The results of the manipulation were significant. The teachers who were aware of the effects of an expectation bias paid more attention to their students than did teachers who were unaware. They also provided more qualitative feedback to the students who were supposedly dull than did the unaware teachers. It would appear that such awareness training effectively reduces the negative effects of teacher expectancy. Similar work has yet to be done in the area of attributions but the potential is apparent.

A series of investigations would be required to pursue the possibility of an attribution-awareness-training approach. The first would involve an exploration of the manner in which significant others explain the variable performance of handicapped children. This would involve determining the validity of the four factors used in most of the current research: ability, effort, task difficulty, and luck. Perhaps there are other more important factors that are used to explain such outcomes, as suggested by Elig and Frieze (1975), who stated that "this does not necessarily mean that these [the four factors] are the causal attributions made by subjects in their daily lives" (p. 3). The second stage would involve establishing the effects of certain causal attributions on the significant others. Primary concern would be with exploring the relationship between attributional patterns and the development of differential expectancies for the child on the part of the significant other, as well as any effect reactions to the child that are associated with certain attributions. The third stage would be to determine if and how various causal cognitions are communicated to the child and, more important, if they have an effect of performance, either positive or negative. Without a clear linkage between the attributional pattern of the significant other and behavior change in the child, it is pointless to further pursue this area. The fourth phase would then be to determine if some form of attribution awareness training would result in changed behavior of both the significant other and the handicapped child.

Concurrent with these four steps would be the need to explore the manner in which handicapped children themselves explain variable performance. To date there are few investigations in which attributional concepts have been explored with special populations. Two recent studies, both done with adults (Horai & Guarnacci, 1975; Menapace & Doby, 1976), provide contradictory findings. Horai and Guarnaccia reported that mentally retarded adults responded to success and failure outcomes with attributions similar to those typically reported for nonretarded individuals. Success was attributed to ability and failure to effort and luck. Menapace and Doby compared the reactions of normal adults and psychiatric rehabilitees to success and failure outcomes. They found that the psychiatric rehabilitees attributed failure more to task difficulty and poor ability than did the normals, and success was attributed to effort while the normals attributed their success to ease of the task. It would appear that handicapped persons may indeed make different attributions than do nonhandicapped persons for variable performance. However, experimental manipulation of success and failure with people who have been historically characterized as experiencing inordinate amounts of failure experiences presents an ethical problem. Perhaps now is the time to turn toward more naturalistic methods of investigation.

Preliminary data in support of the concept of attribution awareness training are provided by two studies. Although the conceptual framework of the teacher expectancy and attribution theory research had generated the hypotheses that formed the basis of the studies, the data were not reported in terms of these hypotheses. Since the concept of attribution awareness training is a new one, particularly for the sport-recreation context, it seemed more productive to handle the data in a descriptive and exploratory manner. The hope was that asking some general questions would direct greater attention to the meaning of the preliminary information than would stating specific hypotheses to be accepted or rejected. Three major questions were investigated.

1. What types of attribution do significant others make for low performance by a handicapped child?
2. What is the apparent relationship between a significant other's attributions for low performance and their future expectancy for the child?

3. What type of feedback is provided to a low performer and how do significant others explain the purpose of this feedback?

Questions 1 and 2 investigated in the first study, and data for the third question were obtained in the second study.

Study 1

Participants and setting

The participants and setting were identical for both studies. A total of 39 persons, 17 males and 22 females, provided the data source for the current investigation. They ranged in age from 16 to 26 years, with a mean age of 19.6 years. These persons were staff members at a residential summer camp serving physically handicapped children and youth. Although most (79.5%) had some previous experience in physical education-recreation, approximately one-half of the staff (53.8%) had no prior experience with handicapped children. The subject population is not atypical for a large number of situations where sport-recreation experiences are provided the handicapped. In many instances, due to shortage of money and trained professionals, it has been necessary for such programs to rely on young and inexperienced personnel.

During the course of the summer, the camp staff experienced close contact with young people from 7 to 18 years old who were mildly to severely hampered by a variety of disabling conditions, ranging from muscular dystrophy and cerebral palsy to blindness. The staff-camper ratio was approximately 1-1½, providing for intensive interactions during any of the 2-week sessions that were the usual length of stay for most campers. The data were collected over a 5-day period after the staff had experienced several weeks of contact with the campers.

Cooperation from the staff was facilitated by having the camp director inform them that the information requested from them was to be incorporated in the next year's camp program. Thus, the staff had been prepared for their participation from the outset of the summer and had completed a form providing background information. All were assured of anonymity, and only code numbers identified their responses.

Low-Performance Stimulus

Two children who had recently attended a camp session were selected to be the low-performance stimulus for the study based on the following criteria: (a) consensus among the camp program directors and senior staff that these children had performed much below the levels expected of them during the camp session, and (b) all camp staff had had contact with both children during their camp session. Both children were boys, ages 7 and 8 years, and each was enrolled in the camp with a diagnosis of muscular dystrophy.

The camp staff was given written material on each child (child stimulus). The child's name appeared in a paragraph that explained the fact of the child's low performance during the camp session. It was further stated that a variety of reasons could have accounted for the low performance and that three of these were the child's ability level, how hard he tried, and the difficulty of the tasks he faced. Members of the staff were required to respond to both structured and open-ended questions involving the reasons why each child had performed lower than expected during his stay. All members received explanation sheets for both children with the order randomly assigned.

Measures

Many factors could hypothetically influence the response of a significant other to a handicapped child. Four factors were selected for the preliminary investigation; they constitute the independent variables: sex, past experience with handicapped children, perceived effectiveness in working with handicapped children, and the children themselves (child stimulus).

For purposes of statistical analysis, the dependent variables were the staff member's attributions to ability, effort, and task difficulty as well as his prediction for the child as to future success in similar activities after leaving the camp. Participants responded to each of the four dependent variables on a 7-point scale. In addition, they responded to open-ended questions pertaining to low performance. These responses were analyzed based on the coding scheme of Elig and Frieze (1975); however, the data were treated primarily as descriptive, and no statistical analysis was conducted.

Results and Discussion

A 2 (Sex) X 2 (Child stimulus) analysis of variance, with the second variable treated as a repeated measure, was performed on the three dependent variables related to attribution. Table 1 presents a summary of the analysis of variance. As a main effect, ability and task-difficulty attributions for the two children (child stimulus) differed significantly. Child B was consistently rated higher on these variables than was child A. That is, the staff attributed child B's performance more to low ability, $F(1, 37) = 70.21$, $p < .01$, and to difficulty of the task, $F(1, 37) = 44.63$, $p < .01$, than they did child A's performance. In general, the low performance of both children was attributed to low effort, although a marginally significant trend was observed toward perceiving child A as trying less hard, $F(1, 37) = 6.78, p < .09$.

On the basis of the present findings, it is difficult to explain why staff members made differential attributions for the two boys. As the stimulus

TABLE 1 Analysis of variance of sex X child stimulus for attributions

Source	df	Ability			Effort		Task	
		ms	F		ms	F	ms	F
Between-subjects								
Sex (A)	1	1.85	< 1		0.13	< 1	3.23	1.02
Subjects	37	3.24			3.67		3.15	
Within-subjects								
Child stimulus (B)	1	70.21	40.19*		6.78	3.05	44.63	26.67*
A X B Interaction	1	0.16	< 1		6.34	2.85	0.96	< 1
Subjects X B								
interaction	37	1.75			2.23		1.67	

*$p < .01$.

information was identical for both children, the staff must have gone beyond the general information of low performance and cued in to factors unique for each child. This is consistent with findings of Frieze and Weiner (1971), who reported that subjects use a variety of cue configural patterns to explain performance. Therefore, the differential attributions suggest that significant others use different cues for different children in forming their attributions.

Second, the different attributions give rise to concern over the usefulness of the traditional attributional factors as a basis for understanding real-life attributions in general. It is possible that the consistent difference in the ranking of the two boys indicated a recognition on the part of the staff that an attributional factor (i.e., ability) meant different things for each child. Whatever the reason for the difference, the three traditional factors of ability, effort, and task difficulty do not seem to account for the complexity of the attributional process. Attribution Awareness Training would require more information regarding the actual perceptions of significant others.

Finally, the different ratings of the children leads to yet another speculation. If the staff did defer to the individual child in applying the attribution factor, would a limited selection of factors limit the discrimination between children in a potentially detrimental way? That is, if attribution awareness training entails altering stable attributions of failure, would it not be better to have a more complex and discriminating range of attributions more adapted to real individuals in real situations?

Based on the finding of differential attributions for the two children, separate two-way ANOVAs (Sex X Previous experience; Perceived effectiveness in working with children X Previous experience) were performed on each of the dependent variables. Table 2 presents the means of effort attributions by significant others with varying experience with the handicapped. The findings

TABLE 2 Mean attributions to effort by significant others
with varying experience

Child	No experience	Previous experience	p^a
Child A	2.4	3.5	$< .05$
Child B	2.8	4.3	$< .01$

[a]Based on separate ANOVAs for each child. The higher the score
the less importance assigned to effort.

are consistent for both children; persons with no previous experience working
with the handicapped attributed low performance to low effort more than did
people who had some previous experience [child A, $F(1, 35) = 5.58, p < .05$;
child B, $F(1, 35) = 9.02, p < .01$].

The difference in the attributions of experienced and inexperienced
personnel might reflect a difference in generalized expectancy for the two
groups. It is possible that in the process of acquiring knowledge and
experience about the handicapped, great attention is focused on the
psychological effects of an individual's diagnosed disability. These characteristics could be interpreted as being stable performance factors for an
individual or class of individuals, and particularly so for the physically
disabled. If the more experienced staff members focused on the characteristic
effects of a disability when faced with low performance, they would tend to
perceive effort as less of a factor than would inexperienced subjects. While the
inexperienced persons might believe a child could perform better with
increased effort, the more experienced might perceive disability characteristics
as obviating any effort made on the part of that child. The discrepancy
between the two groups holds possible implications for differential feedback
being provided the handicapped child. As such, the generality of this finding
needs to be established along with its potential for biasing the significant
other's feedback to the child.

To this point it appears that staff are generally disposed to attribute low
performance to stable factors of ability and task difficulty and that the
unstable factor of effort is invoked more by inexperienced than by
experienced personnel. By themselves, such results provide only limited
information about the way in which significant others explain low
performance of handicapped children. However, additional information is
available from content analysis of the open-ended responses (see Tables 3 and
4).

Open-ended Responses

If the three attributional factors of ability, effort, and task difficulty are
sufficient for a person to explain variable performance, then one would

TABLE 3 Comparison of attributional responses to low-performance stimulus on structured and open-ended questions

Type of question	Ability		Effort		Task Difficulty	
	Child		Child		Child	
	A	B	A	B	A	B
Structured[a]	9	28	30	28	11	28
Open-ended[b]	12	19	4	1	0	0

[a]Based on frequencies for values 1–4 on a 7-point scale: 1 (very much a reason) through 7 (not at all a reason).
[b]Figures represent only 1 response per category.

anticipate great similarity of responses on both structured and open-ended questions. That is, if people actually think in terms of these factors when explaining variable performance, then these explanations should be prominent in their open-ended responses. However, such was not true. Table 3 presents frequency data comparing structured and open-ended responses on the three attributional factors. A large discrepancy exists in the use of the three factors, depending on the type of response format required of the staff member.

One obvious discrepancy between these tables and Table 1 is that though differential attributions are still made on the ability factor, with child B's performance attributed more to low ability, there are no open-ended responses that were coded as task difficulty. This difference suggests caution in

TABLE 4 Attributions of significant others for low performance of two children

Attributional category	Child A	Child B
Ability	12	20
Effort	4	1
Stable effort	0	2
Mood	4	1
Intrinsic motivation	5	11
Personality	20	8
Another answer—uncodable	6	6
Ability-Task interaction	0	2
Others' stable help or hurt and effort	3	0
Others' personality, background, and interests	1	4
Personality interaction	7	7

Note. Based on open-ended responses, analyzed using the Elig & Frieze (1975) coding scheme.

propagating task difficulty as an explanation for low performance of the handicapped. Although task difficulty may well be one reason for low performance, staff members appeared to choose other perhaps more salient explanations when their responses were not structured. One of the possible consequences of accepting task difficulty as a major factor explaining low performance might be to foster a practice of restructuring tasks so as to increase the liklihood of the child's success the next time. This would be logical. However, by restructuring the task, one might be depriving the child of the opportunity to experience levels of task difficulty, which might be more critical for developing maturity. In any event, the discrepancy suggests that factors other than task difficulty might account for the low performance and that a forced-choice format such as the structured questions might encourage personnel to use "task difficulty" as a convenient label to express factors that, in themselves, might not be readily interpreted as task difficulty.

A second major difference revealed in Table 3 is a marked reduction in effort attributions by staff in their open responses. Because effort is perhaps the key attribution employed in the recent investigations dealing with attribution retraining, this discrepancy underscores the need for closer examination of the types of explanations that may supercede the effort factor and even modify its meaning. Discrepancies, as presented in Table 3, raise questions as to whether the structured attributional factors are in fact the generic explanations arising out of real-life situations involving significant others and handicapped children. Perhaps there are other more salient factors that must be accounted for before any sensitization of cognition is to be attempted.

A more definitive breakdown of the open-ended attributional factors used by the personnel is presented in Table 4. It is evident that staff members' explanation of low performance is much more complex than originally portrayed by the structured responses. Although the ability category is frequently mentioned, other factors such as personality, intrinsic motivation, and personality interaction are equally common. Of particular interest is the personality category, which is interpreted as a stable, internal factor (Elig & Frieze, 1975). A combination of the ability and personality categories for each child results in approximately 50% of the open-ended responses being made to stable, internal factors. Whereas responses to the structured questions indicated that attribution of low performance to stable factors was more pronounced for child B than for child A, the performance of child A was also attributed in large part to stable factors in the open responses.

It is interesting to note the common use of clinical disability characteristics as causal factors for low performance. Frequent, direct reference was made to short attention span and difficulty in understanding or following instructions for both children (these references were considered related to ability). Several of the staff indicated that they felt that child B was slow or retarded in some respect. Regarding the personality category, both children were characterized as overdependent and manipulative. Child A was identified as having emotional or psychological problems. Thus, personnel tended to interpret the low performance of the handicapped children in terms of clinical disability characteristics. No reference was made for either child to the lack of sport ability per se, nor to any other skill-related aspect of performance. Rather, the personnel tended to explain low performance in terms of fundamental abilities or disabilities related to performance in general. This information was totally unavailable from the structured responses, where the ability attributions could have been interpreted to mean that personnel perceived the children to have limited sport ability.

An equal number of references to the personality interactions category was made to account for the low performance of children. This is an important factor in explaining sport performance of the handicapped. Elig and Frieze (1975) defined this category as including "those situations attributed to the interaction of the stimulus person's personality and the personalities of others" (p. 9). For both children, a majority of the responses coded in this category referred to problems of group interaction, cooperation, and rejection by peers.

Personality interaction provides significant others with an attributional category that goes beyond the individual performer in explaining variable outcome. Because most sport situations are based on interaction between two or more participants, useful feedback to an individual should reflect this dimension.

In summary, It is clear that open-ended responses provide more information about the explanations of significant others for low performance of handicapped children. In addition, it would appear that the expanded list of attribution categories is more useful both for explaining actual attributions and in indicating categories of relevant feedback.

Attributions and Future Expectancy

One of the more important assumptions of this chapter was the relationship between stable attributions and future expectancy. If in fact stable attributions for low performance (low ability; high task difficulty) influence the expectancy a significant other develops for a child, one should find a strong relationship between such attributions and future expectancy. However, Table 5 presents data somewhat contradictory to this assumption. The relatively low but significant correlations between expectancy and low-ability attributions for child B ($r = .26$, $p < .05$) and expectancy and low-effort attributions for child A ($r = -.30$, $p < .05$) are in the opposite direction from those suggested by the attributional model. There are two possible explanations for these findings. First, the attribution-expectancy relationship as suggested by Weiner, Nierenberg, and Goldstein (1976) was based primarily on data from subjects considering their own personal

TABLE 5 Correlations between attribution scores and future expectancy for two low-performing children

Child	Ability	Effort	Task	Amount of contact with child
A	.21	−.30*	.18	.06
B	.26*	.09	.17	−.01

*$p < .05$.

expectations and not on expectations held by an involved-observer for another individual. It is therefore possible that the model has not been tested sufficiently for the latter situation and in fact does not reflect the dynamics involved.

The alternative explanation is based on an analysis of open-ended responses for a question pertaining to the staff member's expectancy ratings of the two children. Persons whose response pattern was low effort-low future expectancy based their low-expectancy ratings on a variety of reasons. Among these were that the child failed to show any improvement during camp, the very limited 2-week camp session, and the child's need for close supervision that would not be available outside camp. Thus, though the effort factor is considered an unstable attribute, the reasons given for setting low future expectancies referred to other stable factors that were deemed more salient. This would suggest that the link between effort attributions of significant others and the expectancies they hold for the child is modified by other considerations and may be rendered tenuous as a result.

In a similar fashion, analysis of the open-ended responses associated with the low-ability-high future expectancy pattern revealed that the high expectancies were based on explanations that were conditional in nature. Personnel made statements such as "if he were given the chance" and "if a person could be more imaginative and creative in working with him."

Although the relationship between structured attributional responses and future expectancy appears to be rather tenuous or confounded, the open-ended responses seem to be more consistent with the attributional model. Table 6 represents frequency data on the open-ended attributional responses and future expectancies for both children. Based on a 7-point scale, only high (1-3) and low (5-7) expectancies are included. For both children, causal explanations that are relatively stable (ability, personality, and ability-task interaction) were associated with low expectancies, whereas higher expectancies were associated with more unstable responses. In particular the explanations for child B categorized as Other's Personality, which carried with them the conditional "if," might be considered unstable and therefore would be consistent with the person's setting higher future expectancies for the child. Staff expected the child to do better outside of camp provided other people would be available who would exercise patience and work closely with the child.

In summary, the discrepancy between structured and open-ended answers illustrates the need to go beyond the traditional factors that have been used to explain variable performance. In addition, the relationship between the open-ended attributions and conditional future expectancy is particularly in need of further clarification. It is possible that the conditional expectancy is in actuality a mask for low expectations that are based on stable attributions. The implications for attribution awareness training are twofold. First, the stable explanations being made should be the starting point for any attempt to modify perceptions of significant others. Second, the communication of these low expectations to handicapped children should be considered from the perspective of the teacher expectancy studies to recognize the various forms of negative feedback that might be directed toward the child.

Study 2

Concurrent with developing an understanding of how significant others explain low performance by handicapped children should be an examination of the way in which such people might communicate this understanding to these children. This is based on the assumption that the way in which significant others explain the child's performance to themselves will affect the evaluative feedback they provide the child. As stated earlier, such feedback is used by the child in responding to future situations (Parke, 1976).

In the learning or performance of various sports skills, some type of

TABLE 6 Causal explanations for predicting future performance of two children

| | Future expectancy | | | |
| | Child A | | Child B | |
Causal explanations	Low	High	Low	High
Ability	5	3	14	1
Intrinsic motivation	3	0	1	0
Personality	6	1	3	1
Another reason	0	2	0	0
Other's personality	2	0	0	7
Personality interaction	1	2	2	4
Ability-Task difficulty interaction	3	2	0	1

formal or informal reinforcement or reward and punishment system is typically in operation. This reinforcement could be viewed as a form of evaluative feedback. Since reinforcement requires some type of behavioral output on the part of a significant other, it could serve as a stimulus situation for an examination of reactions of significant others to low performance.

Reinforcement Stimulus

A simulation paradigm was used in which staff members were required to imagine that they had been working with a child in a recreational-sports skill development program where a variety of skills were being taught. They were to imagine that a learning session had just been completed and that some type of reinforcement was to be provided the child. They were informed that the child had not performed well in past sessions and had done poorly in the present session. They were required to provide feedback to the child in both a structured and open-ended reinforcement situation.

The structured situation required the personnel to assume that one type of reinforcement being used in the skills program was in the form of gold or red stars given out at the end of session, and that the child had learned to associate gold stars with positive reinforcement and red stars with negative reinforcement. Based on the information about the child's performance, the staff were to indicate the type and amount of reinforcement they would use for the child. In the open-ended situation, they were simply asked how they would respond to the child's poor performance if it were up to them to decide on the feedback system to be used.

The staff members were randomly assigned to one of three hypothetical children whose primary disability was stated as one of the following: cerebral palsy, muscular dystrophy, and mental retardation. Each child was portrayed as being ambulatory; as being able to feed and dress himself with effort; and as being able to engage in such activities as throwing a ball, climbing up and over objects, carrying light weights, and walking at a fast pace. The two types of physical handicap were included to control for any possible response set. The mental retardation stimulus was included to explore the possibility of persons' responding differentially to a child with a categorically different disability.

Measures

Six variables were investigated in this study, three of which were used in Study 1—sex, past experience with the handicapped, and perceived effectiveness in working with handicapped children. The remaining three variables were type of disability (muscular dystrophy, cerebral palsy, and mental retardation), type of reinforcement (positive, negative), and amount of reinforcement. After having read the stimulus information, the staff members first selected the type of reinforcement they would provide and then circled a number corresponding to the amount of reinforcement. Therefore, two dependent measures were the type of reinforcement (positive, gold star; negative, red star) and the amount of that reinforcement (1-10 stars). Perceived effectiveness in working with handicapped children was measured on a 7-point rating scale. In addition, the staff members were asked to explain their responses to the structured reinforcement situation. These explanations were content analyzed, as were the responses to the open-ended reinforcement situation.

Results and Discussion

Two-dimensional crossbreaks were examined, with type of reinforcement and amount of reinforcement[1] separately crossed with sex, past experience with handicapped, perceived effectiveness in working with handicapped children, and type of disability. Chi-square analyses were then performed on each of the two-dimensional crossbreaks. No significant chi-square values were obtained for any of the crossbreaks. This is of interest, because approximately 75% of the personnel (29 out of 39) preferred to give positive reinforcement and the remaining staff (10 out of 39) opted for negative reinforcement. The lack of significant findings suggests that perhaps the tendency to give positive or negative feedback is a characteristic of personality that is randomly distributed throughout the population.

Analysis of the open-ended responses provides more interesting information regarding the response tendencies of significant others. Table 7 presents a breakdown of the reasons the participants gave for providing the low performer with positive or negative reinforcement. It is apparent that those who use positive and

[1] Based on frequency distributions, the amount of reinforcement variable was recorded into three categories: negative, high positive (3-10 stars), and low positive (1-2 stars).

TABLE 7   Significant other's explanation of providing variable reinforcement for low performance

Significant other's reason	Frequency of reinforcement	
	Positive	Negative
To make the child feel good	13	0
To provide incentive, encourage effort	10	3
To inform the child that he is doing poorly and what he is doing wrong	1	7
To control child's behavior	1	1
To encourage participation	1	0
Noncategorical	4	0

negative reinforcement perceived the function of such feedback in different terms. Whereas positive-feedback personnel are concerned with the child's feeling good and with encouraging him to try in the future, negative-feedback personnel view the feedback as more informational in nature. That is, they see the need to inform the child of poor performance and also provide some cues as to how the child can improve. Panda and Lynch (1972) commented on this discrepancy and suggested that the informational aspect of reinforcement is frequently sacrificed in favor of the affective or motivational function. If this is true, the behavior of the present personnel favoring positive reinforcement might be called into question; performance improvement depends more on the availability of informational cues than on motivational-affective cues (Panda & Lynch, 1972). The feedback of a significant other is one of the most direct ways a handicapped child acquires information regarding performance. If significant others provide feedback that is primarily affective or motivational, as suggested by the data in Table 7, then the handicapped child is possibly deprived of important information that could improve subsequent sport performance. This points out the need for more closely examining the types of feedback provided the handicapped child in real-life sport situations.

A variety of approaches emerged in response to the open-ended question as to how the personnel would reinforce the child if it were primarily up to them. The approach most frequently mentioned was the use of verbal feedback (praise, exhortation), which was primarily positive. Virtually no staff members suggested using tangible reinforcers. The reasons offered for positive verbal reinforcement again focused on the affective or motivational purpose of feedback, with virtually no reference to an informational function. Several staff members indicated that the reinforcement should convey recognition of effort and the link between effort and improvement. This is similar to the attribution retraining approach (Dweck, 1975). Staff members also suggested that verbal reinforcement should be given to develop intrinsic motivation and should emphasize participation over performance. One participant stated simply, "In whatever way possible I would just try to have him [child] believe he is doing as well as anybody else. Even though he performed poorly, that's no reason to let him know it and make him feel like nothing."

It is evident that the personnel held a variety of beliefs regarding the communication of performance outcome to the low-performing child. To the extent that such communications are biased, as indicated by the preceding direct quote, significant others may be adversely influencing the development of the children with whom they are in contact. The range of reasons behind proffered feedback, coupled with the tendency to use reinforcement for affective or motivational over informational purposes suggests that significant others who work with the handicapped in a sport-recreational context could benefit greatly from some form of systematic training to make them aware of the implications of their thoughts and words.

GENERAL DISCUSSION

It is apparent that significant others tend to make stable attributions for low performance by disabled children and that there is a link between their attributions and their expectancies for those children. Applying the teacher expectancy data (Brophy & Good, 1970; Meichenbaum et al., 1969; Seaver, 1973), one would expect significant others to respond to the low-performing child with less positive attention and feedback as well as with less patience and persistence. In turn, one would anticipate lowered or more variable performance by the child in response to such feedback. Thus, both the evidence and theoretical lines of inquiry indicate that the attributions and feedback of significant others who work with the handicapped in sport-recreation contexts should be examined more closely.

The need for closer scrutiny is reinforced by the data from Study 2, which suggest that the camp personnel were neither fully aware of the reasons behind the differential feedback they provide a low performer, nor conscious of the possible consequences. Moreover, the differences between the attributions made by experienced and inexperienced personnel in Study 1 suggests a possible conflict of feedback, especially in situations where both are working with the same child. These findings point to the need for a method of standardizing the perceptions and communication of various levels of significant others who are involved with the socialization of the handicapped child in sport. Without such standardization, it would be difficult to move toward the goal of having handicapped children demonstrate desire to participate in sport-recreation activities of their own accord. This tendency, which Maehr (1976) labeled "continuing motivation," should be the major socialization goal for handicapped children in sport.

The use of diagnostic criteria as causal factors for low performance has some potentially serious implications for the type of feedback provided the low performer. Many of these factors are stable in nature, and as such can influence the expectancy developed for the child's future performance. This seemed to be evident in the open-ended responses. The use of diagnostic factors indicates a tendency for the personnel to explain low performance more in terms of fundamental processes (i.e., short attention span) as opposed to more specific factors related to sports ability per se. Such attributions possibly might have evolved from participants' experience with the handicapped in other areas of functioning, and have been generalized to the sport situation. The possibility of such transference across behavioral contexts merits further investigation.

The obvious discrepancies between the data provided by the structured and open-ended formats also needs to be examined in greater depth. There was a tendency for the open-ended format to generate a more expansive list of factors, which provided greater insight into the nature of the attributions than did the structured factors. Weiner (in press) indicated the need for investigating real-life attributions, as follows: "The comparative importance assigned to ability and effort in evaluation and selection, and the perceived underlying causes of these causal factors, are essential areas of investigation" (p. 22). To pursue the notion of Attribution Awareness Training, it is essential to identify the population of causal factors used by significant others to explain variable sport performance and, more important, to understand the reasons why these explanations are used. Only then will one be able to sensitize people to the potential import of their perceptions and behavior. The data reported in this chapter provide the initial groundwork in support of the conceptual framework proposed for the development of the Attribution Awareness Training procedure. Future investigations are being planned to more clearly delineate the population of attributional factors as well as the presence of such factors in the communication of significant others with handicapped children. The conditional nature of the expectancy observed, as well as the link between attributions to low ability and the development of lowered future expectancy for the child, will be two other foci for future research.

REFERENCES

Beckman, L. J. Effects of students' performance on teachers' and observers' attributions of causality. *Journal of Educational Psychology*, 1970, *61*, 76–82.

Beckman, L. J. Teachers' and observers' perceptions of causality for a child's performance. *Journal of Educational Psychology*, 1973, *65*(2), 198–204.

Beckman, L. J. Causal attributions of teachers and parents regarding children's performance. *Psychology in the Schools*, 1976, *13*, 212–218.

Bem, D. J. Self-perception theory. In L. Berkowitz (Ed.), *Advances in experimental social psychology*. New York: Academic Press, 1972.

Braun, C. Teacher expectation: Sociopsychological dynamics. *Review of Educational Research*, 1976, *46*, 185–213.

Brophy, J. E., & Good, T. L. Teachers' communication of differential expectations for children's classroom performance: Some behavioral data. *Journal of Educational Psychology*, 1970, *61*, 365–374.

Chapin, M., & Dyck, D. G. Persistence in children's reading behavior as a function of N length and attribution retraining. *Journal of Abnormal Psychology*, 1976, *85*(5), 511–516.

Churchill, D. W. Effects of success and failure in psychotic children. *Archives of General Psychiatry*, 1971, *25*, 208–214.

Cromwell, R. L. A social learning approach to mental retardation. In N. R. Ellis (Ed.), *Handbook of mental retardation*. New York: McGraw-Hill, 1963.

Dweck, C. S. The role of expectations and attributions in the alleviation of learned helplessness. *Journal of Personality and Social Psychology*, 1975, *31*, 674–685.

Dweck, C. S. Children's interpretation of evaluative feedback: The effect of social cues on learned helplessness. *Merrill-Palmer Quarterly,* 1976, *22*(2), 105–109.

Elig, T. W., & Frieze, I. H. A multi-dimensional scheme for coding and interpreting perceived causality for success and failure events: The coding scheme of perceived causality (CSPC). JSAS *Catalog of Selected Documents in Psychology,* 1975, *5,* 313. (ms. No. 1069)

Foster, G. C., Schmidt, C. R., & Sabatino, D. Teacher expectancies and the label "learning disabilities." *Journal of Learning Disabilities,* 1976, *9*(2), 58–61.

Frieze, I., & Weiner, B. Cue utilization and attributional judgments for success and failure. *Journal of Personality,* 1971, *39,* 591–606.

Gergen, K. J. *The concept of self.* New York: Holt, Rinehart, & Winston, 1971.

Heider, F. *The psychology of interpersonal relations.* New York: Wiley, 1958.

Horai, J., & Guarnaccia, V. J. Performance and attributions to ability, effort, task and luck of retarded adults after success or failure feedback. *American Journal of Mental Deficiency,* 1975, *79,* 690–694.

Johnson, T. J., Feigenbaum, R., & Weiby, M. Some determinants and consequences of teacher's perception of causation. *Journal of Educational Psychology,* 1964, *55,* 237–246.

Jones, E. E. How do people perceive the causes of behavior? *American Scientist,* 1976, *64*(3), 300–305.

Jones, E. E., & Nisbett, R. E. The actor and the observer: Divergent perceptions of the cuases of behavior. In E. E. Jones, D. Kanouse, N. H. Kelley, R. E. Nisbett, S. Valins, & B. Weiner (Eds.), *Attribution: Perceiving the causes of behavior.* New York: General Learning Press, 1972.

Kelley, H. H. Attribution theory in social psychology. In D. Levine (Eds.), *Nebraska symposium on motivation,* Lincoln, Neb.: University of Nebraska Press, 1967.

Keogh, B. K., Cahill, C. W., & MacMillan, D. L. Perception of interruption of educationally handicapped children. *American Journal of Mental Deficiency,* 1972, *77,* 107–108.

Lewko, J. H. Specialized knowledge and the delivery of leisure services to the disabled. *Leisure Sciences: An Interdisciplinary Journal,* in press.

MacMillan, D. L. Effect of experimental success and failure on the situational expectancy of EMR and nonretarded children. *American Journal of Mental Deficiency,* 1975, *80,* 90–95.

MacMillan, D. L., & Keogh, B. K. Normal and retarded children's expectancy for failure. *Developmental Psychology,* 1971, *4,* 343–348.

Maehr, M. L. Continuing motivation: An analysis of a seldom considered educational outcome. *Review of Educational Research,* 1976, *46,* 443–462.

McMahan, I. Relationships between causal attributions and expectancies of success. *Journal of Personality and Social Psychology,* 1973, *28,* 108–114.

McPherson, B. D. *The child in competettive sport: Influence of the social milieu.* Paper presented at the AAHPER symposium, The Child in

Competetive Sport: Readiness and Effects, Milwaukee, Wisc., March 1976.

Meichenbaum, D. H. Cognitive behavior modification. In J. T. Spence, R. C. Carson, & J. W. Thibaut (Eds.), *Behavioral approaches to therapy.* Morristown, N.J.: General Learning Press, 1976.

Meichenbaum, D. H., Bowers, K. S., & Ross, R. R. A behavioral analysis of teacher expectancy effect. *Journal of Personality and Social Psychology,* 1969, *13,* 306–316.

Menapace, R. H., & Doby, C. Causal attributions for success and failure for psychiatric rehabilitees and college students. *Journal of Personality and Social Psychology,* 1976, *34*(3), 447–455.

Mendels, G. E., & Flanders, J. P. Teachers' expectations and pupil performance. *American Education Research Journal,* 1973, *10,* 203–212.

Monson, T. C., & Snyder, M. Actors, observers, and the attribution process: Toward a reconceptualization. *Journal of Experimental Social Psychology,* 1977, *13,* 89–111.

Orlick, T., & Botterill, C. *Every kid can win.* Chicago: Nelson-Hall, 1975.

Panda, K. C., & Lynch, W. W. Effects of social reinforcement on the retarded child: A review and interpretation for classroom instruction. *Education and Training of the Mentally Retarded,* 1972, *7,* 115–123.

Parke, R. D. Social cues, social control, and ecological validity. *Merrill-Palmer Quarterly,* 1976, *22*(2), 111–118.

Richardson, S. A. The effect of physical disability on the socialization of a child. In D. A. Goslin (Ed.), *Handbook of socialization theory and research.* Chicago: Rand McNally, 1971.

Rosenthal, R., & Jacobson, L. *Pygmalion in the classroom.* New York: Holt, Rinehart, & Winston, 1968.

Ross, L., Bierbrauer, G., & Polly, S. Attribution of educational outcomes by professional and nonprofessional instructors. *Journal of Personality and Social Psychology,* 1974, *29*(5), 609–618.

Seaver, W. B. Effects of nationally induced teacher expectancies. *Journal of Personality and Social Psychology,* 1973, *28*(3), 333–342.

Smith, F. J., & Liginbuhl, J. E. R. Inspecting expectancy: Some laboratory results of relevance for teacher training. *Journal of Educational Psychology,* 1976, *68*(3), 265–272.

Snow, R. E. Unfinished pygmalion. *Contemporary Psychology,* 1969, *14,* 197–199.

Thorndike, R. L. Review of *Pygmalion in the Classroom* by R. Rosenthal and L. Jacobson. *American Educational Research Journal,* 1968, *5,* 708–711.

Valins, S., & Nisbett, R. E. Attribution processes in the development and treatment of emotional disorders. In J. T. Spence, R. C. Carson, & J. W. Thibaut (Eds.), *Behavioral approaches to therapy.* Morristown, N.J.: General Learning Press, 1976.

Weiner, B. *Achievement motivation and attribution theory.* Morristown, N.J.: General Learning Press, 1974.

Weiner, B. Motivational psychology and sports activities. In T. T. Craig (Ed.), *The humanistic and mental health aspects of sports, exercise and recreation.* Chicago: American Medical Association, 1976.

Weiner, B. An attributional approach for educational psychology. In L. Shulman (Ed.), *Review of Research in Education,* in press.

Weiner, B., Heckhausen, H., Meyer, W., & Cook, R. E. Causal ascriptions and achievement behavior: A conceptual analysis of effort and reanalysis of locus of control. *Journal of Personality and Social Psychology,* 1972, *21,* 239–248.

Weiner, B., Nierenberg, R., & Goldstein, M. Social learning (locus of control) versus attributional (causal stability) interpretations of expectancy of success. *Journal of Personality,* 1976, *44,* 52–68.

West, C. K., & Anderson, T. H. The question of preponderant causation in teacher expectancy research. *Review of Educational Research,* 1976, *46,* 613.

Zigler, E. F., & Harter, S. The socialization of the mentally retarded. In D. A. Goslin (Ed.), *Handbook of socialization theory and research.* Chicago: Rand McNally, 1971.

AUTHOR INDEX

SUBJECT INDEX

Aggression:
  instrumental, 96
  (*see also* Violence in hockey)
Anxiety:
  A-State, pre- and postcompetition, 117–120
  competitive trait, 114–115, 117–120
  fun and, 118–120
  self-esteem and, 113–114, 118–120
  success-failure and, 115, 118–120
  trait-state theory, 112–115
Attribution, 124–131, 138–144, 145–169, 253–274
  discounting principle, 130, 142
  ego involvement and, 168
  information processing approach to, 148–151, 158
  locus of control and, 146
  mini-max principle of, 168
  and motivation, 124–131
  retraining, 256
  self-serving strategies, 148–151, 158
  after success and failure, 145–169
  for team and individual performance, 153–158, 164–169
  Weiner's model of, 146, 255
Attribution Awareness Training, 250, 258–261

Behavioral assessment, 6, 175–180
  of coaching behaviors, 175–180
  of cooperative behaviors, 206–209, 213–215, 221–223

Behavioral instrumentalities of coaches, 187
Biological maturation, 20

Cardiovascular function (*see* Physiological effects of physical training, cardiac output)
Coaches' beliefs about player goals, 195–198
  (*See also* Special Olympics)
Coaching behaviors:
  assessment of, 175–180
  cognitive-behavioral model of, 174
  factorial structure of, 182–184
  in Little League baseball, 173–201
  and players: attitudes, 189, 190–193
    perception of, 181, 183–186, 187–189
    self-esteem, 190–194
Coaching Behavior Assessment System, 175–180
  training of coders for, 178–180
Coaching goals, 180, 187
Coaching Philosophy Questionnaire, 180–181
Coach training, 198–200
Community psychology, 9–12
Competitive sport situation:
  emotional effects of, 26–27
  factors influencing perception of, 108–110
  social evaluation and, 108, 119

285